NEITHER NOWT *NOR* SUMMAT

NEITHER NOWT NOR SUMMAT

IN SEARCH OF THE MEANING OF YORKSHIRE

IAN McMILLAN

EBURY
PRESS

1 3 5 7 9 10 8 6 4 2

Ebury Press, an imprint of Ebury Publishing
20 Vauxhall Bridge Road
London SW1V 2SA

Ebury Press is part of the Penguin Random House group of companies
whose addresses can be found at global.penguinrandomhouse.com

First published by Ebury Press in 2015

Passages from 'Home Rule for Yorkshire?' by John Rowan Wilson,
17 October 1968, used by kind permission of *The Spectator*

www.eburypublishing.co.uk

A CIP catalogue record for this book is available from
the British Library

ISBN 9780091959951

Printed and bound in Great Britain by Clays Ltd, St Ives PLC

Penguin Random House is committed to a
sustainable future for our business, our readers
and our planet. This book is made from Forest
Stewardship Council® certified paper.

To 'Mad' Geoff Utley, who cut Darfield's hair
and told Darfield's stories

CONTENTS

IN MY END IS MY BEGINNING

W E'RE IN DARFIELD, a village in the heart of the old South Yorkshire Coalfield, about five miles from Barnsley and ten miles from Doncaster on the old salt route that became the A635; a settlement that was recorded in the *Domesday Book* as a field full of deer near a river, a place that has gone through changes so incremental as to be barely noticeable and so sudden as to be like that moment when a car windscreen shatters as a chucked rock slaps it. Put it another way: the Saxon stones in the tower of All Saints' Church have weathered quite a bit over hundreds of years, and all the local pits closed in the space of a turbulent decade between the 1980s and 1990s, leaving a moonscape that was quickly grassed over or left to rust.

It's that time of year when autumn waits round the corner like someone who's going to jump out and surprise you. Summer is ready to stumble and fall, gasping for breath.

I wake up early, like I always do, and I remember my scary and repetitive dream:

I'm ambling down Wombwell High Street, two miles from Darfield, on a dramatically foggy morning; I've been to the butcher's and I'm carrying a pork pie like a servant of the royal family might carry a golden and symbolic gift at a ceremony. Suddenly, as is the way in dreams, I'm surrounded by a menacing group of people in ragged clothes who, as though they are the chorus of a musical, are singing, 'Not Yorkshire Enough! Not Yorkshire Enough! Tha might think tha'r Yorkshire, but tha'r Not Yorkshire Enough!', like a crowd at a Conference North game.

I'm disconcerted in my dream. I hold up my pork pie as a badge of Yorkshireness. 'It's a Potter's un, tha knows!' I say in what southerners call my Fruity Yorkshire Brogue. I take a huge bite from the pie to show how very Yorkshire I am. Yet the crowd are not impressed; they advance towards me, their eyes shining with a terrible light, shouting, 'Not Yorkshire Enough! Not Yorkshire Enough!' The words make my head ring like a ship's bell and pie-detritus escapes from my mouth, twisting and turning in the air like smoke, because this is a dream ...

I glance at the clock: 04.06. Pit time, my wife would call this. It used to be time for the early shift, the shivering wait for the miners on the corner of Nanny Marr Road and School Street, hoping the Houghton Main Colliery bus would turn up soon. This dream, and variations on it, is one I've been having on and off for months now. Like all dreams, I guess it's a distorting mirror of my real thinking, which is: am I Yorkshire Enough? Am I really, truly Yorkshire Enough? And what would it mean to be

Yorkshire Enough, anyway? How do I get to the bottom of the idea of what Yorkshire is, and where I fit into its ever-shifting mosaic?

Now, though I was born in Darfield and I've lived here all my life, I've got a confession to make: I'm keeping a secret as dark as this bedroom. I'm only a half-tyke; my mother was from Great Houghton, the next village to Darfield, but my dad was Scottish. He was from a place called Carnwath in Lanarkshire, a village so obscure that when Carnwathians went into town they went to Biggar. My parents met as pen-pals in the war, got together a couple of times for nervous afternoon tea in settings like the Queen's Hotel in Leeds and then, in October 1943, got married on a 48-hour pass in Peebles before my dad disappeared to the Far East with his Royal Navy ship and my mam, who was in the WAAFs, went back to base at RAF Blackbrook where they arrested her for going AWOL. AWOL for love: it's our family's abiding myth, of the Yorkshire lass and the handsome tartan sailor boy, love across the border, across the water.

And maybe because of that enduring story I sometimes feel that the county is somewhere to visit like my dad did, somewhere to go to rather than somewhere to be from, somewhere to romanticise and make fabulous. I feel like I'm an outsider, someone who will forever be standing in the slightly overheated conservatory of the house called Yorkshire, tapping on the window, wanting to come in and sit down on the settee.

Never a sofa in Yorkshire, of course: always a settee.

And maybe this is what makes me want to describe the

county, as much to myself as everyone else. Maybe this is why I want to write this book.

I'm often called upon to write about and comment on Yorkshire as some kind of home-grown expert but it strikes me that I don't really know the whole of it at all, I'm just familiar with my wrinkled neck of the woods: villages like Darfield, Great Houghton, Wombwell, Elsecar, Goldthorpe, Grimethorpe, Thurnscoe and Jump, towns like Barnsley and Doncaster, regions like the Dearne Valley and the old metropolitan county of South Yorkshire but there's so much more to Yorkshire than this, and I'm going to try and find it. I'm going to define the essence of this sprawling place as best I can, to me and to anybody else who'll listen. I can't really be a Professional Corner-of-Yorkshire-Man, after all. I've got to be a Professional Yorkshireman, if you'll pardon the cliché. Normally I don't like that phrase when others use it of me, but if I use it of myself that'll be okay. As I often say, when prodded, I'd rather be a Professional Yorkshireman than an Amateur Lancashireman.

Only joking. No, I'm not joking.

I'm going to confirm or deny the clichés, too, holding them up to see where the light gets in.

You know the ones I mean: Yorkshire people are tight. Yorkshire people are arrogant. Yorkshire people wear blinkered Yorkshire glasses that see places like Lancashire as a fetid swamp. Yorkshire people eat a Yorkshire Pudding before every meal, including Christmas dinner and Chinese takeaways. Yorkshire people solder a t' in front of every word they use. Yorkshire people are rarely called Alphonse and if they are they shorten it to Alph. Yorkshiremen call their wives and girlfriends Our Lass unless they're in Sheffield in which case they call them Our Gert. People from Yorkshire start every sentence with, 'Well, speaking as a Yorkshireman/woman...' Empty lies, the lot of them.

Most of them.

I'm going to start here, in this village, and radiate out like a ripple in a pond. I don't want to go to the obvious places, either; I want to be like a bus-driver on my first and last morning on the job, getting gloriously lost, turning up where I shouldn't. That's what Dr Johnson and James Boswell did, of course, when they went on their trip around the Hebrides in 1773; they had an itinerary but they kept, literally, getting blown off course because they did the trip on the grip of winter. If you can be blown off course on a train that's what I want to happen to me.

I want to have chance encounters of the sort I had when me and my mate, the late Martyn Wiley, recreated Johnson and Boswell's trip for a radio programme in the early 1990s. We'd ended up on the Isle of Coll in the Inner Hebrides and we'd approached the anti-nirvana that all makers of travel programmes end up in sooner or later: Interesting Character Fatigue. We'd interviewed so many amusing crofters with excitable dogs and eccentric ancients in Cro-Magnon cardigans that we didn't want to talk to anybody ever again for the whole of our natural lives.

We left the recording equipment in the room of the pub we were staying in and went to the bar.

'Two pints of bitter!' I said, using a loud voice like Johnson used to when he burst into smoky hovels to harangue the Gaelic speakers huddled round a dying peat fire.

A man on a high stool looked at me. He was completely covered in soot because he was the island chimney sweep, I learned later.

'I can guess where you come from in three guesses,' he said, a cloud of soot escaping from the area around his mouth into the afternoon. 'Just order that beer again.'

I did so, then I looked at him.

'Barnsley!' he said.

'Close,' I replied, pretending to be distant and cool, but secretly impressed.

He stared into space, thinking hard. More soot-flurries escaped. 'Wombwell,' he announced with a hint of triumph.

'Closer,' I said. He drummed his fingers on the bar. He scratched his stubbled chins. Finally, he spoke.

'Darfield. You come from Darfield.' I was amazed.

'How on earth can you do that?' I asked. He shrugged.

'It's just something I've always been able to do,' he said, and glugged his half-and-a-dram.

'Can I get my tape recorder and interview you?' I asked.

He said that I could, but that I'd have to meet him in the churchyard in half an hour because he was just off to cut the grass around the gravestones. I went to the room to check the batteries were working.

Half an hour later, Martyn and I wandered to the churchyard where we found him slumped on a tomb, limp as a glove-puppet between shows. In the gap between talking to us and performing his grass-cutting duties, he'd somehow got spectacularly and disastrously drunk. I held the microphone in front of his beery breath.

'Just tell me what you said before, about Wombwell and Darfield,' I said, despairingly.

He responded with the old Andy Stewart number, 'A Scottish Soldier', his voice breaking with emotion.

I asked around afterwards and people said he'd never shown that skill before but it made me feel obscurely proud of the way I spoke, and of the way it could be so easily identified with a square mile or so.

The ferry came and we left the island, so I never had chance to ask him anything else, which is a shame but it's also a relief because maybe, as I surmised years later, he'd just read my address on the hotel registration card. Still, it was a neat trick.

I want to be like my Uncle Charlie who couldn't read or write so couldn't follow signs and was flummoxed by maps but would drive for miles in his green Ford Anglia, registration number 4095 HE, relying on guesswork, dead reckoning, and the kindness or wickedness of strangers. When he got bored he'd jerk into reverse for a laugh, which frightened Mrs Fareham when she was walking to the dancing club. I might try that, too.

Today, though, I'll do what I always do: go downstairs and venture out on my early stroll. I've been walking these streets for more than half a century, and I've been shaped by them in more ways than I care to remember. My stroll always take me down to the newsagent's and then down Snape Hill past the place where the post-box used to be that I dropped a threepenny bit in as a child because I thought it was a rebellious and transgressive thing to do, and past my old junior school, which was called Low Valley Primary, and is now rebranded The Valley Primary. Low has gone.

I was born in 1956 so that means I went to school in the West Riding of Yorkshire, a glorious education authority run by a god-like genius called Sir Alec Clegg who said that all children were creative; he wanted the young people in his schools to feel that education was about making them better human beings, more rounded citizens, often through the media of poetry, art, music and contemporary dance to music clattered out by enthusiastic infants on shining glockenspiels.

Sadly, Clegg wasn't a Yorkshireman; he was from Derbyshire, but he was transplanted here and flourished like a pot plant placed with love on the right sill. We accepted him, though. He became ours, another outsider who shaped the county in his own image from 1945 until his retirement in 1974 when the West Riding was screwed up and thrown away.

A string quartet came to our school each term, made up of peripatetic music teachers; each time they came they played a piece by Haydn that stops and starts again, and each time it fooled us, even the kids in the top class who'd heard it many times before. They'd stop: we'd clap. They'd start again: we'd go, 'Awwww,' and wait until the end, when we weren't sure whether to clap or not. Mrs Roche always had to start us off, slapping her leg like a principal boy.

A van would arrive packed with abstract art and stuffed animals. We'd gaze at the pictures and someone would ask what it meant and Mr Manley would say, 'It means what it looks like, lad, and this afternoon you'll be drawing something like it,' and that's exactly what we did. We didn't know it at the time, but this was an education driven by something you'd have to call Love.

In a speech given at Bingley College of Education just before he retired, Sir Alec Clegg quoted a reference Michelangelo had brought with him to show the Pope before he got employed to paint the Sistine Chapel: 'The bearer of these presents is Michelangelo the sculptor ... his nature is such that he requires to be drawn out by kindness and encouragement – but if love be shown him and he be treated really well, he will accomplish things that will make the whole world wonder.'

I'm very lucky to have been educated like that, even if my rendition of abstract collage did make Mrs Yelland shake her head and purse her lips. Yorkshire for me has always meant love, though. But don't tell the lads at Oakwell next time Barnsley are losing 3-0 to a team from south of the Trent.

Clegg also had some odd ideas, mind you: we had a few visits from a temperance activist who warned us of the dangers of alcohol. I knew all about these dangers because my dad was a lifelong teetotaller who had signed the pledge as a young man in the Royal Navy in the late 1930s, giving up the tot of grog that they still handed out in those days. Indeed, in the tiny upstairs room in our house on Barnsley Road that he called the lobby, I once found his framed copy of the pledge, with a frightening picture of the great god Neptune stabbing a sea serpent with the words THE DEMON DRINK etched on its scaly flanks.

Two of the temperance man's illustrated arguments stick in my mind. He would hold the audience, even the squirming infants, with his gaze of tempered steel and say in a deep voice that rumbled and rolled and has lingered in my audio memory: 'A friend of mine went for a long walk on a summer's day and at the end of the walk he was hot and tired so he went into a pub and asked the publican, "My man, could you give me a cheese sandwich and a pint of beer?" and, do you know, boys and girls, I can understand the cheese sandwich but I can't …' And here he would slow down and each of his next few words would be beaten out with a steady rhythm '… understand. The. Pint. Of. Beer.'

He stopped with a flourish and I tried to understand why you had to understand a pint of beer.

About halfway through his talk, he did something startling and radical. He put his hand in his pocket and pulled out what was obviously, even to our junior school eyes, a piece of brown wool. He shook the wool dramatically.

'This, boys and girls, is a worm.' I could see Mrs Hudson trying not to roll her eyes. 'I'll drop it in this glass of water and, look, it's happy to wriggle around and swim in it because …' The percussion began again. '… Water. Can. Not. Hurt. The. Worm.'

I thought Mrs Hudson's eyes were going to roll out of their sockets and round the corner to Pitt Street. He fished the wool out of the water and dropped it into a second glass.

'Now, boys and girls, in this glass we have beer. Bitter beer.'

Mr Owen was trying not to smile. He was probably reciting the names of the kings and queens of England and the manner of their deaths in his head.

'And look: The. Worm. Is. Dead.' He pulled out the wool and it lay limply over his hand. 'Boy and girls. That is what beer can do.'

He nodded to Mrs Hinchliffe and she began to play 'Hills of the North Rejoice' and we filed out, unsure whether to sing or not. I turned round and saw that he was putting the wool into a tiny cardboard box. Maybe it was a worm after all.

A wonderful example of the West Riding's immersive attitude to the curriculum was The Day Mrs York Chased the Goat. It would have been 1963 and I was in Mrs Hudson's class. A note came round from Mr Owen as we were doing our sums. Mrs Hudson read it to herself and frowned. She folded the note away and slipped it into her drawer.

'We won't be going out to play today, children,' she said, 'We'll do some drawing in the classroom instead.' We could detect an unusual note of nervousness in her chapel-alto voice.

Suddenly we heard a clattering kerfuffle and we saw Mrs York, the considerable school secretary, charging across the hall brandishing one of those long wooden poles you opened the window with. We crowded to the window, misting it up with our trembling breath. Mrs York, like Don Quixote in a skirt and top from Thurnscoe market, was tilting at a goat. The goat scuttled away, its feet rattling and slithering on the floor that the caretaker, Mr Rothin, had polished to perfection the night before. Mr Owen appeared, waving a vivid red fire extinguisher, even though neither Mrs York nor the goat was alight. However, the combination of the window-pole and the fire extinguisher subdued the goat and it was hustled outside where it ran off towards the Drapery Co-op, scattering some women who were just making their way to the Knit'n'Natter at the church hall.

The whole class sat down again, reluctantly, trying to prolong the magical moment for as long as possible.

'Well,' said Mrs Hudson, 'we know what we're going to write about today in our news books, don't we? And why don't we see if we can write a poem about what happened out there with the goat and Mrs York and Mr Owen? If you need help with your spelling, come and see me, but let's get some ideas down on paper first.'

I think that the man I am now was born then, in the distant 1960s at Low Valley Primary School, in a goat's sharp absence and my recreating of it in a WRCC exercise book, my concentrating tongue protruding. In a room that was briefly noisy with the sound of the Camplejohn's bus taking the afternoon shift to Darfield Main, changing gear as it turned the corner by the Astoria Ballroom. In a room that smelled of crayons and brimmed with the idea that to write experience is to make it real.

Not Yorkshire Enough, eh? Let's see.

THE DISTANT PAST
AND ME

SOMETIMES I'M ARROGANT and stupid enough to imagine that Yorkshire somehow didn't really exist until that snowy day in January 1956 when I slithered into the county crying in a Barnsley accent. I don't think that's just me, it's everybody: we find it hard to slip from memory to history and to see the links between the two. A lot of us find it hard to imagine a world without us; we're solipsistic beings. I imagine it's something evolution has painted into our corners to help us survive. If you don't think you're important you won't worry about the sabre-toothed tiger as it approaches through the trees, as Darwin should have said if he'd come from Yorkshire.

I need to step outside this self-made temporal corral to show myself and others exactly how small I am on the map of the Ridings, and to understand what Yorkshire is and how I fit into it I'm going to start in my own back yard.

I'm going to meet John Tanner. You see, John works for Barnsley Museums, and he's got history running through his veins. Well, we all have, but you know what I mean. If you cut him he'd bleed history and then he'd mop it up and put it on display with interpretative signboards in several languages including Braille. I first came across John when he started working as Museums Officer in Barnsley and was instrumental in opening the new Experience Barnsley museum that sprawls excitingly across a floor of the town hall and reflects Barnsley people back to themselves. And there's a great café where the cakes aren't historic and the espresso is tack-sharp.

He's going to take me on a dawn meander around some ancient and more recent sites across the Dearne Valley, an area that was until recently topographically shafted by the coal industry but which has now settled into a kind of uncertain warehouse and call-centre present. If I want to get to the bottom of this county I need to begin here, the place that nurtured me, and John's an excellent guide. He's always breathless with history. I once sat with him in a place that was to my simple mind devoid of any cobwebbed hinterland but, as far as John Tanner was concerned, we could have been sitting in one of the mausoleums of the ancient pharaohs. It was a Portakabin on the site of Experience Barnsley as it was being constructed and John metaphorically peeled away the layers of chipboard to reveal the lurking and informative treasure below, riffing on the idea of old Portakabins and linking the idea of the Portakabin with the idea of the first shelters people made from wattle and daub. And speak of this quietly, but John isn't from Yorkshire at all. He's from the Lancashire mill town of Rochdale; a place that's a bit like Barnsley with looms. There's a pattern here: me, Sir Alec Clegg, John Tanner. None of us are fully from Yorkshire. Maybe you have to be an outsider to completely understand the glory of a place. Perhaps that's why Buzz Aldrin liked the moon so much.

I clamber into his car and, oddly, we shake hands. I think I'm shaking hands because I know I'm at the start of a great adventure which will take me towards the meaning of a place I think I know. Autumn has slipped me into a jumper and the morning is chilly. We set off towards the secret location of a Romano-British site that's not too far from my house in Darfield and we get lost trying to find it. Presumably because it's secret.

'I should have brought a better map,' he says as we swerve and almost make history of a rotund man on a suffering bike.

The poet in me notes that phrase: 'I should have brought a better map.' It is a metaphor for writing and discovery, but then an obvious question occurs to me: if it's secret, how can it be on the map?

John explains in the patient voice of a man who's gone over this many times before in many different settings, that a number of years ago, before he came to work in Barnsley, an archaeologist came and identified the site and put it on a map which, in John's carefully chosen words, 'may not be 110% accurate', perhaps for reasons of continuing security.

'I think this is the layby,' John says and we grind to a halt, and that's not really a metaphor for anything; it's the fourth time he's said it of the same and different laybys and one patch of gravel that had never been a layby and would never ever be a layby; it could have been a child's drawing of what a layby might look like. The bloke on the bike passes us, gesturing timelessly. The layby is next to some thick tangled woods of the kind you encounter in a folk tale. A crow sits in a tree like a Goth in a bedsit.

One of John's verbal signatures is the phrase, 'How are you for … ?' and he certainly doesn't disappoint today.

'How are you for walking through brambles?' he says, and before I can answer we're doing the front crawl through what appears to be a huge green and prickly cardigan. On John's map the Romano-British settlement is a faint ghost of a perfect circle, as though somebody has rested a coffee-cup on the paper.

'It's very close. How are you for walking through gorse?'

He looks in all directions, rotating in the style of a traffic cop at the start of his shift in a huge city.

I get a sense of the layers of history I'm walking on in my muddy boots; these woods would at one time have been the wildwood that covered most of England like a hair-shirt. Hundreds of years ago people must have roamed these spaces, the ones that we now call Yorkshire, hunting but mainly gathering like those swift-limbed women at the Rag and Louse Market in Barnsley on a Tuesday. For years and years nothing much would happen and hardly anything would change. Seasons would roll by unannounced but acknowledged by either visible breath in the air or sheens of forehead-sweat, and yet this feels like a special place. If Yorkshireness is something that evolved then it might have been in anonymous spots like this where it began it crawl out of the swamp. Yorkshire is a place built on arrival, on off-comed 'uns making their mark and making a home. The Romano-British people would have tramped over a hill and made a circle in these trees for reasons even John can't work out. They'd have settled here, close by the Rivers Dearne and Dove, not too far from roads that were elderly even then. They'd have made fires that flickered in the evening and, almost imperceptibly, with a flattening of a vowel and the spark of an attitude, they would have started to become Romano-British-Yorkshire people, a real step forward for civilisation, in my opinion. I realise I'm probably the only person alive who finds the idea of this moving, but I do.

Later, this settlement would be abandoned, and the descendants of those early tykes would have moved into the farmsteads and hamlets that dotted the hills and flat spaces near here. Again, nothing much would have happened for a long time, except that they would have started to dig coal out of the ground; permission was given to the local landowner Earl Fitzwilliam in 1367 to mine in the area, and a number of tiny pits scraped coal from the unforgiving ground to heat houses and smelt iron.

As the Industrial Revolution in the eighteenth century moved from a canter to a gallop and covered this part of the country in smoke and steam and sparks and people shouting, there would have been a moment replicated in all the big houses across the valley, when a bloke with big mucky hands would have rushed into the dining room as the local landowner was eating his lunch.

'Coal, sir, we've found coal!' he would have yelled in the voice of a Brian Blessed alarm clock and the landed gent would have whooped because he knew he would be made for life and the man who found the coal would have been kept in turnips in perpetuity or until he died in a pit accident, whichever came first. This was happening in my part of South Yorkshire because of the rapid expansion of the canals that ensured the coal could be got to the ports more quickly and pits sprang up, if a pit can spring up, everywhere.

John and I are standing very still. This really is a moment. We can feel those ancient Yorkshire people all around us; we can almost hear the songs they must have sung to keep away the night. We are standing in their footprints and, as my eyes become used to the trees' half-light, I can see that we're in the middle of a hesitant circle that's almost like a ring drawn in the mist on a bathroom mirror. Or on a classroom window as a goat hurries by.

We don't speak as we walk back to the car. The secret location has remained secret, just, but I've got a sense of the history of Yorkshire layered like a cake, like a wallpaper palimpsest in a 1930s semi. The morning is expanding, as though we're unfolding it.

Time to move on, towards Elsecar, one of the cradles of the Industrial Revolution. Lots of places claim to be this cradle, of course, but Elsecar's right in the middle of the nursery.

This industrial and post-industrial part of Yorkshire is well used, let's face it. Any sheen has been rubbed off years ago. The aforementioned besuited gentry who danced jigs and gavottes when the coal turned up really did shape and reshape the land round here, and nobody more so than Earl Fitzwilliam. He was the uber-toff, descended from a long line of landowners and the pits he sunk on his land, Elsecar Old Colliery, Elsecar New Colliery and Simon Wood

Colliery, helped to make his family one of the richest in Europe, giving him vast wealth and his own private railway.

To understand a little of the influence of the Fitzwilliam family on this part of South Yorkshire you should drive through their picturesque estate village of Wentworth, not far from Elsecar, with its astonishing big house, Wentworth Woodhouse; two stately homes back-to-back, the longest single-fronted house in Europe, a place that once had a window for every day of the year, where you had to have a box of confetti to sprinkle on the corridors to find your way back to your room if you went for a ball. Building began in 1725 and wasn't completed for decades. As you trundle down the main street, you'll notice that a lot of the drainpipes and letterboxes and fences are painted a kind of pea-soup green because Earl Fitzwilliam liked that colour; he liked the cottages in his village to wear a smart uniform and metaphorically doff their caps to him as he passed. There was always a rumour when I was younger that the Yorkshire Traction buses that went through Wentworth on the main road had to have a pea-soup stripe on them too, and I hope it's true.

So now John and I are driving across the valley towards Earl Fitzwilliam's industrial powerhouse, Elsecar. In the early 1990s the old National Coal Board workshops at Elsecar were turned into a heritage centre and tourist attraction by the borough council and it's true to say that not everybody was convinced. You could go to the Dales, yes, or Whitby, they were places that sold Yorkshire postcards of picturesque views, but Elsecar? So soon after the miners' strike when vanloads of coppers roared through your village at four in the morning with their sirens going just to wake you and the kids up? So soon after the union man brought the food parcels to your father-in-law's house just as he was having what he called A Good Wash at the sink in his vest?

The heritage centre opened and flourished briefly and brightly in the 1990s. I took my kids there a lot on long Sunday afternoons and we once stood next to a trad jazz band as an exasperated granddad tried to tell a boy who in my memory is called Rollo that the trombonist's straw boater was not a miner's summer helmet.

At around the same time, I remember meeting some Japanese tourists in Wombwell who held up brochures from Elsecar and raised quizzical eyebrows. I mimed elaborately that they should turn left, go up the hill to the station and take the train in the Sheffield direction. I thought I'd done well until they turned right and walked confidently towards the Summer Lane Fish and Chip Shop.

For a while at the turn of the millennium and into the new century, the heritage centre just trundled along but now thanks to people like John Tanner and his phalanxes of workers and volunteers it's beginning to blossom again.

John speeds into the car park and stops suddenly as though he's run out of petrol. He's already been excited today at the secret location and now he's really excited. If he was a kettle he'd be coming to the boil. We leap from the car, cop-show style, and trip briskly towards a structure festooned with scaffolding.

'How are you for climbing up scaffolding?' John asks.

I'm fine, I say.

He gestures at the scaffolding. 'The Newcomen beam engine!' he intones, like a butler announcing a celebrity at a black-tie dinner.

The Newcomen beam engine is John's pride and joy because it's the only one of its kind that's still in its original setting and still, potentially, in working order. Thomas Newcomen invented his eponymous engine in 1712 and as the eighteenth century progressed, thousands of them were in constant use throughout Europe, principally pumping water out of mines and making them safer and, perhaps more importantly, more profitable. Newcomen ended up seeing his creation overshadowed and usurped by James Watt's more sophisticated steam engine but, like Ducks Deluxe and the Sex Pistols, you couldn't have had one without the other. Sadly, Newcomen was another builder of our identity who wasn't from Yorkshire; he was what my dad used to call a 'stout denizen of Devon'. I think there's an unYorkshire pattern developing here.

From the late 1700s until the early 1900s, the Elsecar Newcomen pumped water out of the nearby pit, pounding away for 12 hours each day like a martial drum or, more fittingly, a beating heart.

'It must have been great when it stopped!' I say to John, imagining the equivalent of that special silence you get after noise, like when a car-alarm cuts off.

I can tell by his face that he isn't so sure; he likes the idea of the noise saturating the village, slicing up local time into bumps and thumps, and I realise that if I want to make sense of Yorkshire I've got to listen as well as look. There are several ways not to be Yorkshire Enough, and

I'm slowly beginning to learn them. For John, history is noisy, and in that noise you can begin to fathom how Yorkshire people lived. Listen and learn, kid, as some mythical mill owner might have said in volume four of a family saga.

Thanks to the Newcomen engine, Earl Fitzwilliam entrepreneurially had mines sunk and railways laid and canals dug and the noise level rose and the money rolled in; for a county that's got more than its fair share of collectivism, much of Yorkshire has been constructed by individuals wanting to make things and money. However, most Newcomen engines were eventually dismantled and chucked away or left to rust or reused for their metal while their stories were ignored, but the one in Elsecar is unique because it's still proudly in the same place it's always been. It could be the start of yet another reinvention of this area.

John hands me a hard hat and hi-vis vest. We climb the ladders and negotiate the scaffolding that encases the engine and I know that for John this is like scaling the walls of the tower they keep the Crown Jewels in.

'Are you sure you're all right with heights?' he asks as, mesmerised by the vista, I almost step back into the small, local abyss I've just ascended from.

The view from the top is a kind of artist's impression, a map of possibilities. John guides me through them.

'So, you've almost got the perfect set-up,' he says. 'The canal basin, the ironworks, the railway, the pit; one man's vision of what a place can become.'

This is what Yorkshire is, I guess: a series of overlapping visions, a bouquet of ideas of exactly what a place can be, from those secretive Romano-British people to here and now.

We climb down again and hand in the safety equipment. Thanks to the hard hat my grey hair is more of a surprise than a shock.

I want to believe in this place; I want the coachloads to come and marvel at Earl Fitzwilliam's vision and the sweat of the people who built this place and their green drain-pipes. I feel like I've won this morning in a competition. First prize. Time to move on. Time to move away from The Mothership.

GOING TO EXTREMES

I'T'S A CHILLY autumn morning on platform 2 at Barnsley Interchange and you can see my breath. A tabarded cleaner moves deftly around me sweeping crisps up, and a young woman on platform 1 lights a cigarette and blows a shivering ring of warm smoke into the chilled air. I'm surrounded by familiarity, by the blanket of the place that nurtured me and made me who I am. And salt'n'vinegar detritus. If I really want to home in on the idea of what Yorkshire is, then I've decided that I should abandon my original plan of moving outwards from Our Darfield or perhaps just vary it a little.

I now think that I really need to start by working out what Yorkshire isn't, where it begins and ends, where it shades into somewhere else. Maybe in the borderlands I can begin to sense the county's essence.

I'm going to go on what, in my opinion, is one of the world's great railway journeys. You can keep the Orient Express and the Trans-Siberian, with their endless, numbing forest views and the murder suspects gathered shiftily in the buffet car as the music swells. Give me the 0801 from Barnsley to Huddersfield every time. This line cuts through South and West Yorkshire, from brick-built terraces to stone-built cottages, sliding, as a man said to me once as we bought our tickets, between anthracite and shoddy. The line managed to survive Beeching's axe but was then almost closed in the 1980s and only remained open thanks to dogged campaigners and official pragmatism. Now it's a busy route taking students to Huddersfield, shoppers to Meadowhall, and a poet part of the way to the edgy place where Lancashire and Yorkshire spark against each other.

The ancient Northern Rail pacer train rattles in, like a home-made lean-to on wheels. It's a good job I've got my ticket because the guard, in his broad Sheffield accent, keeps telling everybody that his ticket machine isn't functioning.

'Might be working by Stocksmoor,' he says, always naming a place several stations along.

I like the guards on this line: if you were a visitor to Yorkshire, they'd be the first ones you encountered, the doormen beckoning you into t'club, and they'd make you smile and want to stay. I remember the one who used to play a kazoo when you went into a tunnel to scare the toddlers and who would shout, as we approached Castleford, 'Welcome to Cas Vegas, gateway to Ponty Carlo!', and who would mutter as he passed me in the aisle, 'I don't have to do this job, you know, I'm a trained golf course designer.'

He won an award once for customer service but then the story was that this went to his head and he was verbally disciplined for over-enthusiastic use of the kazoo. Apparently there were times, as the train rumbled into Sheffield late on winter nights, that the sound of it almost approached 1960s New York free jazz.

He once said to me, 'Tony Hancock got on at Dodworth. I got his autograph.'

He meant Nick Hancock and I think he really knew that.

The Cannon to his Ball was the big-necked conductor who never spoke but had the words GIZ YER BRASS AND SHURRUP written on his change bag.

The train rolls through Dodworth and the older people (headscarves and trilbies) nod their approval when the guard announces Doduth and Silkstun Common. God help the RP automated station tannoy person who still, to this day, calls Elsecar Elsie Carr, conjuring up a sepia image of a perfumed lady who sews the buttons on the dresses of the dancing-school girls in her spare time.

Language is vitally important in Yorkshire's Tower of Babel, as anybody who's asked for a teacake and got a breadcake will testify. The guard on this train is a DeeDar, which is what Barnsley people call Sheffielders because of their habit of hardening the 'th' in 'thee' or 'tha' to a 'd' so it becomes Dee and Da. It's a tiny linguistic point, where language changes in a small geographical space; it's known as an isogloss and it's one of the building blocks of identity in these parts. The guard would call me a Dingle because that's what Sheffielders call people from Barnsley because they see themselves as big-city sophisticates and they believe that we're slack-jawed cartoon primitives like the Dingle family on *Emmerdale*.

The sun breaks out across the grassed-over pit-stack of Dodworth Main and we begin to move into gentler country. Barnsley Metropolitan District was built on coal and the getting of coal, but more or less all that's left of that industry are the artificially green hills where woolly sheep graze and trail bikes etch lines. Unless you count Glasshoughton Pit, near Castleford, which, in an irony-failure of epic proportions, is now a dry ski-slope.

By Penistone, that fiercely independent town that won't admit it's part of Barnsley or Sheffield, the fields are widening, the stone farmhouses are the colour of roast parsnips, and the huge mast at Emley Moor dominates the windows of the train. I'm never really sure why Penistone sees itself as a separate self-contained kingdom. Maybe, in an area dominated by heavy industry, it's because it's a market town full, on market days, of farmers wearing tweed jackets that seem so heavy that they almost need a hoist to lift them round their shoulders. It's returned Tory councillors, too, and they're as rare round these parts as the mating song of the angel fish.

Emley Moor mast is still the UK's tallest man-made feature, beating the Shard in London by several feet, much to the satisfaction of Yorkshire folk; it's the conduit for broadcasting television signals across the region and it's been doing so since 1966, beaming pictures of the World Cup to front rooms all over Yorkshire and beyond. In 1969 it fell down, spectacularly, like a drunk uncle at a wedding, because of a build-up of ice rather than a build-up of best bitter. It was rebuilt later that year and was broadcasting again the following spring, a tribute to Yorkshire grit and engineering knowhow and people's visceral need for *Coronation Street*. When you're flying south from Leeds-Bradford airport it often pokes up through low clouds, reminding you exactly where you are.

A lot of people say that Yorkshire is a British version of Texas, a Lone Star State where everything is bigger, higher, longer, deeper, and Emley Moor mast proves that point, pointedly.

It's a strange thing, this Yorkshire one-upmanship, but it certainly continues to flourish; at a cricket match at Headingley between Yorkshire and Leicestershire I once saw a balloon-like man stagger to his feet and shout, 'Come on, Yorkshire! They only make shoes!'

You can buy T-Shirts that say 'CHEER UP THA'S FROM YORKSHIRE' and car stickers that simply show Billy Casper from *Kes*'s raised two-finger salute to the world.

My brother got me a mug for Christmas that said 'YOU CAN TAKE THE LAD OUT OF YORKSHIRE BUT YOU CAN'T TAKE YORKSHIRE OUT OF THE LAD' and I glugged tea from it without irony as we sat and laughed about the fact that Lancashire people would say they were taking cattle to'th abbatoir to get slaughtered, rather than the much more sensible 'to't abbatoir', which to the trained Yorkshire ear sounds very different.

'To' th'abbatoir!' we kept repeating, laughing until we couldn't talk any more.

I like Northamptonshire but I can't see this sort of county-patriotism happening there. After all, they only make felt hats. They say that Yorkshire people are boastful, and we often hear the line 'you can tell a Yorkshireman but you can't tell him much' and then we have to pretend to laugh or make a little smile-pout with our lips but really we're thinking, Of course you can't tell a Yorkshireman much: what is there to say, apart from 'I think your county is the most beautiful of all!' I've thought about this a lot, and in the end what other people see as showing off is just accepting the inevitable. It's a realistic attitude, not any kind of construct or exaggeration. It's not a post-impressionist painting, it's a photograph. Yorkshire is the best and that's all there is to it. If you want empirical evidence, it's all around you: the wide skies, the perfect tea, the waves crashing symphonically on the shore, the lyrical language that seems to dance its way to your ears, the sheer beauty of a sunset on fire over Holme-on-Spalding-Moor. You may as well say that an elephant is boasting about being big. It simply is. Like Yorkshire: it simply is. I won't go on about it or people might think I'm boasting. But it simply is. It really is. I'm biased, of course. But in the right direction.

I'm not sure where the idea of the overconfident Yorkshire person comes from, historically, but I like to pretend that it was crystallised into the public mind by a late nineteenth-century music hall that I've just invented called Boasty Yorky Frum't Top End of Tong. Here's the opening of one of his monologues, rendered in the vernacular:

'Hello the good people of NAME OF TOWN and let me offer me sincerest condolences to you all because you're not clever enough or lucky enough to come from Yorkshire; never mind, when the wages in the mills go up to a penny an hour you'll all flock there, I dare say. And I dare say this: I say I say I say, why did the Yorkshireman cross the road? Because several well-meaning people told him not to! I thank you! Now it's time for a song: Don't Go Down The Mine, Daddy, Your Head Won't Fit in the Cage...'

Shame he doesn't exist. Still, he fills in an idle few minutes on a journey.

The train seems to fly over the fields on the Penistone Viaduct and the crop rotation of the wind farm's blades slice the air; now the cast-list of beautiful station names begins. Denby Dale, where the local community centre is called the Pie Hall in honour of the giant pie they used to bake in the village every decade; Shepley, with a Yorkshire flag, the proud white rose on the blue background, hanging limply in the absence of a breeze in a neat back garden; Stocksmoor, where nobody gets on and nobody gets off and the train doors close with a forlorn elegiac hiss; Brockholes, where high above a wooded valley a kestrel hovers; Honley, where a man in a jacket stands and stares at the ground and doesn't get on the train; Berry Brow, where a wild-eyed chap carrying a standard lamp gets off and runs into the distance, and finally, the last station before Huddersfield, Lockwood. I've never got off at Lockwood but one day I will, just because it's said that around these parts the withdrawal method of contraception is known as 'getting off at Lockwood' because you don't go all the way. And just to be able to say I'd done it would be something else to tick off in my personal Yorkshire t'bucket list.

To be honest I usually get off at Brockholes having got on at Penistone.

We roll through another tunnel and arrive in the cathedral-light of Huddersfield's magnificent station; this is what I think an opera house would look like if it had trains running through it. It's very easy to imagine steam here, and people in top hats and flat caps dashing across platforms, newspapers under their arms with headlines like WAR DECLARED on the front as a man with a huge moustache shouts, 'All aboard!' These days it seems to be a centre for the buying of coffee, too; there are four outlets, independent and corporate, and I settle with a cuppa in the tiny, dark and welcoming establishment on platform 4, where a man is eating a bacon sandwich stolidly, two sequins of brown sauce on his white shirt. He winks at me.

'Best butties for miles!' he says, talking with his mouth full, chuckling. Three sequins of brown sauce and a medallion.

I've always thought of Huddersfield as a prime example of those self-contained towns that dot the county: city-states like Doncaster, Hull, Barnsley, Bradford, Sheffield, Rotherham, Beverley, Malton and many more, places with a passionate local civic pride that outsiders can mistake for stand-offishness, for a deliberately insular outlook on life. An inlook, in fact.

This is partly to do with language and culture, of course, even within the same county, where each valley or village or street almost seems to have its own fiercely contested grammar and syntax. I once wrote a play in an extremely local dialect about pigeon racing where, in the clumsily climactic third act, all the birds died because they were allergic to a younger character's Brylcreem. At Gawber Club, on the outskirts of Barnsley, the audience were laughing so much the actors kept having to stop while people sucked desperately on inhalers to get their breath back and borrowed hankies to staunch their streaming eyes; by contrast, at a community centre ten miles away in Fox Hill, near Hillsborough, the following night, there was rapt silence as the crowd on the wooden seats concentrated on the action, treating the drama as an Ibsenesque glance into various dark nights of the White Rose soul. The actors kept having to stop to let the crowd sigh.

Years ago, in the tap room of a pub near Wakefield, I overheard an old man say to an older man, 'I've not laughed so much since they bombed Sheffield.'

People around them winced and tutted but they knew what he meant. Rivalry with your neighbour is always the most intense, the most bruising.

Perhaps what divides Yorkshire is that its fragments don't really empathise with each other but what unites us is that we don't feel fully English so we feel embattled and proud and Other.

The writing of this book is taking place in front of a backdrop of the possible atomisation of the United Kingdom, in which the regions claw autonomy and pride and self-worth back from a government that feels remote.

At times Yorkshire seems like Italy, which for centuries was a loose bundle of city-states and made its way up a kind of shaky geopolitical ladder via republics and kingdoms and grand duchies until it became an autonomous country in 1860. In Yorkshire's case, this is probably to do with local government, with the fact that until the 1970s even places as small as Darfield had their own Urban District Council which set a rate and cleaned the slide in the park. Overlaying this fragmentation like a template of a county map is a burning desire to belong to Yorkshire, above and beyond, or rather slightly to the side of, any more local allegiances.

When my Yorkshire brother-in-law took on a pub in a village near Stranraer, nobody came in for the first three days.

On the fourth day, a man with a Saltire on his tie came in and said, 'Are you an Englishman?', and Terry, thinking quickly, said, 'No, I'm a Yorkshireman.'

The man nodded, went out and brought his mates back to sup.

'We don't like the English,' he explained later.

And somewhere hidden not too far from the surface of all these stories, all these limited or limitless horizons, is the heart of what Yorkshire is; it seems to me that the desire for independence at the level of a country is replicated and fuelled at what scientists would call a molecular level of civic pride. This both feeds Yorkshireness and keeps it tense. In other words, never marry a lass from Methley unless tha'r a lad from Methley. Or, at a push, Skelmanthorpe.

I scuttle from the buffet and catch my train, which goes all the way to Wigan Wallgate, but I'm getting off in Greenfield, which could also be a slightly more westerly version of Getting Off At Lockwood.

Greenfield is a place which either is, or isn't, in Yorkshire depending who you ask and when you ask the question. I want to test Greenfield and the whole of Saddleworth out. I want to see if, like me, they're Yorkshire Enough.

Until 1972 Greenfield was contentedly part of Yorkshire but, when local government was reorganised in the mid

1970s, they had a referendum. The people voted over-whelmingly, in their thousands, and put a cross next to the 'stay in Yorkshire' section but their wishes were ignored and it became part of Oldham Metropolitan Borough, which definitely isn't in Yorkshire. It's in Lancashire. I get off as people pile on excitedly, attracted by the idea of Wigan. The autumn sun I'm bathed with feels like a Yorkshire autumn sun, but of course I'm biased.

I go to check the times of my return train and ask Rochelle behind the booking-office glass if we're in Yorkshire or Lancashire. She's been asked this before, I can tell, and she replies, diplomatically, 'Oldham'. I leave with a timetable full of ambiguities.

They're more forthright in the Post Office when I ask. 'Lancashire. Definitely Lancashire,' says the lady who sells me a pen because the one I nabbed from a hotel has run out, scratchily.

The woman buying stamps isn't so sure. 'I think it's still in Yorkshire,' she says, interestingly referring to Greenfield as a separate thing rather than the village she's standing in; she could have said, 'I think *we're* still in Yorkshire,' but she didn't.

The way she says 'Yorkshire' is fascinating, too; she makes the 'shire' into a 'sheer', saying it in a Lankysheer way, the isogloss hanging in the air by the rack of birthday and anniversary cards.

'It was in Yorkshire till a few years back,' says the Post Office woman, losing interest, 'but it's been Lancashire for ages. Anyway, I'm a Manc. And that's in Lancashire.'

'This feels like Yorkshire though,' says the woman,

sticking a stamp on a letter, and maybe that's exactly what I want to hear.

I've thought about this a lot, in idle moments on trains and on station platforms as I wait for trains, and I can't really fathom why Yorkshire people are more passionate about their county than Lancashire people are; Lancashire has the same shimmering internal rivalries, between great cities like Liverpool and Manchester, it has a certain pride-of-place, it has huge industrial and post-industrial areas and fantastic Lancascapes that you can wander in. They just don't seem to want to shout about it as much as we do.

I buy broad beans in Stamford's grocers and the lady from the Post Office follows me in.

'You still here?' she says.

'Still in Yorkshire!' I say.

I'm joined by the photographer Ian Beesley, born and bred in Bradford yet living in Saddleworth, and one of the country's leading documentary photographers. I asked him to come along and help me in my search for the heart of Yorkshire because he's in no doubt about which part of the atlas his feet are planted on.

'But this really is Yorkshire!' he says as he buys the sea bass that was brought fresh from Fleetwood, Lancs, this morning, and amongst the veg and the fruit and the fish, we're all in broad agreement. Broad bean agreement. For a moment. More or less. It's not certain, I can tell.

I've known Ian Beesley for years and I'm always fasci-nated by the fact that such a fiercely patriotic Yorkshireman should live in the back yard of the enemy, so to speak. I'd like to go and chat to him in his house but he's got a dog as big as a holly bush and I'm allergic to dogs. Five minutes in his house and I'd swell to three times my normal size and float round the room like a dirigible. If we have a cup of tea it'll have to be in his garden. On chairs, of course; we've got to set an example to the Lancashire people.

Outside, Ian points out a sign that seems to settle, or half-settle, or even open up, the argument.

'WELCOME TO GREENFIELD IN THE ANCIENT COUNTY OF YORK' it reads, above the words 'OLDHAM METROPOLITAN BOROUGH'. For a moment it feels like I'm surrounded by Basque separatists or people who speak Kernow in Padstow pubs.

We ask a man with a yapping dog where we are.

'The West Riding of Saddleworth!' he says, confidently and confusingly, before the dog leads him away.

A postman passes and he's deliberate and thoughtful in his reply to the question about our location, as befits somebody whose job it is to consider location by royal decree.

'I think this is Lancashire now,' he says, in an accent that passes over both counties like a cloud, 'but there are still bits of Yorkshire that hang on.'

He stands and chats about the nuanced differences between Rastrick and Elland, both places he's lived in; after a while I can see he's getting impatient to go and deliver envelopes and padded bags and acres of Amazon cardboard, and I'm all for letting him get off, but Ian has another question, a vital one.

'What's the difference between Lancashire and Yorkshire people?' he asks.

The postman thinks hard and casts for the word he needs, waving letters to conjure it up.

'Yorkshire people are more, they're more ...' He's furrowing his brow. He's determined to get it right. He tries again. 'They're more ... philanthropic,' he says, triumphantly.

It's a word worth fishing for, especially as I don't think it's quite what he meant. I'll settle for it though, in a place and a time where, as T.S. Eliot (not a Yorkshireman) said, there's 'an intolerable wrestle with words and meanings'.

The newsletter of the Saddleworth White Rose Society is much more emphatic about the Yorkshireness of the place:

Although entirely on the western side of the Pennine Watershed, Saddleworth's links to the County of York can be traced back to Norman times. Saddleworth, or Quick as it was alternatively known, was throughout the Middle Ages a township in the West Riding of Yorkshire and had from the twelfth century been part of the Honour of Pontefract, the Yorkshire fiefdom of the de Lacy family, granted to them by the Conqueror.

And you can't say fairer than that. It's a shame it's not called Quick anymore, though. It could be twinned with Dedham in Norfolk.

In a café, we try to work out the story of how Yorkshire became the place it is and where Greenfield fits in, and a lot of it is to do with that Pennine Watershed. Like spies in a 1950s film about the Cold War, we use the coasters, spoons and other table furniture to make lines and landmarks.

The young lad behind the counter eyes us over his football magazine.

Geographically, the county's boundaries are drawn on three sides by the Pennines, the North Sea, and the wide Humber.

'You can't get further than the sea at that side, and the Pennines are a barrier at this side', Ian says, laying sachets of sugar out.

Looking south there's the River Trent, looking north there are the harsh moors that form a kind of theatrical safety curtain between us and the north east, and then there's the River Tees, a kind of half-and-half stretch of water, half-Yorkshire, half-somewhere else.

The lad behind the counter has nudged his mam and she's staring at us. She doesn't like us messing with her cruet. She doesn't realise it represents Yarm and Middlesbrough. It's time to pay and go, putting everything back in its rightful place because we're proper Yorkshire gentlemen.

I realise that many of my insights are going to come in cafés and pubs because that's where Yorkshire people gather to set the world to rights and discuss items of philosophical importance like Geoff Boycott's Hundredth Hundred for Yorkshire, and how long Yorkshire Pudding batter should stand before you pour it into the hot fat. The cafés should always be like this one; independent, with odd cups and saucers, the calendar a month or a season late, and askance glances when you ask for a ristretto.

Greenfield is one of the villages that are the constituent parts of the area known as Saddleworth; the others, of varying sizes, are Diggle, Delph, Dobcross, Denshaw and

Uppermill and, as I glance at the notes I'm making for my journey of discovery, it strikes me that lists of place-names are starting to feature prominently, partly because in Yorkshire, like anywhere else, they're little biographies, almanacs and encyclopaedias of the places they're describing, and partly because they can be a framework for this tale, scaffolding on my Grand Tour. I mean my Reyt Grand Tour. I mean my Champion Tour. I'm trying too hard.

Greenfield and Uppermill have names that feel self-explanatory; I've found out that Delph would have been a place of digging, and Dobcross was a settlement where wool was walked across to thicken, or full, it. It was also the place where John Schlesinger filmed *Yanks* in 1979, the epic about American airmen serving in England in World War II.

In Greenfield we pay homage to the flat-capped statue of Ammon Wrigley, the great Saddleworth poet and spokesperson for this neglected corner. He was born in 1861 in Denshaw and never moved far; his work dances with the rhythmic language of these valleys, sometimes in dialect, often in an inflected version of Standard English. His work has a combination of fragility and strength that I find nostalgic and uplifting in equal measure. A good example of this is his poem, 'The Watermill', which captures the idea of industrial power and the post-industrial neglect that has always gone hand-in-hand with it.

Down in the clough there stands a wreck,
a worn old watermill
where slimy pools of mud and reeds
lie in the wheelrace still

their broken walls, forlorn and weird
are black with age and grime
a lonely grave where buried lies
the toil of olden time.

As a poet he was loved and respected in his community and the publication of his second book was marked by a dinner at the Globe Inn in Uppermill where Wrigley was presented with a cheque for 100 guineas while his wife was given a watch; something for my wife and I to aspire to, especially the bit about the love and respect of the community.

And the watch. I've lost mine.

According to the local *Saddleworth Independent* newspaper, in 2014, on Yorkshire Day, 1 August, the Yorkshire Declaration of Integrity was read, or probably intoned, by Wrigley's statue at 11.39am, marking 1139 years since Yorkshire was created. The declaration, a stirring (in many senses of the word) invention of the Yorkshire Ridings Society, reads:

I (name) being a resident of the (West/North/East) Riding of Yorkshire (or City of York) declare: that Yorkshire is Three Ridings and the City of York, with these boundaries of 1134 years standing; that the address of all places in these Ridings is Yorkshire; that all persons born therein or resident therein and loyal to the Ridings are Yorkshire men and women; that any person or corporate body which deliberately ignores or denies the aforementioned shall forfeit all claim to Yorkshire status. These declarations made this Yorkshire Day (year). God Save The Queen!'

The chairman of the parish council, who was originally from Wakefield, laid a wreath of white roses at the foot of the statue and, again according to the *Saddleworth Independent*, someone who had been auditioned for *Britain's Got Talent* sang her own song, 'Live My Life In Yorkshire', despite suffering from a debilitating illness.

I stand beside Ammon and have my photograph taken; two Yorkshire bards together in perfect harmony; the Allus Right brothers. T'Shelley and T'Keats. This is definitely Yorkshire, no doubt at all. I think I can still smell traces of those white roses in the air, hear the echoes of the Yorkshire Declaration ringing in my ear.

Ian and I walk by the canal and suddenly we're surrounded by a gaggle of orange-suited council men, four of them in a loose configuration. They look like a tribute band to a forgotten group who had one novelty hit and then faded away.

'Have you seen a mattress?' one of them asks, his voice urgent with enquiry.

I shake my head. Ducks pass: animated versions of a mural on a terraced-house wall.

'Are you sure?' the tallest one says. 'Only we've been told there's been a report of a mattress.'

Ian Beesley reassures them. 'There's no mattress, but we did see a blanket further down.'

'Definitely a mattress that was reported,' a third man says.

It's as though an absurdist playwright has given each of them just one line to speak.

'I've got a question for you,' I say, looking at the one who hasn't opened his mouth yet. 'Are we in Yorkshire or Lancashire?'

They gaze at the canal. The tall one clears his throat and says 'We're just looking for a mattress,' and the unspoken words 'we don't want any trouble' glow.

Ian and I and the council men all look shifty, for no reason at all.

I knew it was going to be puzzling and problematic, this question of identity; I know that when you wander around disputed territory you have to mind your language, choose your words carefully. Here on the fringes of Yorkshire there's a sense of embarrassment. I wish I'd never opened my mouth. I was wrong; I'm not definitely and absolutely in Yorkshire at all. I'm somewhere hazier.

The one man who hasn't spoken yet speaks.

'We're here, aren't we?' he says, his voice louder than I thought it would be. 'We're here and we're looking for a mattress.'

More ducks pass, quacking this time. In accents that I really can't decipher.

It's time to move on, go back to Huddersfield and then home. I wonder if the man with the lamp will get back on at Berry Brow. I do hope so; I want Yorkshire to be a strange and poetic place. That should be part of the Yorkshire Declaration of Integrity.

THIS SKERN TASTES LIKE A STERN

RAIN. HARSH, UNYIELDING Yorkshire rain, siling it down in stair-rods and flamenco dancing on my conservatory roof. The forecast has gone from bad to worse and the zip on my cagoule is temperamental; indeed it's having a laugh at my expense. I pull it up and it stops like a lift between floors. I tug at it and it shudders a little bit and moves a little bit. There's no way it will keep the rain off me; indeed it might attract more rain to me.

I'm still determined to go to Hull though, the other Yorkshire extreme to Saddleworth on the far eastern side of the map, the other place where the core of the county may be found on its edges. I want to walk on the wild side of its boulevards and tenfoots and ring my wife from a white phonebox just because I can.

I've been to Hull a lot and I like it in the same way you like a cantankerous uncle who always tells the same anecdotes and inevitably buys joke rubber jam tarts to fool you with when you go to tea.

'Hey, Jack, these tarts are a bit rubbery! And are those glasses false?'

'Not at all, kid. I seem to have got a nail through my finger, though.'

I like the way Hull still believes its own myth that it's a remote place that you can only get to after days of hard travelling or weeks waiting between trains on lonely stations with no timetables and harsh flickering lights. Only the latter is true, of course.

Hull can often be defiantly part of Yorkshire, too: stand at a bus stop and listen to the way Hullonians say 'Humberside', like it's something on the end of their shoe, and you'll know what I mean. And, gloriously, it's going to be City of Culture in 2017, which I think is a wonderful thing. I did play a small part in Barnsley's bid for nomination in 2013, an honour that eventually went to Derry/Londonderry. We're not a city, which didn't help, and maybe the arty promotional T-shirt clung too well around what some journalists would call my ample contours during that photo-opportunity in the old market.

'Stand away from the tripe sign!' the photographer shouted. Not loudly enough, as it turned out.

I'm early for my train to Hull, so I splash up to the Frenchgate Centre in Doncaster between the railway station and the bus station for a cuppa; a man in a soaking suit passes me on the stairs, carrying a bike wheel and looking into space with almost architectural nonchalance. I sit and take in Doncaster's postmodernism; for a Roman settlement there's a heck of a lot of bright lights and strident fonts.

I'm fascinated by Doncaster like I'm fascinated by individual pieces of jigsaws seen in isolation and possibly from different jigsaws, and if I can fathom the town I can go a long way towards working out what Yorkshire is. Part of the enigma of the place is the reason I'm here now, waiting for the 08.24 to Bridlington via Hull; Doncaster's always been a place of transit, a stopping-off point for the trains to all directions of the compass, and for the A1 which used to arrow straight through the town. As a result, Doncaster has always felt to me a little more cosmopolitan than most of the rest of South Yorkshire.

At secondary school, a posh kid said to me, 'My mother says that Doncaster market is the only place round here you can get decent coleslaw.'

I replied that I preferred my slaw warm and asked him if he'd read the works of Go-eth, because I had.

Crossing-points like Doncaster attract transitory people and when I worked as Literature Development Worker (I soon sacked that title, and became Words Worker because the idea of literature can scare people off) I made poems with a group of young and not-so-young sex-workers who gathered round an education and advice centre called Streetreach that flourished down a side street far away from the racecourse. One of the women said she wrote poems, and that sometimes she read them to herself when she was out on the streets. I asked her if she was ever scared out there in the dark, and she replied with a beautiful and poetic phrase: 'the moon looks after me'. I asked her to write it in a poem, and she did, sharing it with me and the girls round a table at Streetreach.

There was a silence and then someone said, 'If somebody takes me to the pub today, I'll shoot myself.'

The kettle boiled, thankfully.

As a family, unaware at that time of Doncaster's frilly demi-monde, we always saw it as the sort of place you went to once or twice a year if you wanted to do a really big shop, one that involved Sellotape and string and a pit-stop for a sandwich in a steamy café. The 37 bus would chug slowly, glacially, through innumerable pit villages and the 14 bus would go on almost the same route in a slightly higher gear; the choice wasn't always ours to make because then, as now, the timetable had its own mind and played to its own changeable and shifting rules. Odd to write it now, but Doncaster felt slightly exotic: like Barnsley, it had coal mines, but it also had a place called the Plant where they made beautiful steam trains and it had a Rugby League team and a racecourse. The Plant was built by the Great Northern Railway in 1853 and, as a snapshot of productivity, in 1891 no less than 99 locomotives, 181 carriages and 1493 wagons were built to transport the workers generated by the Industrial Revolution to work and to Cleethorpes for fun. A number of famous railway engines were built in Doncaster, names whose whistles sound through the tunnels of the years: the *Flying Scotsman* is a native of Doncaster, as is the *Mallard*, which still holds the record for the fastest speed ever clocked up by a steam train, reaching an amazing 126mph in July 1938 on a stretch between Grantham and Peterborough. I pass that stretch often, and I always lift a metaphorical flat cap to those clever, clever engineers as I pass by.

Doncaster racecourse has held races since the 1500s and it's one of the largest in the country; it's a big part of how Doncaster presents itself to the world and in 1997 I was asked by Doncaster Libraries to present the winner of the Doncaster Libraries handicap with their trophy. I foolishly thought I had to write and recite a poem for the occasion and carried the masterpiece (it rhymed and scanned, as I remember) around all day in the pocket of my ill-fitting suit. When it came to the time to present the cup I grabbed the poem, reading it through a couple of times to get the rhythm right but the children's librarian, spotting me rehearsing, whispered in my ear that I didn't need it, I just needed to give the cup away. I did this, towering over the jockey, and then hurled my poem into a bin.

'I've backed them hosses and all,' a bloke in a comedy hat said. I nodded and walked away.

On race days, you see well-dressed people who have drunk so much that language and co-ordinated movement are only a faint muscle-memory, staggering through town as though they've just taken part in a mass trespass at Moss Bros. They've got suits on so their behaviour is considered eccentric rather than criminal and anti-social, of course.

The X19 is the express bus from Barnsley to Doncaster, launched in the early 1980s when one of the many property booms that bubbled to the surface of capitalism meant that somebody could sell the promise of a walk-in wardrobe in London and buy a castle in South Yorkshire, with a live-in underbutler and a jump-in moat. Early publicity material for the X19 advertised Darfield as being two hours from King's Cross, which amused my Uncle Charlie who said, 'Well, it's three hours to chuffing Grimethorpe,' exaggerating for comic effect, but only slightly.

Once, upstairs on the X19, a young lad turned to his granddad and announced that he felt sick. The silver-haired gentleman didn't help at all by continually reiterating to the rest of us what the boy had had for breakfast.

'I told you you shouldn't have given him jam and crackers!' he said to the boy's stoic mother. 'Jam and crackers! What kind of breakfast is jam and crackers? I ask you: jam and crackers!'

The boy then reiterated the jam and crackers in big aromatic crop circles all over the bus floor, much to the horror of some Seventh-day Adventists who were sitting behind him.

The Romans called Doncaster 'Danum', and they settled here because of the place's centrality; it's more or less in the middle of England and it's quite high up, and that makes it easy to defend and easy to transport goods to and from. The Normans took advantage of the topography when they built Conisbrough Castle on the outskirts of the town; this fantastic edifice dominates the valley and has survived years of pillage; the Parliamentarians tried to demolish it during the civil war and in the eighteenth and nineteenth centuries people just took stones for their own purposes. It's amazing that it's survived intact, and not as stone confetti.

A local head teacher once planned to take a group of pupils to the castle for a study day but couldn't get in touch with the offices so rang directory enquiries to get the number.

'It's okay, love, nobody lives there. It's a ruin,' the woman said.

Almost time for my train to the City of Culture. A man goes by on a mobility scooter, vaping. Two schoolboys are involved in a frantic gestural epic about buying sausage rolls. I walk down the stairs, ignoring the escalator because I want to add years to my life. Platform 3b, Sheffield to Bridlington. On time.

I board my carriage in the half-darkness and sit facing backwards. A woman aligns a banana on her table as though she's trying to find Magnetic North and another woman assembles a public face with the aid of a small round mirror. The train revs scarily and rattles out of the station towards the Enchanted East. As I gaze out of the window maybe I'm building this trip up a bit too much in my heart and my head. This flat landscape doesn't feel a lot like Yorkshire; the sky and the ground meet grudgingly in a sheen of rain, as another poet almost said. This could be Lincolnshire or Norfolk, those spongescapes that squelch obligingly when you visit them as though they're mattresses you're testing in a showroom.

At Goole, which like Uppermill isn't in Yorkshire any more, there's another white rose flag, soggy in the back garden of a house near the Victoria Pleasure Grounds, the beautifully named home of Goole AFC. Goole was once at the extreme edge of the West Riding and I imagine that here, like Saddleworth, Yorky diaspora feelings run high.

We went on a school trip to Goole docks from Low Valley Juniors, which felt so otherworldly that it might as well have been Paris. Some of the infants believed it was. The boats appeared to be sailing across the fields towards the huge cranes at the dockside, like vessels in a fable. Goole AFC are called The Vikings, after all.

Hull is, in the Yorkshire and non-Yorkshire sense of the word, grand, as befits the twelfth largest city in the UK. It's actually called Kingston upon Hull, possibly to distinguish it from Kingston upon Thames, and it's the only place I've ever been that has a station called Paragon. The station's only called Paragon because it used to be on Paragon Street and not through any kind of inanimate nominative determinism, but I always enjoy arriving at a paragon, even in a cloudburst.

The rain, by now, is asserting itself hugely. It's mocking any attempts by mere humans to keep themselves dry. I imagine that in a moment I'll see somebody ushering household pets into a big wooden vessel, two-by-two.

As you get off the train, you're met by the poet Philip Larkin created in sculptural form by Martin Jennings; he appears to be walking away from you towards a draft of a poem that he may have dropped, perhaps the one where he refers to the adjacent station hotel as being a place where silence was laid like carpet, although I remember it wasn't the night I stayed. It was as loud as the laying of new lino. Hull embraces Larkin awkwardly, like men at a funeral with other men they once borrowed £5 from, and in turn, he said of it, 'I never thought of Hull until I was there.'

In 2003 I was appointed poet in residence with the Humberside Police, a gig which I guess Larkin wouldn't have aspired to; he'd have seen it as more a job for a clown than a poet. Hello. I'm here. That job told me a lot about the police and a lot about Hull and a fair amount about the public perception of poetry, particularly in Yorkshire.

I'd done an after-dinner speech for a gathering of top coppers in the echoing function room of a posh hotel in Scunthorpe and David Westwood, the Chief Constable of Humberside, had confronted me in the car park afterwards. Well, his gloved hand had. I was waiting in the Scunthorpe cold-steel cold for my lift home and his car drove by me and shushed to a halt. The window hummed down and the aforementioned gloved hand appeared, pointing. It was almost the start of a pop video for a remake of Dave Berry's 'The Crying Game'.

From the back seat, he said, 'You could be our poet. You could be ...' He paused to chuckle '... our Beat Poet.'

'What would that entail?' I asked, hoping he wouldn't frisk me and find the sachets of sugar I'd lifted for my mother-in-law to put on her apple pies.

'You can go anywhere you want and write poems about it,' he said.

'Round Hull on a Friday night?' It felt strange speaking to a hand and a window.

'Yes, if you wish.'

And that's how I found myself outside a nightclub at two o'clock in the morning clutching a notebook, surrounded by a camera crew and some girls who were wearing skirts that were shorter than the reign of Edward VIII.

It seems strange, as the new century matures, and actual and intellectual poverty dance together under that cosy word Austerity, that a police force would even want to have a poet in residence, but in the early years of the new millennium it seemed that there wasn't anywhere a poet wouldn't be made welcome. Poets were placed in London

Zoo, at Marks & Spencer's, and on a North Sea oil rig, and expected to inspire and be inspired. It was a Cleggish idea in Pooterish times.

In my residency, as well as going round Hull's baroque and dazzling nightlife, I went out with some traffic cops chasing stolen cars down the M180 with the sirens blaring and the lights flashing, and I was present at a very sensitive interview between an officer and a young woman in a tiny house who'd just been burgled. He held her hand as she stared out of the window with red eyes. I took notes myself for a poem I never wrote.

My poetic craft was tested to the limit when we went on a dawn raid on a terraced street.

At the briefing, which was held in a room on an industrial estate lit by a flickering fluorescent light, a senior copper said to me, 'Well, to put it briefly, we're after a bad lad and a daft lad. We don't really mind if the daft lad gets away but we want the bad lad. We really want the bad lad.'

He later used a phrase that resonated with poetry: 'I say it as I see it. I call a spade a fork,' which is something I've wanted to say ever since.

At the dawn raid I shivered with my notebook, glimpsing a side of Yorkshire I'd never seen before. A dozen uniformed officers ran to a terraced house that had a tired-looking bush in the small front garden. They shouted 'Police! Open Up!' more times than they do on the TV and I briefly and heretically thought, 'This is more exciting than poetry.' One of them smashed the door down and they all rushed in, none of them getting stuck in the door like poets might have. I scribbled furiously, noting the sounds and the sights. I noted that someone who must have been a health-and-safety copper spread a blanket on the floor so the kids wouldn't get glass in their feet.

In the end, they got the soft lad but the bad lad got away. I stared at my poem. Maybe there are some places poetry can't go. In terms of productivity, it wasn't much of a residency. In terms of Yorkshire-enlightenment, it was.

Outside the nightclub, I said, 'Tell me a poem, girls,' brightly. Or rather, I shouted it above the din called City Weekend.

'Stand closer to them,' the director hissed through the drizzle. I couldn't stand any closer to them, particularly the one on the left, or we'd have had to get married as the old music-hall joke goes.

'I like beer and I like wine and I like having a really good time,' the tall one said, then they all said it together, shrieking with laughter. It had echoes of the birth of hip-hop in the Bronx in the 1970s although it was colder and wetter. Larkin would have nodded approvingly, I hope. He liked rhyme and scansion and he liked it when form matched content. Then they rushed off into the club before the cameraman could ask them to say it again from a different angle. It wasn't just the poem, fine and spontaneous as it was, it was the way they said it that was beautiful. Their accents were spectacular and hard to render in print without sounding patronising: 'Ah lark beer an ah lark wahn an ah lark havin a really good tahm,' is as near as I can get.

In the station hotel in the early hours, as I tried to embrace a few short minutes of sleep, people kept thundering by my room shouting, 'Good naht!' 'Good naht!' 'We've had a good naht!' 'We've had a raht good naht!' 'Ah feel a bit sterned!'

At around five o'clock in the morning, I heard somebody from South Yorkshire, probably on a stag night in the big city, shout 'Good neet!', to be met by howls of derision. 'He said "Good neet!"' people from Hull chorused on the crowded 18-30 party venue that was the corridor, although they couldn't quite say 'Good neet!' because they were from Hull and when they tried to say it the vowels and consonants got mixed up and gasped for breath and couldn't move.

For the first and only time in my life so far I wished I'd asked room service to send a socio-linguist up on a trolley to explain the subtle differences between Good Neet and Good Naht.

The Hull accent was born in Scandinavia and refined through the mouths of generations of fishermen shouting to be heard above the howling wind in a Force 11, and from the singing of the women who gutted the fish. It's one of the most gorgeous accents I've ever had in my ears and one of the purposes of my latest rainy trip on the 08.24 was to overhear somebody say 'that skern tastes like a stern', which, of course, translates as 'that scone tastes like a stone'. This would necessitate a visit to a café for a scone. Or a spoonful of jam and some crackers.

I pass Larkin and plunge into the city. Figures hunched against the weather scuttle for buses and into shops, trying to spend as little time as possible in the harsh and wide-open air. I wished I was a socialist-realist artist so that I could capture them in all their glory but in language all I can say is that grimacing figured strongly and umbrellas blew inside out at a rate of one every six seconds, which is almost a record, even in Yorkshire in the rain. I walk down towards the Ferens Gallery, a marvellous temple of art that, on this day of mobile floods dropping straight from the sky, beckons me in. I stand in the foyer dripping like a melting snowman, grinning apologetically at an attendant with a mop.

The gallery is named after another one of those philan-thropic rich men who've made such a difference to the Yorkshire landscape, moulding it to their image, to their enthusiasms and hopes and desires. Thomas Ferens was the founder of Reckitt and Sons, who made, philosophi-cally, cleanliness, and, practically, black lead, starch, household polish and laundry blue. Because the women of the working class were fanatical cleaners, Thomas Ferens made a lot of money and gave some of it away.

I like to think that a small artistic fire ignited in his heart when he gazed at the absence of colour that is black lead. I'd like to think that he was a deep and abstract thinker, making the conceptual leap from the donkey-ston-ing of a front step in the sunshine to the painting of a portrait that would hang on the white wall of a gallery, contemplating the idea that they're both branches of human endeavour, that the possing of vests in a sink in a hot and steaming kitchen was on a par with the creation of a watercolour of a beach scene at Filey as the tide went out. Maybe that's just what I want to believe. Maybe it's Alec Clegg speaking through me.

Ferens was one of those industrialists who believed that he should be fully engaged in civic life; he became an MP and a JP and spoke in the Houses of Parliament on women's suffrage, and perhaps the heart of a scholar and an aesthete did beat under the waistcoat and fob. Maybe his soul was more bright laundry blue than deep black lead. Or maybe he just wanted a big memorial: the gallery is named after him, after all, as are several other places in the city. Perhaps it's just rich man's graffiti monogramming the streets.

I always feel a fraud coming in to a gallery or a museum out of the rain. I want to say to the attendants and to the woman who's mopping up my drips, 'I come in places like this when it's sunny, you know! I like art! You're a temple of culture not a bus shelter!' But I don't. Mind you, I shouldn't stride past old masters but I do. Maybe it's something to do with the heavy frames and the way they often seem to point straight at the past. I know they have much to teach me but I prefer the new and the fresh and the untried and the avant-garde. Avant practised, some people say, but they're wrong. The new is where it's at, man.

In gallery 9, the place in the Ferens where the new lives and breathes, there's a touring exhibition called '3am', based around the idea of that middle-of-the-night no-time. My eye is taken by a simple film of some people walking through a wood in the pitch dark. All you can see are their torches, sometimes a few, sometimes many. They could be coppers chasing pickets in 1984 in Armthorpe. They could be kids from a church youth club out on a midnight hike through Great Houghton Woods in 1974 like me and the girlfriend who became my wife were once. They could be beaters on the Wentworth Estate. They could be the Beat Poet and the Beat Coppers looking for rhymes in some waste ground. They could, simplistically, be me looking for Yorkshire.

I leave the gallery and wander through the storm that's becoming monotonous, persistent and unvarying. My glasses are freckled and weeping and I can hardly see where I'm going.

I'm glad I'm not on a fishing boat having had a hearty breakfast of jam and crackers. Hull's wealth was built on water and fish-scales, on vast fleets of trawlers bouncing and pitching above the so-called 'Silver Pits' of the North Sea, so full of fish that they seemed to want to jump into the welcoming nets. Hard to believe now, but in the 1950s almost 8000 trawlermen worked out of Hull, away for days and weeks at a time, coming back for a weekend to spend money like the 'three-day-millionaires' they became known as. Like the coal and steel industries, the fishing industry declined in the late twentieth century. I remember my dad pointing at a news report of the Cod Wars in the 1970s and saying, 'That'll be the end of them.' The TV was black-and-white and the towering waves were grey. The Cod Wars did indeed speed up the decline of mass fishing and, perhaps because it's raining, I can't help but think that so much of present-day Yorkshire is about regret, a remembrance of times past in an all-embracing Proustian sense that's just a long song for all the things we've lost.

I make my wet way to the Kardomah café, a new venture a scone's throw from the Ferens. It's also a gallery and a performance space and it's part of the buzz that's building around the City of Culture. It's trying, and succeeding in the main, to recreate the atmosphere of the old Kardomah Coffee House in Swansea where Dylan Thomas and his bohemian mates would glug hot drinks and spout arty bollocks long into the South Wales afternoon, saying things like, 'This bath bun tastes like a brick, isn't it!'

The rain has relented a little. It's just pouring now. Outside the Kardomah, two men with designer stubble are looking at estate agent's brochures which are turning to papier mâché in their hands. It may be designer stubble or it may be sticky street droppings blown into their faces by the morning's gale. They stand at the Kardomah's door. English isn't their first language.

'Houses?' one says, pointing at the café.

'Coffee house!' I reply, miming a slurp, pretending to take a cup from a saucer. I realise almost as soon as I'd said it that I shouldn't have included the word 'house'. Maybe I should have said 'coffee shop'.

'Rent a house?' the other one asks. He really is very handsome, despite, or because of, the rain. His cheekbones should have a preservation order slapped on them. Not too hard, in case they break.

'Buy a coffee!' I say, creating an even more elaborate Tati-esque elaborate dumb show of me pouring coffee into a cup and tasting it. I open the door, thinking I've convinced them that double espresso is not the new single-storey property and they precede me into the café. A young woman approaches them and their shoulders straighten perceptibly and their stubble seems to glow.

I feel like I'm in a daytime version of that torches-in-the-wood film I saw at the Ferens and that somehow, in

Yorkshire in the twenty-first century, we're all looking for something that we can't quite grasp. I am, anyway. I should rewrite that Paul Simon song that goes, 'We've all gone to look for America,' replacing America with words like Pocklington and Mytholmroyd. I might have to rewrite the tune a bit as well, mind you.

One of the men says to the young woman, as she tries to proffer them menus, 'House? Rent house?' For some reason, he mimes knocking on a door. I'm in a mime festival; perhaps the endless rain has robbed everybody in Hull of the power of speech. She instantly points them to the estate agents next door. One of them begins to leave. The other takes the menu and looks closely at it, as though he's studying the bottom line of an optician's chart. Maybe thick, unforgiving glasses didn't go with his image and cheekbones. His mate taps him on the shoulder and he steps reluctantly away, smiling dazzlingly at the waitress and saying something in a tongue I can't fathom.

'Table for one?' I say, forlornly, and I sit down. My cheekbones are blunt and my stubble is uneven and early-morning accidental. I order a single espresso and a scone.

'Do you want jam and butter with your scone?' she asks, and I'm disappointed. She doesn't say *skern*.

I say 'pardon?' just to get her to say it again but she repeats the word scone, with the long o. No skerns here.

The espresso lifts my mood, as espressos are hardwired to do. The scone is lovely, if crumbly, and when I get up to pay a lot of it is scattered across my jumper. I try an experiment. I'll thank her in the voice of someone from Hull, just to see if the Hull accent is really unique and unrepeatable by somebody like me, from Yorkshire but not born within sight of the Prince's Quay Shopping Centre.

I'm not very good at doing accents except my own so of course my view is that there's no point doing any accent apart from a Darfield one. It would be like trying to get a nightingale to sing like a corncrake.

I was once making a radio series which involved eating and describing a lot of pies. I wanted to call it *Crust Almighty* but the BBC wouldn't let me because it went out on a Sunday afternoon so we called it *Who Ate All the Pies?* and I had to go into a shop in Dundee and order a pie. In Dundee a pie is called a peh and in order to say 'Could you make that an onion pie, my good man?' you have to say 'an an inyin yin an aw'. I was fitted, round the corner from the shop down an alley next to an overflowing skip, with a hidden microphone that nestled under my McMillan tartan scarf, the one with the yellow streak down the middle.

I walked purposefully to the counter and said, 'Ah'll hae a peh, pet. An an inyin yin an aw.'

She looked at me witheringly and said, 'Ye're no frae roond here, are ye?'

I pay in the Kardomah and say, 'Thanks, pet, that skern was one on its ern.' The girl looks at me as though I want to be directed to the estate agents with the Stubble Brothers or a bank to get a lern.

'Thank you,' she says; her Hull accent has been educated away, perhaps. A degree from somewhere like UEA or Durham. A crowded bar during Fresher's Week and a couple of snide remarks from people who think they have no accent at all about the first-year student who sounds like she's just stepped off a trawler and the accent begins to wither and die. That's just speculation, of course. She might be from Hessle.

I walk back to Paragon station with the rain behind me, slapping me on the back, crackling on my cagoule hood like I'm a tent. A one-man tent. Wonderfully, I see the two house-hunters again, gazing in the window of a bookshop, holding the estate-agent literature above their heads to fail to ward off the rain.

MAD GEOFF AND MAURICE

AFTER THE HULL visit, my quiff is more or less destroyed; the constant striding into the belting rain has beaten it up and left it for dead, mewling feebly for help. I like my grey quiff; it feels like a symbol of who I am, in the same way that some people identify with their vintage cars or the model of York Minster they've made from used matches. It's aged with me and as the world has turned and turned its shape has stayed constant although its colour has faded. The quiff was very much a part of the Yorkshire hairstyle-scape when I was growing up; miners on days off would painstakingly sculpt theirs in front of cracked mirrors in pub toilets before going out into the tap room to croon along with the turn's version of 'It's Now Or Never', swivelling their hips as much as years of hard manual work would allow, their knees creaking like stairs. The quiff felt Exotic, a rebellion against the short-back-and-sides and the pudding-basin cut, so that when the never-ending cycle of the alarm clock and the job and the deep sleep on the armchair after tea got too monochrome and dull, there was always your self-standing quiff to remind you of a world beyond. 'Slicked-back slabheeads' my friend

Ray Hearne from Rotherham calls them, and that'll do for me. I feel, as I rub my hands through my slabhead quiff, that every Yorkshireman and woman who's ever been bequiffed is standing behind me in a long, long line, adjusting their topiary too. I'm living history, an exhibit in the Museum of Me.

Hull, though. Hull. Flipping Hull. It's rendered the quiff ungafferable or, in the language of hairspray ads, unmanageable. It's time for a visit to Mad Geoff's for a tidy up.

Mad Geoff has been a fixture on the Darfield hairdressing scene for over a quarter of a century; he'd been a barber when he was younger but, in his words, 'long hair finished me off', and he went long-distance lorry driving. As fashions changed, he emerged from behind the wheel and tried his hands at hairdressing again, and he's never looked back. In his little shop you'll find conclusive evidence that the idea that Yorkshiremen are dour and uncommunicative is a downright lie. It's a noise-filled meeting-place, a pub with no beer, a haven for those who have never adjusted to a world with BBC2 in it and a version of those sunlit open spaces where ancient Greek philosophers used to meet to invent things like democracy and verse drama before tea.

Mad Geoff's nickname is lost in the echoes of South Yorkshire time, perhaps dwelling in the same shimmery and indecisive place as the reasons why Little Houghton is called Plevna, and the knowledge of the origin of the phrase, 'He were stood there like Clem or Souse'. Some say he's called Mad because when he first appeared at the back of the adjustable barber's chair all those years ago he would appear to physically go crazy, taking off more hair than you wanted him to at lightning speed, his fingers a blur, so that all the men of the village quickly learned to say, 'Just a trim, Geoff. A light trim. A very light trim. Hardly do anything at all,' and Geoff would reply, 'Ah! Tha means a glancing blow!' and hair would cascade to the floor and scatter across the lino. The newly shorn would go home and members of their family would say, using non-PC language, 'Who's tha been to see? Cochise else Geronimo?'

Others say he was given the name because he habitually wore moleskin trousers and a bow tie which, in the sartorially conservative Dearne Valley, is madness, the equivalent of sporting a diamante-studded ball gown and a fascinator made from Yorkshire Pudding crusts rampant. As someone once said to me on the last 226 bus, 'Who would have thought we'd ever be wearing pink shirts and drinking water we've bought in a bottle from a shop?' The fact is, though, that Geoff is a great raconteur and if the walls of his shop could speak they'd keep after-dinner crowds entertained until long after the dessert had gone cold and the waitresses had begun clearing up.

I've gazed at myself in Geoff's unforgiving mirror for decades as he snips and watched my jowls fall along with the region's prospects; it's hard to believe now but when Geoff first arrived in the late 1980s, my hair was as dark as shoe polish, my kids were little, and some of the local pits were still open and doing all right, considering.

I've always been lucky enough to have a good head of hair, unlike all the other men in my family who follow a more predictable male pattern towards baldness. One meaning of McMillan is 'son of the tonsured one', after all. My hair grows straight up from my head like the bristles of a shaving brush or the false locks of a fright wig. My mother used to despair of my privet-hedge barnet and tried, over many years, to get it to go in what she called 'a proper style' with a regimented side parting but, like Robert Mitchum in *The Night of the Hunter*, it would never be tamed.

The first time I went to Geoff's, he asked me what I wanted and I said, 'Do your best,' which has evolved over time into 'the usual tidy up, please' because we understand each other well and we both know that, in the end, not that much can be done with it.

Geoff's shop used to be the Co-op chemist and the drawers where he keeps his scissors were full of bandages and bottles of Indian Brandee and Something for the Weekend and this little space continues to exemplify the changes in this part of Yorkshire in miniature, from one service industry to another. When I first went, the remaining pitmen and the recently redundant would come in to swap tales of life underground at Houghton Main and Darfield Main and faraway exotic pits like Kimberworth and Ledston Luck. Now those ex-miners are coming less often because they've got less hair or they don't get out of the house or they're simply not with us anymore, and the talk is of football and cruises and what the grandkids are doing.

When I walk in, though, on this day, I'm in luck: two old faceworkers have come to have their comb-overs enhanced.

It's an Oral History degree with local radio murmuring in the background about travel and time and the consequences of inclement weather.

The man sitting in the chair is talking about a day when the pit manager was showing a visitor around.

'He sez to me, "How many men work in this mine, my man?", and I sez to him, "Not enough, feller!" Look on his face! Tha'd think ah'd shit in his snap tin and pissed in't Dudley!'

The room murmurs and shudders with laughter at this oft-told tale, so the man in the chair shares the line again as though he gets paid for repeats, standing slowly up from his seat and turning to address the audience.

'Tha'd think ah'd shit in his snap tin and pissed in't Dudley!'

There is slightly less laughter the second time, as there always is. One or two people look at their shoes. A chap in a cardigan reads an old copy of a magazine about vintage buses. The man in the chair delivers his gag again. It's as though a battery is fading on a torch that's shining from the past. The laughter shuffles away, towards the door. It doesn't stop him saying it again.

The other old pitman says, with a wheeze of finality, 'Some on 'em still think they're darn t'oil.'

That little tale highlights for me the dangers inherent in attempting to write down the glorious linguistic and cultural triumph that is Yorkshire language, a language that flourishes in the air and on the ear but less well on the page. You'll have read my previous stabs at Hullonian and you'll perhaps have decided that the main place people get lost in Yorkshire is In Translation. There are unfamiliar words and concepts, of course, but they're easy to illuminate.

A snap tin, often made in metal by ACME, was what miners took their sandwiches down the pit in. As an insufferably pretentious sixth-former I took my packed lunch to school in one to show solidarity from the poets to the working class. I cringe and want to origami myself into a blushing paper bird and fly away when I think about it. Especially when I remember the little two-finger KitKat and the satsuma. A Dudley was a water-bottle for quenching thirst at the face; the derivation is unclear but it gave its name to a pub in Goldthorpe, the Rusty Dudley, which achieved national and international notoriety when the regulars there paraded a burning coffin of Margaret Thatcher on the occasion of her death, singing and shouting slogans like 'the Iron Lady will rust in Hell'.

Names of things are easy; they can be explained, given context and history. On the other hand, t'elephant in't room is the t followed by the apostrophe which is always used to represent a particular trope of Yorkshire dialect but which solidifies in unforgiving print something that hardly ever happens in real life. Nobody lining Mad Geoff's on his benches and chairs has ever said, on a Saturday afternoon when Barnsley are playing at home, 'I'm off to't match,' with the t' hanging in the air, sharp and gleaming as a tack. If you listen carefully, as I have done for many years, you'll notice that the t and the apostrophe are merely hinted at, almost unsaid like the letters of those ghost signs you see advertising things like Bile Beans on the gable ends of that house in York. The sound, the inflection and the intention should perhaps just be represented by the apostrophe alone, or maybe just by a gap in the sentence, a hole in language's carefully constructed wall. I will, at times in this book, use the t', but I'm doing it until I can invent something else.

It's my turn in the chair.

'Tidy him up?' Geoff asks, and I nod.

The anecdote-salesman pays his £5, in a handful of coins; it's recently gone up from four.

'I'm a pensioner, tha knows. I'm sponging off you lot. Five pounds!' He repeats the amount as though this will lessen the pain and perhaps get Geoff to offer him a discount.

Geoff responds by passing him a shiny brochure from a women's hairdressers in Barnsley, saying, 'You can go there if you want. Dry cut for 15 quid.' There's a barely audible gasp from the room. A car horn hoots outside.

'That's my son come for me in the estate,' the old man says and exits Mad Geoff's in a flurry of guttural and phleghmy farewells.

The man who was reading the vintage bus magazine is now studying the price list from the hairdresser's with vague disbelief. Suddenly, like Columbo, the man who's just been out comes back in. His son toots forlornly. Twice, three times. It could almost be Morse Code.

'I've got a question for yer all,' he says, surveying the hairy waiting audience. 'Who knocks up the knocker-up?'

And then he's gone again, slamming the door.

There's a momentary pause and then the cape is whisked over me and the snipping begins.

'At least you get a young lass pressing against your back in them places in town,' somebody says, 'that's worth paying extra for.'

Cyril walks by in his trilby; a man shouts, 'How many?' and Cyril replies, 'Two this week; both pink. I hung 'em on't bowling club gate.' Everybody knows he's referring to the discarded bras he finds on his morning walk through the park to the paper shop.

The park was opened in 1923 as a miners' welfare park and my earliest memory of it is getting my head stuck in the railings of the Big Slide.

'Too many brains,' said Geoff Stables's dad, also called Geoff, as people first eased, then dragged, me out.

Cyril often finds underwear near where the crazy golf used to be and tells me about it early in the morning when he's lighting his pipe outside the paper shop, his hat emerging through the smoke.

The man's question, as he knew it would, gets everybody going, and the consensus is that, at least round here, it would be the Valley Ghooast, a shadowy figure who was seen, or half-seen, in the 1950s, roaming the area between Darfield and Wombwell between midnight and the time the knocker-up had to go and perform his morning duties which consisted of hitting upstairs windows with a long stick, a satisfying yet limited career path. Yorkshire is laced with legends and fables of this kind, lighting up pub-talk and bus-stop rattle and bar-room chit-chat; maybe the essence of the county falls somewhere between the Valley

Ghooast and the knocker-up, between the fable and the verifiable truth.

George adjusts his hearing aid until it emits a sharp and piercing whistle and says, 'What about the Owl in the Tower?' Everybody nods apart from a younger man who's only lived in the village for 25 years. George is giving what amounts to a celebrity lecture at a submission to UNESCO's Intangible Heritage Committee.

'We all thought it were a giant owl hiding in the church, sitting in the mechanism of the clock and slowing it down. People would stand around at the foot of the church tower and you could hear it breathing. Or maybe it was the clock, slowing …'

There is a silence that hangs like memory. The local radio is playing 'Simply The Best' by Tina Turner, very quietly. It could almost be a choir of toddlers in the café next door.

'They reckoned that owl flew down and took a babby out of a pram,' somebody says. The silence grows. 'A big babby and all. Not a little 'un.' I never want to leave this place. It's like *1001 Nights* in here.

A week passes and I'm wandering by Mad Geoff's on my way to Darfield Museum or, to give it its full and glorious title, the Maurice Dobson Museum and Heritage Centre. I glance into the barber's and, because we're at a certain end of the week, it's not Mad Geoff behind the chair, it's his mate Bu; he beckons me in and shows me an enormous and ugly, unless you're a fish, stuffed cod on the wall. 'What's tha reckon to that?' he says, and I stand on tiptoes and take a photograph of it.

'Tell him about it, Bu,' somebody says from the recesses of a flat cap, and he does, but as he's recounting the story, the talk in the shop is also about the new chair Geoff and Bu are trying to buy on eBay as the business expands and Geoff's grandson is taken on as an apprentice, so the fish-tale is interspersed at times with chair banter and, as an unexpected sidebar, a gently delivered self-contained George and the Glasses Anecdote which arrives unannounced at the party. It's an exercise in complex Yorkshire polyphony.

Bu begins. 'See that date on that plaque under't fish?' he says, and I put my glasses on and stand in front of it; I can just make out a faded 1998. Barnsley were still in the Premier League. Just. Fading. Three sent off against Liverpool and Jan Aage Fjortoft tackling a pitch-invading fan.

'Geoff's lad caught that in Whitby and it were't biggest fish landed in Whitby that year.'

A man with bright white teeth asks, 'Why can't tha get a brand new chair? Be better than an old 'un.' Bu isn't put off.

'Because the one he's sitting in is 70 years old, it's vintage. It used to belong to Scrivener and then Shaky Pete bought it.'

The man in the chair wheezes, 'Scrivener. He used to cut my hair, but I never let Shaky Pete near it.'

Bu continues. 'And we want to get one to match, or as near as we can. So he took the fish home and said to Geoff, "Let's put it in't freezer, and then when we fancy a bit of cod, we can hack a bit off and have it for tea and it'll be a reminder of the day I caught the big fish in Whitby."'

The man with the gleaming teeth is ruminating. 'Scrivener. He could cut hair. He could cut it. Never went to Shaky Pete.' Bu glances at him, ignoring the fact that he keeps saying the same thing in slightly different ways.

'Well, this is Scrivener's old chair, like I said. So Geoff waits till his lad's gone out and he gets the cod out of the freezer and takes it to his taxidermist mate and said, "Stuff that for me but don't tell our lad."'

The idea that a barber has a taxidermist as a mate doesn't strike anybody else in the room as unusual; I feel as though I'm being pitched a new animated version of *Sweeney Todd*.

'He goes out and buys a big bit of cod off Wombwell market and puts it in the freezer. And every now and then they have some, and his lad says, "Eee, you can tell it were caught off Whitby!" And, do you know, that lad knows nowt. He knows nowt at all.'

He pauses for dramatic effect. A man in a blue coat of the sort non-league football managers used to wear before the advent of the Premier League says, in a quiet but insistent voice, 'I bumped into George yesterday on Nanny Marr Road. I was testing out my new glasses. I was trying to read a number plate 25 yards away. George looks at me and says, "What does tha want to see that fer for?"'

Bu continues. 'Then, after a bit, when they've eaten most of the cod out of the freezer, Geoff comes in one day and gives him the stuffed fish, mounted and all. I bet his face was a picture. I bet he looked like that theer cod.'

I want to stand up and applaud.

Another man says, 'I never went to Scrivener's, but I did go to Harry Holden's for years.'

A car pulls up outside and after a slamming of doors a man comes in. 'Yes, but who knocks up the knocker-up?' he says, brightly. It's time to go. I emerge into the chilly Darfield autumn; blown and swirling leaves are almost a murmuration of starlings, but not quite.

I'm on the way to the museum for my monthly volunteering stint as a meeter-and-greeter. In times of a thin public purse in Yorkshire, my wife and I reckoned it was time we stood up to be counted: 1, 2. So once every four weeks I stand in the shop and tick people off as they come in and take them round and she makes teas and coffees and toasted teacakes in the café-gallery.

The Maurice Dobson Museum and Heritage Centre is, as I proudly tell anybody who will listen and some who don't want to, the only museum in the world named after a gay cross-dressing ex-Scots Guard. As far as I know. During my childhood Maurice and his partner Fred ran the corner shop at the end of Church Street that is now the museum; my mother would tell me tales about them walking hand in hand, looking like Barbara Cartland and Joanna Lumley with Adam's apples, down the lane to Houghton Main passing the pitmen and courting couples along the way. They didn't always wear frocks, of course, only on special occasions. When I went into the shop as a boy on a Friday night on my way to the Church Lads' Brigade for a Jubbly, Maurice would often be sitting in front of the counter on an elegant high stool, wearing a powder-blue suit and smoking a cigarette in a long holder.

Fred would be behind the counter, quiet and almost invisible in the kind of brown smock that *Open All Hours*-type shopkeepers wore in those days.

Maurice would lean forward on the stool at a dangerous and precipitous angle and say, in a voice that was part Barnsley, part Noël Coward and part Kenneth Williams:

'If you say bugger I'll give you a Spangle. Go on: say bugger and I'll let you have a Spangle.'

Fred would shake his head in mock-despair and the light from the bulb hanging from the low ceiling would dance on his gleaming pate. I settled for a quarter of rhubarb-and-custard and got away without swearing because, even though there was no CCTV in those days, my mother would have known.

'Well,' Maurice would say, pouting, 'I'll tell you this: if you had a job and you worked for me I wouldn't pay you in bloody clear mints. Bloody clear mints. And that's swearing.'

I often think that Maurice and Fred are a great example of Yorkshire tolerance, but I have to admit there was an ounce or two of fear mixed in with the respect they were shown because, being ex-army men (rumour had it that Fred had been in the marines), any bequiffed youth-club goers or lairy kids on their way to the chip shop would get a clip if they tried chucking homophobic insults before or after they got their change. It's true, though, that they were a fully accepted part of the Darfield tapestry when I was younger, alongside Mr Coward the milkman and Mr Leech the other milkman and Billy McHale the Darfield poet and Mrs Dove the fearsome librarian who introduced me to

Henry Rider Haggard with the words, 'Ian, I think you're ready for this.'

The old West Riding County Council library used to be at the bottom of Snape Hill, near Low Valley school in what's now a chip shop where, if you buy enough fish and chips, they give you a free bottle of pop. The old library was previously a corner shop and, if you could get Mrs Dove to stand and lean in the right position by the Junior Fiction, you could get the faded words RINGTON'S TEA back to front on her forehead. That gave you a lot of points.

Maurice and Fred were great collectors of antiques and when Maurice died, Fred having gone to the great cash-and-carry in the sky some years before, he left the house and the contents to the Darfield Amenities Society to create the Darfield Museum. After years of form filling and grant applications and grant re-applications, as the old millennium turned into the new millennium with an audible click, the Maurice Dobson Museum and Heritage Centre opened.

Maurice would have been proud, I reckon. As you walk in, I'll be standing (without the suit and the cigarette in the holder) where he used to stand. I'll write down the numbers as people enter and, once they've had a cuppa and teacake, I'll take them round the rooms and tell them all I know, which isn't much. And what I don't know I'll make up. It's only Yorkshire history, after all, and that's part of the glory of this place. We know that sometimes, more than sometimes, we exaggerate to make a point and we emulsion the truth in glossy paint-by-numbers colours that make the facts seem shinier and, paradoxically, more real. Perhaps we really are a Yorkshire of the mind, a Yorkshire that each of us, whether we're from here or not, can invent. Who knocks up the knocker-up? Well, anybody you like.

We open at 10am and there's a flurry of visitors to the café to start with, and then a family arrive. They're staying with relatives in the village and they've come for a look round. It's my job to take them upstairs and talk them around the exhibits; we go up past the poster for the last ever programme at the Empire Cinema in 1956 when they bowed out with *White Christmas* and I like to think of a top-coated scattering of Darfield residents shuffling out into a freezing night with dandruffs of sleet in the air, wishing each other 'Merry Christmas' and 'Good night', and popping into Maurice and Fred's for a little bottle of whisky and some TUC biscuits to take home.

I'm both a good museum guide and a bad museum guide at the same time; I think I'm good because I'm enthusiastic but I'm bad because my garrulous enthusiasm keeps running away with me and I want to tell them stories; perhaps they're more interested in those old and unidentifiable farming implements than they are in my recounting of the story of Mad Geoff and the Stuffed Cod, which in the short time since I left the barber's has become an epic, but I doubt it. A man from the cricket club down the road comes in and sits stolidly all day, going through the club's archives which are held in trust, or rather held in a cardboard box, upstairs at the museum. The family are gazing at the display about the football factory which for some people is the name of a film about hooligans but for us is a vital source of employment in the village.

I recall Mitre Sports being halfway down Snape Hill, next to the Victoria pub which later, after the strike and with the aid of payoff money, became a tiny brewery called the Hewer & Brewer. In the football factory case at the museum there's a photograph of what looks like an implement of torture; it's a device that women would clutch between their knees as they put the sections of a football together. As I talk to the visitors and gesticulate to animate this tiny slice of history, I see my face reflected in the glass of the case. Frankly, I look like I don't know what I'm talking about, but I look like I'm carrying it off with aplomb.

'Was there ever anybody called Young worked at the football factory?' the man of the family asks.

Ah, that's a specific enquiry. I'll pass him on to Geoff or the bloke from the cricket club who's making a slow trawl through the archives and a slower trawl through the second of two toasted teacakes served by my wife. I'm better with general or, preferably, fictional enquiries.

The church bells begin to ring for a wedding, rope, wheel and metal music dancing in the air. I don't want to think that Yorkshire is just a museum, but that's how it's starting to feel: all these old stories, all these memories, all these industries done and dusted.

As I've hinted before, maybe I'm too caught up with the place. All this 'In search of Yorkshire' stuff maybe really means 'In search of Ian McMillan'. Perhaps me and Yorkshire are the same thing, neither nowt nor summat. I couldn't live without Yorkshire, that's a fact. Yorkshire could live without me, though. Very happily. In fact I bet it wishes I'd stop bothering it and let it carry on.

ENJOY THE GAME

I F YORKSHIRE ISN'T just a celebration of the past then I need to find something that can be an emblem of the past and the present and the future. It seems to me that one of the main things Yorkshire defines itself through is sport: football, rugby, cricket, solitary hours fishing, the rapid castanets of dominoes, the darts that leave your hand as winners and then the air decides otherwise, the pigeon flyers that take their baskets to remote spots and practise the art of liberation, the cyclists who, particularly since the Tour de France, whirr up hills in the wrong gear or whizz down resisting the urge to whoop. Maybe Yorkshire itself is a game; a board game where Mayfair is Harrogate and Old Kent Road is wherever you remember as scruffy before you moved away to the suburbs.

If I'm looking for a metaphor for Yorkshire, then sport is it, and that's because competitiveness pounds in the Yorkshireman and Yorkshirewoman's veins, running as fast as it can alongside our blood to keep up, and sometimes overtaking it. We like to win and don't mind, in the current sporting parlance, 'winning ugly'; and if I dig a little deeper then it becomes obvious to me that I'm not just talking about sport. Our marrows and our leeks and our onions have to be the biggest and the best; our station platforms have to be the coldest; our caps have to be the flattest; our accents have to be the closest to the way the whole of the country spoke in a mythical past; our polished anecdotes of poverty and despair have to wrench more tears from the listener than any slapdash Lancashire tale of cold and misery.

Let's face it: the famous Monty Python 'Four Yorkshiremen' sketch was a fly-on-the-wall documentary rather than a piece of observational comedy.

Our love for organised sport is partly to do with our industrial past, when cricket and rugby and football teams were organised alongside the brass bands and the choirs by the factory and the steelworks and the pit. I don't like the cliché 'work hard, play hard' but that's what it was. After grafting next to someone for eight hours on the coal face you tried to score a penalty past him or knock a six all the way into his allotment. After all, sport is about competition and communality and self-expression, and that could be the Holy Trinity of Yorkshireness.

The idea that you have to be born in Yorkshire to play cricket for the county has more or less evaporated now, but the sentiment hangs on, often in tap rooms on long autumn afternoons at the end of the season, or at bus stops at the opposite point of the year, populated by knots of men and women who carry flasks and plastic sandwich boxes like badges of honour.

So if sport is the sweaty and liniment-soaked prism through which Yorkshire views the world and its place in the wider universe and, as a season-ticket holder at the mighty, mighty, Barnsley FC I can agree with that, then where do I start with Yorkshire sport?

At times it feels like this county is glued together by a sporting event that has happened, is happening, or is just about to happen, and that's fine by me.

No Yorkshire person will allow any other Yorkshire person (or anybody else in hearing distance for that matter) to forget that, if Yorkshire was a country, it would have come twelfth in the medal table at the 2012 Olympics; Yorkshire feet pounded tracks and part-sturdy, part-fragile boats were rowed through water with the aid of Yorkshire shoulders and Yorkshire legs cycled till their thighs burned and Yorkshire arms flung sharp javelins and Yorkshire bottoms rode on their horses through the warming air and Yorkshire fists knocked opponents for six. The golden names ring out like bells: Ennis, Adams, Campbell, Brownlee, Clancy, Triggs-Hodge, Copeland. Their golden pillarboxes light up the Yorkshire-scape, reminding us of glory as they catch the evening light and the morning sun. Eat that, Lancashire! Chew on that, Sir Bradley Wiggins, you off-comed 'un! And, as the *Huddersfield Examiner* reminded us recently in a chortlingly joyous article, Yorkshire even won the space race, with Helen Sharman from Sheffield being the first British person to orbit Yorkshire and the earth. How's the Lancashire space-race going? Can I lend you some rubber bands and string? Gaaaaah!

(That last word embarrassed me. I'm sorry. I didn't mean to go Gaaaaah! and stick my face right next to yours, my eyes bulging and my chin, and then yours, flecked with spittle. After all, this is a respectable socio-cultural book. It's not a crowded pub half an hour after the match has finished. It's just that sport makes all Yorkshire people very, very competitive indeed. I'm not normally like this, Officer. This is the first time it's happened to me. It won't happen again.)

Yorkshire is crammed to the gills with sporting excellence and endeavour, though, you've got to admit it. At random, plucked from the last few years, let's mention the Tour de France in 2014, embraced by vast crowds of Yorkshire people replacing 'Allez Allez Allez!' with 'Gu On Theer!' Let's talk about the way we marvelled at the world marvelling at us, at the way we pushed right to the front to see a colourful shadow whizz by faster than you'd ever dare. Let's talk about the way we somehow felt that, in an odd rewriting of history, the race had come home, and that we'd only loaned it to France and it was time they gave it back to us. After all, there's a great Yorkshire cycling heritage that often gets forgotten with people like Barry Hoban, who rode 47,500 kilometres a year racing and training, and Victor Sutton, whose thighs were honed on the unforgiving fells.

Let's mention the great cricketer, Sir Geoffrey Boycott, standing at the crease like a tree, occasionally deigning to swipe a branch at a ball then settling back into stillness and contemplation and waiting, waiting, for the moment to send the ball over the pavilion for six. The moment will come, eventually, for Sir Geoffrey, but he doesn't want to hurry it and Yorkshire fans who demand action would slow their heart rates down to a crawl in the knowledge that Sir Geoffrey would take his time until the shadows were long over Headingley and it was almost time for stumps and the light was almost too bad, almost undeserving of the name light, and the bowlers were tiring and suddenly there would be the moment and the ball would be stroked into the middle of next week where nobody could ever catch it.

Sir Geoffrey is Yorkshire personified, and not just from a sporting point of view: this comes from the combination of stoicism, self-confidence and the coining of metaphors that would seem ludicrous coming out of anybody else's lips. His grandma could have caught that in her pinny, you know. The greatest of these qualities is the self-confidence, the unshakeable conviction that you are right and everybody else is wrong, even if they haven't said owt yet. It's as though being from Yorkshire is a gift only bestowed at birth on those who feel they can talk about it in any setting and at any time of the day or night. If you are silent about your Yorkshireness then the gift will be withdrawn. Painfully, with a bradawl. A friend of mine from Cheshire once commented that Yorkshire people begin every sentence with 'Speaking as a Yorkshireman (or woman)' as though this declaration of where you're from and who you are sets the scene for what you're about to say. And what you're about to say will make complete and utter sense because you have bracketed it with that idea. My Cheshire friend was trying to ridicule me by saying this but, again, it made sense to me, although I have to admit to occasional mini-moments of self-doubt, and we know what that means. NYE.

Let's mention Rugby League, that intricate ballet of muscle and numbers, of sidesteps and grubber kicks. League was invented in August 1895 in the George Hotel in Huddersfield, just across the road from the station and the square where Harold Wilson now turns as if moving away from the white heat of technology in case his Gannex mac catches fire. The Rugby League was created when 21 Yorkshire and, I'm sorry to say, Lancashire, clubs voted to leave the southern-dominated Rugby Football Union and start their own union. I imagine that the Yorkshire clubs had most to do with it and the Lancashire delegations just enjoyed being in rooms with glass in the windows. The Stockport Union was, in a splendidly Victorian mixture of early modernism and pragmatism, accepted into the league by telephone. I guess that the Yorkshire people would be gathered round the instrument making sensible comments and guiding the arguments and negotiations and the Lancashire folk would be looking into the air and peeping behind the pot plants to see where the voices were coming from.

'Am skeered, am I not?' one or more of them would pipe tremulously, on the verge of tears.

Imagine that, though: imagine inventing a new sport in a crowded room in a hotel. Imagine taking on the establishment and coming out with something worth fighting for.

I very rarely get drunk but many years ago I got drunk in the George Hotel in Huddersfield and ended up trying to impress the night porter with my knowledge of both Rugby League and the science of numbers. Both were found very wanting that night, I'm sorry to say. My first mistake, in my beery haze, was to think that the STD code on the hotel number on the ironing board-sized key was the number of my room. Huddersfield's code is 01484 and I thought that was the room I was in. Because there were two fours in the number I surmised that I was on the forty-fourth floor and spent at least the length of the first half of a Rugby League match going up and down in the lift and failing to get off there because there was no forty-fourth floor. Eventually I docked at the fourth floor and sailed into the rolling seas of the thickly carpeted corridor looking for room 484. I wandered around like t'Ancient Mariner for hours, hoping to find somebody to tell my tale of being lost to. I vividly remember a man in a suit walking past me carrying a heavy case; he was off to catch the first train. For him it was tomorrow and for me it was still yesterday. Today was fast asleep in the lift, snoring.

After a while I discerned that there was no room 484, so I went back down to the reception desk and held the key up to the night porter. I spoke with the robotically baroque precision of the kaleyed.

'Sir,' I said. I sounded like a lush in a 1940s *New Yorker* cartoon. 'Sir, this is the number of my room and I cannot find said room. Said room does not exist.' I was dimly aware that I sounded like a Yorkshireman trying to put a posh accent on; my voice echoed in my ears, reverberating until it came to a halt like a coin spinning on a sideboard. I hate it when people say 'said' this or 'said' that and at that moment I hated myself. He looked at my key.

'Twenty-three,' he said. 'Twenty-three.' I must have looked askance. 'You're in room 23,' It was as though my dialogue was written by F. Scott Fitzgerald and his was written by Ernest Hemingway.

I suddenly changed the subject to hide my shame at trying to enter, wizard-like, an imaginary room.

'Rugby League started here, you know,' I slurred. 'Well, not in this spot, not at this desk but 1895 was the date and the blokes, the northern, well Yorkshire, lads wanted to get, they got rid of the southern toffs with their 15 or was it 13 or was it 15? Anyway. It. Started. Here. Rugby. League. A man's game played by men.'

My monologue was fractured and had more or less replaced words with music.

'It's almost morning, sir,' he said kindly. 'Maybe you should go to bed. In room 23. I'm sure it's really comfortable.'

It was as though my dialogue was written by James Joyce and his was written by whoever writes the training manuals for long-suffering hotel workers. Samuel Beckett, maybe.

Let's mention Barnsley's, indeed Cudworth's, finest runner Dorothy Hyman, who won Commonwealth Gold in the sprint relay in 1958 at the age of 17 and went on to win more medals at Commonwealth and Olympic games and who, because she used to have to travel eight miles on two buses after work to the nearest track, gave her name to the sporting facilities that still hang on in her home village. She was Sports Personality of the Year in 1963 but in a recent interview she thinks she might have given the trophy away. I like that. It seems to speak of a time when taking part was good, and winning was great, but awards like the Sports Personality of the Year just cluttered your mantelpiece up and were a devil to dust.

Let's mention a Yorkshire sport that has more or less disappeared but which hangs on in pockets of the county and in the memories of older men: Knurr and Spell, otherwise known as Nipsy. It's a shame that Knurr and Spell sounds like a made-up Yorkshireism, like J.B. Priestley's imaginary Cleckhuddersfax or that line in the film of *Billy Liar* where Rodney Bewes says to Councillor Duxbury, 'Eee, I'm reyt thraped, Councillor.' When the film was on TV it always made my Uncle Charlie laugh so much that he began to cough and then he had to spit symphonically in one of the empty crisp packets he kept by the settee for that purpose.

If the Olympics ever come to Yorkshire we'll at least have to have Knurr and Spell in the opening ceremony, even if we can't shoehorn it into the games proper. Maybe synchronised swimming can make way. If the games come to Barnsley we'll call Knurr and Spell by its local name, 'Potty Knocking', which sounds like a toilet cleaner coming back from the dead.

It's a sport that originated on the Yorkshire Moors in the fourteenth century and by the nineteenth century, like many Yorkshire inventions, it had spread all over the country and indeed across the world, if you count the indie band in Chapel Hill, North Carolina who share their name with the game.

The idea of Knurr and Spell is to hit an object as far as you can. I like this game because there's no subtlety to it and that feels, as Uncle Charlie would say, 'Proper Yorkshire'. It isn't Go or Curling. Sir Geoffrey wouldn't have been much good at it because he'd have thought that waiting was part of the game and the crowd and eventually his fellow players would have packed up and gone home or died of old age.

In Knurr and Spell you hit something and it flies. The further it flies the better. It isn't like golf where you have to aim a ball at a hole and it isn't like skimming pebbles across a bay because you get no points for aesthetic charm, you only get points for distance. The knurr is the tangerine-sized object that you hit after it's been levered briskly into the air by means of a wooden trap. The spell is the bat you hit it with, after swinging it round your head as though you're trying to get intruders off your allotment before the police come for the daft lad and the soft lad. You play it on your own and you advance across a field. You take territory and claim it as yours. After five thwacks, the person who is furthest away wins. Simple and beautiful as a sunset.

And let's mention Barnsley FC again, and the year 1912 when they won the FA Cup 1-0 after a replay against West Brom at Bramall Lane, the home of Sheffield United, the goal being scored by a man with a proper early-twentieth-century footballer's name, Harry Tufnell. Tufnell is a true Barnsley hero and, like many of the people who are making an appearance in these pages, as well as the man who's writing it, he's NYE. He was born in Burton upon Trent in 1886 and died in 1959 in Oldham. He scored in the 1910 final against Newcastle United from a Wilf Bartrop cross but Barnsley lost the replay. His goal against

West Brom is still talked about at Oakwell by people who were far too young to have been there; it's as though spectral film of it flickers above the stadium like a version of the Angels of Mons.

The idea of sport makes me examine myself and my Yorkshireness. I find that even when I'm at my most involved, when Barnsley are hanging on to a one-goal lead in the third of six minutes of extra time and the opposition are piling forward like ants across a dropped lemon curd sandwich, I still feel that I'm watching the game a little ironically, that part of me is watching me watching the game.

Tuesday evening games in February are best for philosophical self-examination, I find. Your breath hangs in the air; the pitch is illuminated by the floodlights and it glows an almost impossibly green colour: Jewelled Peas on a colour chart. The word 'sen' is a beautifully Yorkshire one, a corruption and shortening of 'self' that feels more intimate, more like the 'agenbite of inwit' that the first English poets talked about. On nights like this you can almost become a Sen Buddhist, looking deeper than deep into your very deepest Sen as a man sitting behind you in the stands shouts at the incredibly youthful-looking assistant referee, 'Get back on thi mother's tit, lino!', and the Bovril-lite warms you a little, just a little, even though that's not really top-quality pepper you put on it from the condiments station.

As a seven-year-old at Low Valley Juniors, I had my first encounter with football. Or, rather, I had my first encounter with *a* football, which is one small grammatical alteration for a lad but one giant leap for mankind. I'd gone to watch a game between a pit team and a pub team with my mate Chris Allatt in the field at the back of the Astoria Ballroom. I can't remember anything about the match until at a point towards the end when the ball flew through the air at what seemed to be a record-breaking speed and thwacked me full in the face. That moment is etched in my memory like the pattern of the football, no doubt made a few hundred yards away, halfway up Snape Hill at Mitre Sports, was etched on my ample chops for quite a while after the final whistle.

The ball began its journey that afternoon as a dot in the distance being kicked around by Subbuteo figures then, as though it was an object in a speeded-up film about the solar system, it grew bigger and rounder and vaster and more enormous in a very short space of time.

Somebody shouted, 'Watch thissen little 'un!', but I could watch nothing but the approaching orb. It held me in some kind of spherical power.

When the ball hit, meteor-like, I staggered backwards and fell in a heap. A helpful spectator shouted, 'He's deead!', but I wasn't. I was lying on the ground hoping that I still had a usable nose. I was put off football for years after that. I became marinated with a fear that if ever I went to a match it would only be a matter of time before the ball found my face and there was a ball/face moment that would sting like heck fire. Sport and pain became mixed up in my aching head at that moment and for the future, which prepared me for my life as a Barnsley fan and for which I should be eternally grateful.

At Wath Grammar School, I could easily avoid football because it clashed with my sessions editing the school magazine and choosing how prominently to display my poems and stories and how big and bold a font my name should be in, but I was dragooned into the under-13s rugby team by a teacher who had a very high voice.

'McMillan, lad,' he piped, 'I'm going to put you in the scrum because you've got the face for rugby!'

So I lined up, with my rugby face, on the Saturday morning after Jimi Hendrix was found dead in a hotel room, to face a team who'd come on a creaky school bus from Ecclesfield Grammar near Sheffield. It was odd, in the middle of a county dominated by Rugby League, to be playing Rugby Union, but this was because we wanted to ape the public schools, which was very much the way in those Yorkshire grammar schools at the time. We were the chosen ones, the ones who wouldn't go down the pit but might work in the pit offices, who might go to that fabled place called 'University', where, according to my English teacher Mr Brown in his green corduroy suit, girls called Felicity and Tamsin would walk around in straw boaters and little else and you could sit up all night talking about Kant. Kevin Sands asked if you could sit up all night talking like a Kant and Mr Brown gave him what they used to call an Old Fashioned Look. Many of my class-mates had arrived at the grammar school via the A road called the eleven plus, but at Low Valley Juniors we had a system of continuous assessment called the Thorne Scheme which deposited me into the arms of selective secondary education in 1967 without having to take an exam. Not only am I Not Yorkshire Enough: maybe I'm Not Clever Enough.

It felt odd that my mate Geoff, with whom I'd spent a glorious last summer before we both went to the big school making the Ants' Destruction Diary by flattening them with a coal shovel and filling the body count in in a notebook from Mrs Parry's, went to the secondary modern and then down Darfield Main, while I went to a place that did Latin and Greek and had a debating club and a school song that began, 'Through Vale of Dearne …'

We even had a school motto in Latin, emblazoned on our jackets beneath an image of a flaming torch rising from the waters of the River Dearne: *Meliora Spectare* or 'look to better things'. Mr Dunsby, the Latin teacher, told us that meant Mexborough.

That Saturday morning the Ecclesfield under-13s all looked like middle-aged men who'd just come straight from a shift at the steelworks. They stood in a circle scratching their half-beards and perusing a magazine that featured grinning women whose breasts were as big as mine but a lot pointier.

I was a reluctant prop-forward and in the hellish smelly makeshift tent of the first scrum of the game the opposition prop said to me, 'You're really ugly, aren't you, my ugly friend?' in a tone of mature and threatening intimacy, as though we'd known each other for years, and he was the villain in a film, and then began to try and remove my left eye from its socket with surgical precision and a big sharp thumb. I really should have been able to think of a witty riposte but instead I panicked and tried to escape upwards, leaping salmon-style into the morning air. I felt my neck turn anticlockwise noisily.

I'm not a medical man and I wasn't a medical boy but it felt serious. I lay on the ground with my neck at an awkward angle looking the opposite way to the game along the muddy grass, but I could tell they'd scored. My dad ran towards me, his Saturday hat blowing away in the breeze, his scarf flapping. He half-lifted me to my feet as the game carried on around him and together we staggered to the car. The high-pitched games teacher seemed unconcerned and the lad who'd tried to blind me gave me a cheery wave and a sharp thumbs-up. I'm sure I saw him recently in the background of a British gangster film on late-night TV, taxing somebody's balls with a warm egg-whisk.

I writhed in agony on the back seat of my dad's Zephyr 6 and urged him to drive as quickly as possible, to break the speed limit or at least get out of second gear, and at the same time I urged him to drive as slowly as possible and stay in first gear to try and lessen the appalling pain I was in. Eventually we trundled, not to the Barnsley Beckett Hospital as I'd hoped, but to the doctor's surgery in Mrs Harley's house on Church Street in Darfield.

Mrs Harley, a statuesque woman in a flowery pinafore, would stand with her arms crossed in the waiting room in her front parlour and keep a beady eye on the lame and the halt who populated its chairs and settees. This Saturday morning the room was full of people who looked like I felt, and worse. A man held his hand to his bright red ear, calmly. A child played with a jar of marmalade from his pale mother's shopping basket, rolling and re-rolling it up and down a chair arm. A woman wept loudly, blowing her nose into a flag-sized hanky. A man coughed and coughed and then coughed some more; he leaned over to spit in the fire like he did at home but a glance from Mrs Harley stopped him in his tracks. I felt like I'd never be able to straighten my neck again, felt like I'd always be looking round corners or shiftily gazing to one side. I was a sign-post pointing back the way I'd come, back to the game and the boy-man with the deadly attack-thumb.

Eventually Dr Scott called me in and I sat down uncomfortably on a high wooden chair. My teeth were more or less permanently gritted so my dad explained what had happened, with a number of details Dr Scott didn't really need: the scrum, the ungainly attempt at flight, the sudden angle of the neck, the score, the colour of the opposition's shirts, the weather, the death of Jimi Hendrix. Dr Scott didn't seem perturbed by any of this; he'd seen and heard it all before. Apart from the bit about the death of Hendrix. The harsh strip light gleamed on his glasses as he said those five words you never want to hear a doctor say: 'This might hurt a bit.' Years later, when I knew what a euphemism was, I wished he'd used a euphemism.

He stood over me, casting me in deep medical shadow. He leaned over and put his arms under my jaw and the back of my skull, where the knowledge bump protruded. He lifted me up by my head and I swung like a pub sign. He was right: it did hurt a bit. Clever, those doctors. All those years at medical school. As I hung suspended in the air I felt my neck begin to click like my alarm clock does just before it rings. Dr Scott and me and my dad were by the window of the surgery in an unholy trinity built of wincing and we all saw a woman in a headscarf walking up the short path. She glanced into the window, saw the awful dystopian triptych in front of her, gaped in horror, her mouth open wide in a silent scream, and rushed away in the direction of the Cross Keys. I may have imagined that she was making the sign of the cross.

I didn't go back to the under-13s rugby team, suitable face or not.

This afternoon, though, I'm going to watch a football match between Barnsley and Bristol City, who are top of the league, as they will keep reminding us throughout the match with the vocal power of a ball hitting a face. After my experiences with the flying ball and with Dr Scott, I didn't go to, or take part in, any kind of sporting activity for years unless you count blind man's buff and reading the lingerie section of my mother's catalogue. Indeed, I became snobbish about sport and dismissive of it, seeing myself as being in a camp with fellow hipsters and bohemians far from the musclebound clods who lived their lives to a soundtrack of whistles and grunts.

'It's just 22 men kicking an inflated bladder around a patch of grass,' I would pontificate to anyone who would listen, pretending that I was coming up with an original thought rather than a threadbare cliché.

Then, in the autumn of 1996, after the successful Euro 96 tournament had convinced lots of people like me that football could be part of our cultural palette, I began to go and watch Barnsley FC and I quickly became hooked and reeled into the keep net. Now, instead of peddling my line about the 22 men and the bladder, I extolled the virtues of football as the Working Class Ballet. I'm surprised more people didn't try to hit me.

'You can always guess the end of a play or a film,' I'd say, 'but you can never guess the end of a football match,' which is true, of course. I took my kids to home and away games and the ones against the other Yorkshire teams were the most intense and frightening.

At Sheffield United we parted as a phalanx of riot coppers ran through us towards some people who were lining up against each other at opposite sides of the road like scary Morris Men. A bloke called Charlie who even went to reserve away games said, 'Them's strike bobbies, kid. Strike bobbies.' At the same game I bought a pile of pies to calm me and kids down with comfort food and dropped one down the back of a fellow fan who was sitting in front of me. He turned round and said in a resigned voice, 'Good job we're winning.'

At those Sheffield games we were hurled into a linguistic maelstrom that any aliens visiting from one of the outer moons of Jupiter would have found strange and baffling. The massed Barnsley fans sang, all the way through the match, 'The referee's a DeeDar,' and the Wednesday fans sang, 'The referee's a Dingle,' and somehow I felt like I'd been singing the song for years. I felt like I'd come home, like football did in 1996.

It seemed fitting that in April 1997, Barnsley were promoted to the Premier League against a fellow team from Yorkshire, Bradford City. We won 2-0 in a game that will resonate through the history of my small town for many, many years. When the referee blew the final whistle, you would have imagined that there would be a sudden explosion of sound and there was, eventually, but it only came after one of the most profound moments of silence I've ever heard as, all over the ground, people remembered their dads who brought them and who never gave up on the idea that one day we would be in the highest league possible, who came to the match straight from the pit, who collected programmes and studied results and league ladders and who took the long view. Well, this was the long view come home to roost and lay red and white eggs. And then the noise began, the noise that lasted a season and that you can still hear, somehow, in deserted corners of freezing fields, somewhere by the goalposts.

At Oakwell, Barnsley FC's ground, I always sit in front of a man called John who comes down from his house, which I always hope is named after a Barnsley player but I never dare ask, near Newcastle for every home game. It feels like quite a long way from Oakwell to Darfield when we lose, but I bet it feels like a journey of Marco Polo-esque proportions up the A1 for him through heavy fog after a heavy defeat. John always says the same things at the same points in each home game, a litany of statements that have the cultural weight of the Stations of the Cross but not the spiritual gravitas.

At a certain moment in the game, often after one of our silky passes has gone wildly astray and floated towards the Pukka Pies stand where we both sit, he will shout, 'Ian: get your boots on!' I have to laugh and shake my head because this is part of the ritual, like the congregation replying during eight o'clock holy communion. Then he'll shout, 'On the floor! On the floor!' as though he's an ARP warden in the Blitz. My part of the deal is to nod sagely as though he has just arrived at a hitherto unknown Football Truth. Then comes the final part of the three-movement piece, the last bit of the jigsaw. He'll stand up as the luckless linesman passes us after making the latest in a long series of ill-thought-out and ramshackle decisions and holler, 'Linesman! Stick your flag up your arse!' and over the last couple of seasons my next move has had to be to put my hands over my grandson's ears in a comedy style.

John's there, in his usual seat well before the kick-off. It's not a bad afternoon but we know that as the year turns it will get colder and wetter and windier and we'll waddle to our seats like Michelin men, unable to get our hands in our pockets because we've got too many pairs of gloves on.

'Why do we come, Ian lad?' John will ask at this point, because the long drive down the A1 has made him philosophical; 'why do we sit here, year after year?' I can't explain but, as the cheesy music begins and the team come onto the pitch my heart begins to pound in a way that belies the fact that I'm Not Yorkshire Enough. Maybe I am. Why else would I feel a sense of pride for a team in League One, for a town that has had lots of good kickings over the years, for a region that should, really should, be further up the economic and cultural ladder than it is. That's the ladder with somebody holding it so that you don't fall. Ah, they've not turned up. Ian: get your boots on! Except I'm still watching ironically, still pretending that I'm making an animated video of the match that will have a soundtrack of electronic dance music that I'll source exclusively from charity shop CDs. The ball comes towards me. I duck. John tries to catch it and fails.

INTERLUDE: CUDWORTH PROBUS CLUB

THE CHAIR OF the Cudworth Probus Club rang me one evening in late spring while I was sitting in my dressing gown reading the *Yorkshire Post* and drinking Yorkshire Tea; I'd just thought to myself that I was a living embodiment of a Yorkshire cliché and I'd mused aloud to my wife about what would happen if the Queen walked in and caught me without a flat cap on. I answered the phone, hoping it might be the Queen, but it was the next best thing.

Being a Yorkshireman, the man from the Probus Club launched straight into the conversation: 'You went down quite well at Wombwell Probus Club, I've heard,' he said, his voice crackling on the shaky connection as though he was in outer space rather than three miles down the road. 'Mind you, they're mixed. So would you like to come and talk to us?'

I said I would, adjusting my dressing gown to give me gravitas and dignity.

'What do you normally charge?' he asked, a twinkle in his voice as though he knew this was a ridiculous conversation for two Yorkshiremen to be having, especially in the evening. Especially if one half of the conversation had no trousers on. Or, for all I know, both halves of the conversation. It had been quite balmy.

'Just pay me in chutney,' I replied. In my experience, with groups like this, it's best not to ask for cash and I always ask for chutney; they might make chutney themselves or know somebody who does. Or they might, like one retired persons group did, give me a jar of Aldi chutney in Christmas wrapping paper in June. He ignored the chutney request.

'We meet Tuesdays at ten o'clock in the morning at the West End Club. We do the minutes of the last meeting and then we have the guest speaker for an hour. Then we have a cup of tea.'

How could I resist it? He suggested a date.

'How are you fixed for October 29th?'

I said that I was fine and that, apart from chutney, the only other thing on my rider was that I needed a lift because I didn't drive.

'Yes, a lift. That'll be fine. I know where you live. One of the Wombwell lot told me at the farm shop.' We verbally shook hands over the airwaves and the deal was set. October 29th felt as far away as Devizes.

I like talking to Probus Clubs: their raison d'être is that they're for retired professional people – indeed the name is an amalgamation of the words Professional and Business – and they always do a nice cup of tea. Often with a saucer. Sometimes with a biscuit.

As spring lightened to summer and summer darkened to autumn, he would ring regularly, as the date grew closer, from Devizes to Northampton to Worksop. He became something you could rely on, like a favourite TV pro-gramme or a piece of music that made you want to stand up and sing. Sometimes when he rang I was in my dressing gown, sometimes I was fully dressed. Sometimes I'd just come in and breathlessly ran to the phone as I shucked off my jacket, and sometimes I was just about to go out and the taxi was revving outside.

'Are you still coming?' he'd say and I'd confirm that I was and that I needed a lift. I got used to the calls and quite enjoyed getting them: it was like a long-lost relative ringing from Australia, a Ten-Pound Pom who'd made good, perhaps, or somebody who'd gone to follow their heart and ended up running a pie shop in Brisbane called Of Mince and Men.

He rang one final time the day before the gig. I always call them gigs, wherever I happen to be performing: it keeps my spirits up.

'We'll see you tomorrow,' he said.

'Don't forget you're giving me a lift,' I replied.

'We'll see you tomorrow … at half-past nine,' he said, as though he was redrafting a speech.

The next morning I was standing at the window watch-ing for him. It was quarter past nine. I'm always ready far too early; if the train is due to leave at ten past I'm there at half past the previous hour. If the taxi is due on the hour I'm standing with my bag over my shoulder at twenty to; in its way, this kind of behaviour has the jewelled arro-gance of the fashionably late. I see it as a Yorkshire thing, though, being early. We like to be in charge, we like to be in control; we like to be the first ones in the room so that the people have to come into our space, the one we've been inhabiting and Yorkshireising for a while.

The Sheffield radio writer, Dave Sheasby, once turned up a year early to give a talk to the Huddersfield Authors' Circle. They liked to book people two years in advance and they booked him for 2006 and he turned up in 2005. All the authors in the Authors' Circle were sitting in a circle and the chairperson looked up.

'You're early,' he said, nonplussed.

'Don't you start till half past?' Dave asked, equably.

'No, you're a year early,' the chairman said.

Dave couldn't and didn't believe it. He got out his letter and read it as the authors watched.

'I am,' he said, 'I'm a year early. Can I do my talk now?'

The chairman indicated a novelist sitting beside a pile of paperbacks.

'I'm afraid this year's speaker's here. You'll have to come back next year.'

We even like to tell time what to do. We would happily have knocked up the knocker-up.

I see a small blue car trundle very slowly up the street, climbing the foothills of first gear into the challenging slopes of second. A man with a bald head and glasses is peering out, mouthing house numbers to the driver who is proceeding with the caution of the almost-drunk. He isn't drunk, of course. He's my lift. They drive by at walking pace. They're almost as early as me. I get my coat on and stand by the door. I wait. A window cleaner passes, whistling, and we exchange a few words about Barnsley FC's last match. The Grimsby fish man appears in his green van and a couple of neighbours go out to buy. Have the Cudworth Probus Club got lost?

The green van moves away and I can hear the window cleaner's ladders clanking as he sets them up against a house. The air is clear and crisp and time, like it used to do in those episodes of *The Avengers* I watched as a child, seems to have slowed down almost to a halt. Then the blue car creeps down the other side of the street and stops. I go out and clamber into the back seat.

'We were a bit early,' the man in the glasses says, 'so we sat at the top of the street for a bit and talked about cricket.'

We roll along down Edderthorpe Lane towards Cudworth. It's pronounced Cuderth, of course, just so you know. When I first made my early tentative steps into showbiz in the very early 1970s, I was the drummer in Barnsley's first folk rock band (well, that's how we styled ourselves and now I think back, Seaboots might have had something to say about that) called Oscar the Frog and we used to practise at the house of the Creasey Brothers in Cudworth. I suppose I was technically the drummer, although I had no drums, just Tupperware tubs. Big ones for salad. And I had no drumsticks either, so I had to borrow a pair of my mother's knitting needles. Big ones for cable stitch. My drum solos sounded like a storm on a bratish roof. This sound worked very well on our progressive free-improvisations around old ballads but was less successful on our Yorkshire Dialect version of 'Dream A Little Dream of Me'.

Edderthorpe Lane winds like a memory between Darfield and Cudworth; this really is ancient land. Edderthorpe is an old Viking locution meaning Edda's Outlying Farm and in the years before I was in Oscar the Frog, me and my junior school mates would walk along the lane finding bits of twig and rock that we kept in old biscuit tins marked VIKING ARTY FACTS. It was rumoured that the great 1960s TV traveller, Ian Nairn, came to the nearby viaduct in Storrs Mill Wood when he was making his curmudgeonly and faux-affectionate film about the town and declared it 'one of the best views in England' although maybe that's just wishful thinking.

Once when Martyn, the bass player, and I were walking to a rehearsal we came across what we thought was a dead body under a tree; on closer inspection, after we'd put his jazz bass down carefully, the body revealed itself to be two bodies having enthusiastic sex in the leaves. The man looked up and shouted, 'Gerrooam or I'll tell yer mams!' and we turned and ran, as though the sex and the frighteningly exciting noises they were making were somehow our fault. Later, though, when everybody was out, we recreated the noises in Martyn's mother's kitchen, our faces big and reflective in the shiny kettle. We sounded odd, even to ourselves, as we imagined that we'd crossed a forbidden threshold into adulthood.

Cudworth is, like so many of the villages in this part of Yorkshire, a place that grew with the discovery of coal, although it was never actually a pit village. It was originally part of the diocese of Pontefract and the main road through the village went straight to that ancient town, often carrying salt before the coal was found. A lot of the local roads were salt roads, and I often try to visualise the huge wagons laden down with vast white sacks, some of them leaking, leaving long snowy trails across the mud.

The Probus men drove very slowly down the lane; cars zoomed past us, both ways. We were in a tortoise and hare fable. The journey needed a soundtrack that was part Shaft-like guitar and part comedy trombones. I find it hard to believe now, but when my children were small I'd walk with them down this lane, pushing one of them in a buggy. Now Edderthorpe is a rat-run as people speed along it to find a quick way to get to the warehouse where Houghton Main used to be; some of the dust they scatter is Viking dust.

The Probus men remembered the Creaseys. And their dad and, although there was some dispute about this, both their granddads.

'He's still waiting for that bus,' the driver said as we passed a stooped man on a bench.

'He's missed it,' said the co-pilot, 'he were sat there when we set off.'

It struck me that I was in the presence of Probus Gurus or Probus Shamen who knew everything there was to know about Cudworth and everybody who lived there or who indeed had ever lived there. They were still talking about cricket as children on tricycles passed us.

'We took a bloke from Darfield to a game at Hanging Heaton once. We'd been told he were good. Aye, he was. First innings he got a fucking duck. Second innings he broke his jaw.' The industrial word shattered the peace of the car and we arrived at the club.

'It'll be locked,' the driver said, winding his window down as the other man did the same, 'it always is when we're this early.'

This begged a question. He turned and waved to a man walking down the other side of the street.

'Morning, Bill. How is he?'

'Not out!' Bill replied, not breaking stride.

Cudworth was like Darfield, I suppose. Or rather: it was like Yorkshire. I simply had to try to understand it and I'd be all right.

The door of the club was knocked on, smartly. The door handle was rattled. Nobody appeared. We sat in the car.

I said, 'Tell me again what Probus is. Is it like Rotary?' They shook their heads simultaneously.

'Nowt like Rotary. This is meant to be for professional men, retired professional men.'

'Professional Yorkshiremen?' I asked, wickedly.

'No, not really. Just professional men.' There was a silence like the one just before the parkin is cut at a bonfire party, a silence heavy with the anticipation of what's going to happen next. 'Mind you, some places have gone mixed. Wombwell. Wombwell's gone mixed. It means they get more members. But they've gone mixed; we're supposed to be talking about it here.' He indicated the closed door with a slight sideways movement of his head. 'But we've not got round to it yet.'

A younger man arrived, by which I mean a man as old as me arrived.

'This is't treasurer; he'll get them to open up.'

The treasurer leaped from his car and pounded deafeningly and rhythmically on the club's indifferent door. We could have done with him in Oscar the Frog, especially that rowdy youth club gig where the skinhead stole the fiddle player's dad's best hat. There were, oddly, two letterboxes in the door and he rattled them both. He shouted through them both, one after the other: 'Probus! Probus meeting!' He bellowed it again and then he yelled it.

A young lad in a baseball cap popped his head out of the door of a terraced house at the other side of the road and then rapidly closed the door again. I thought I'd never been on this street before but this swift opening and closure reminded me of the time many years ago when I'd walked down here to visit my mother in a council respite home, now shut, and a man had opened a door and shouted, 'Heyop! Settle me an argument! What day is it?'

I'd replied, with great certainty, 'Thursday!', and he shouted back into the house, 'See! I telld thi!'

After a lot more shouting, the club door opened slowly and we trooped in. The Probus members trickled into the room, taking their time. A man with a smart goatee beard arrived; he asked the treasurer, 'Is he coming?'

'I'm here!' I said brightly, sticking my thumb up like I do in all the local paper pictures that have ever been taken of me.

'No, I can see you're here,' the goatee man said. He turned again to the treasurer. 'Is he coming?' The treasurer shrugged.

'He said he would.'

'I hope he does; I've summat to show him.'

Men of a certain and an uncertain age began to drift into the club. In the main room Sky Sports News filled the air with results and previews as a cleaner wiped tables fiercely. The Probus met in a small room off, of which there were quite a few in the West End Club, chambers of autodidacticism's still-beating heart. This morning's meeting would be a version of Mad Geoff's barbers and the discussion with the council men in Saddleworth. It would be Yorkshire men and men in Yorkshire (two different beings, as we know) talking and listening and working things out. A lot of these men would be committee men, blokes who had spent a lot of their lives organising clubs and societies and trade unions and, in the case of the secretary, brass bands. With their thinning hair and their voices that sometimes teetered on the edge of squeaking, they were part of a narrative of proud endeavour that had almost been ground into the dust by a vindictive history that was determined to see them off. It hadn't, yet.

The secretary took a gavel out of a bag and placed it next to a wooden stand. He tapped the stand experimentally, presumably to see if it and the hammer were still working, and the room hushed like a wedding does when the best man tings a flute.

'Carry on, lads,' he said in a loud voice. 'Just testing!'

The treasurer was taking payment for the Christmas do, a four-course meal and a magician at Burntwood Hall and the complication was that, for the first time, they'd joined forces with the Local History Society.

A man arrived with a bundle of notes in a coin bag.

'This is for me plus eight,' he said. 'Derek can't come. I've added it up reight,' and he showed the treasurer a betting slip with an amount written on it that I wasn't able to see. I could tell, however, that it was written in red ink and underlined twice.

The treasurer glanced at it. 'Tha's totted it wrong.'

There was a silence; in the main room it seemed that even the Sky Sports presenters had stopped talking. The hoover began in a corridor.

'I have not!' the man said, and he and the treasurer began a duel of paper and pens and crossings-out and addings-up.

I was leaning over to try and make out what was happening when the dapper Probus-member with the goatee beard approached me.

'Ah, The Bard!' he said and shook my hand. In these situations I'm often like Prince Charles: I cast around for something generic and anodyne to say.

'It's nice not to have to come far to do a talk,' I say and he nods.

'I used to be the assistant porter at Darfield station. That station master were a warm 'un: he wouldn't let you whistle.'

Behind me the right totting/wrong totting debate is carrying on, ebbing and flowing, adding and subtracting.

A man consults his enormous mobile phone, taking his glasses off and perching them on his head to do so.

'Is he coming?' he asks.

'I'm here,' I say, but I get the feeling they mean somebody else.

'I once had to take delivery of a goat,' the man with the goatee says. There's a linguistic connection here that my brain isn't sophisticated enough to make. The man with the gavel is twisting the end of it as though it's come loose. Nobody is listening to this story except me; it's been told many times, I suppose, to people who know it by heart, who've heard it until it's threadbare and way past its sell-by date, but I've never heard it before and I'm eager for it.

I'm finding this, on my trawl through the county to try and find its heart: Yorkshire is full of stories that need an audience, that need an outlet. The tales we tell ourselves to help us find our way across the world like the old Aboriginal songlines do. Each of our stories is another brick in the edifice that is Yorkshire. Maybe if I hear them and retell them like a troubadour I can become, finally, Yorkshire Enough.

'They lifted a goat off the up train and they told me to deliver it to an address in Low Valley,' he carried on, his eyes sparkling with memory and narrative. 'I pulled it on a string down Snape Hill and people were laughing at me and pointing. I remember blokes on the bus going down to Darfield Main having a right giggle.' He pronounced 'giggle' in the Yorkshire way: *giddle*. The story fitted the teller like a well-worn glove. 'I had to find an address and I went up and down Low Valley and New Scarborough until I found it. I knocked on the door and a feller opened it and he had one arm round a horse and he was playing a piano accordion with the other.'

Momentarily, the West End Club was like the Jemaa el Fna Square in Marrakesh, a place where storytellers plied their wordy wares as they had done for centuries.

More men arrived. There was muted and half-hearted discussion of the possibility of going mixed, with Wombwell being held up as a good or bad example depending who you overheard. Eventually 13 men sat around the room; it felt like a visit to the doctor's or an interview for a job or a version of the Last Supper.

The secretary rapped the gavel on the circle of wood.

'Right then, let's get going,' he said. He glanced at the entrance to the room (there was no door) in case anybody else came in. His opening remarks were spoken to the rhythmic cabaret of the television. I wondered if they'd turn it off for my talk but I suspected not. I wondered if they'd turn it down for my talk but I suspected not. I wondered if they turned it off when the club was shut and everybody had gone home but I suspected not.

'Welcome to the October meeting of the Cudworth Probus Club. We are pleased to welcome our guest speaker, the Bard of Barnsley, Mr Ian McMillan ...' I stood up, expecting to acknowledge applause and then to begin my talk '... and we will be hearing from him when we've read the minutes of the last meeting and discussed the joint Christmas do with the Local History Society.'

I sat down again. The man with the huge mobile phone winked at me.

'Is he coming?' he asked his neighbour.

'I'm here,' I mouthed, winking back.

The neighbour shrugged in slo-mo. A man in a Barnsley FC shirt put his head round the door; we all stared at him. He was considerably younger than the rest of us and he looked fresh-faced and eager.

'What's happening here, like?' he asked. Nobody said anything.

'I'm here to do a talk to these gentlemen,' I said, my voice ringing with welcome.

Outside I could hear a very early ice-cream man, probably Uncle Les, the father of my grandson's mate Bradley, patrolling the streets musically.

'Can I stop?' he asked. I looked at the chairman. He nodded, once with his head and once with his gavel. 'Can I get a drink?' the younger man said.

'If tha wants,' the chairman said impatiently. The interloper disappeared and returned with a foaming pint.

The chairman said, 'I now turn to Frank to present his report on the speaker at the last meeting. A man stood up and read slowly from several sheets of paper to tumultuous nodding and murmuring. Even the whippersnapper with the beer was nodding, and he'd never been before. The report was thorough. Very thorough. The gist of it was that the speaker had gone down well. The speaker had gone down very well with the meeting. The speaker had brought 18 notebooks with him and had read from them all. The speaker had produced 18 notebooks from his person and he had read from them all. The speaker entertained the group with humorous stories and anecdotes. The speaker entertained the gathering with humorous anecdotes and stories. The report was full of repetition but I was enjoying it because the repetition seemed to me to be born of love. The bit about producing notebooks from the person alarmed me, though.

'I hope I don't have to produce notebooks from my person,' I said to silence. I realised that they wouldn't start laughing until I had actually begun what one bloke had called my presentation.

'He was a copper,' somebody said, explaining the note-books.

'Was he?' said somebody else, who must not have been listening, must just have been hypnotised by the appearance of the notebooks.

The younger man went and got another pint. The ice-cream van sounds grew louder then faded away then grew louder again as Uncle Les criss-crossed the expectant streets of Cudworth.

I was introduced to a polite ripple. I started to talk and got laughs. Big fat laughs. This was my kind of room, a small tight one full of men who understood every reference to Houghton Main Pit and the Creasey Brothers and Sir Alec Clegg and Barnsley FC. I baroqued-up the anecdote about the time in Cudworth Library when I'd been doing a story-making session with kids and I'd been introduced by a pasty-faced and trembling librarian who had told me beforehand that she didn't feel well and then had staggered into the toilet which was about three feet away behind a flimsy door as soon as I started talking and began to vomit loudly and terrifyingly, shouting 'OH MY GOD' and 'OH NO' as I began to speak. The splashes were ominous and industrial-strength. The toilet flushed until it could flush no more. I'd thought of a punchline that was relevant to the morning; I was going to say, as I ended the story, that Cudworth was full of people who produce things from about their person. It was going to bring the club down.

Sir Michael Parkinson walked in. He strode over and shook my hand.

'Hello, Ian, how are you?' he said.

My mouth may well have hung open, flapping. I felt like I'd stumbled onto the set of a TV show, which is how people must often feel when Sir Michael Parkinson walks in. The man who'd given me a lift stood up.

'Michael,' he said, 'I've got the pictures.'

Sir Michael Parkinson turned to the gathering and said, 'I'm sorry to interrupt you; I'll be back later,' and both of them went out. Nobody turned a hair. I love Yorkshire because of that. We aren't starstruck by anybody. When I've been on TV people in Darfield will say things like, 'We saw thi. Yappin,' and then they'll carry on buying crisps.

So I carried on talking as though nothing had happened, although of course something had, and the punchline I'd been building up to didn't get the uproarious howls and table banging I previously thought it might. Cudworth had produced its most famous son from about its person. I half expected Johnny Depp to walk in in a moment with Barbra Streisand on his arm, or at least Dorothy Hyman, Cudworth's Olympic medal winner. They'd be welcomed, of course. In Any Other Business.

JESUS NOT HORBURY

I N MY 50-ODD years, I've come across three otherwise ordinary and blameless places with Jesus in their name.

1: The poet Pete Morgan who spent a lot of time attempting to render Robin Hood's Bay in verse but who was originally from Leigh in Lancashire said that his mother always used to call Fazakerley near Wigan 'Jesus Fazakerley' and in their house it became a synonym for Our Lord particularly at Christmas time and other holy festivals. They weren't a particularly religious household.

2: I was once on a train going from Sheffield to London and the man opposite me looked like he'd had what's euphemistically called 'a good night' the night before. His face was as pale as the lining paper you find in chests of drawers in B&Bs. His eyes looked as though they'd been found in a skip. His comb-over had been thrown together amateurishly and as his head nodded and he fell into a deep sleep it began to unravel from his skull. It was as though an octopus was emerging tentatively from a cave. It tumbled down, changing from scribble-on-a-pate to spaghetti-on-a-plate. He snored brassily and urgently. Suddenly the announcer informed us that we were arriving in Loughborough and the slumbering geezer woke up with

a jolt and a miniature yodel. He windmilled his arms frantically. He tried and failed to pick up his briefcase with
doughy hands that were still fast asleep and refused to
obey orders. His comb-over had become a veil. He opened
his tremulous maw and uttered a phrase that's become my
name for this quiet Midlands town, birthplace of Ladybird
books – 'Jesus Christ Loughborough!' – as he ran from the
train, comb-over waving in the breeze.

3: When I worked at Slazenger's tennis-ball factory in
Barnsley in the early 1980s, we all knew of the existence of
the other branches of the manufacturer. There was the
squash-ball factory in Goldthorpe, on the A635 between
Barnsley and Doncaster, and the squash-racquet factory in
Horbury near Wakefield. In those days very few people had
cars so if work was slack and we had to be sent somewhere
else we'd rather go to Goldthorpe than Horbury. Goldthorpe
was a bus, maybe two. Horbury would be a bus or a train
and then another bus and a walk. So the place became
known as Jesus Not Horbury or, in my head, JNH.

At that factory I worked with a man who made his own
false teeth from wood.

'If it's all right for George Washington, it's all right for
me,' he would say, his S's whistling shrilly as the loose teeth
slopped round his mouth and threatened to disengage and
tumble.

A fellow buff-and-dipper three machines down, the one
who always brought six tins of lager to help him through
the endless clanking night shift, said in a voice as unsteady
as his breathing, 'How does tha think he'd fettle in Jesus
Not Horbury?' and he shook his head and the cans

clattered in the duffel bag that was permanently attached to his back. I knew what he meant: JNH was considered posh, as well as being a long way away. They probably wouldn't take kindly to wooden false teeth there. Unless they were artisanal mahogany ones with their own velvet-lined case.

I felt that I had to revisit Horbury, situated between Wakefield and Ossett, to try and exorcise the demon of the squash racquets, which is one of the lesser-known stringy demons, and to see if the place really had the aroma of poshness. Poshness is a bit of a problem in Yorkshire, a pulsing spot on its wide hairy back; I can say with some certainty that no Yorkshire people believe they are posh and yet, and yet, there must be some posh bits, some detached houses, some Conservative voters, some people who call a bath a barth. Not just incomers, either, and not just the old money: proper White Rose toffs with drives that crunch when you walk down them. I want to flush them out for my own satisfaction as much as anybody else's because maybe they give the lie to my one-dimen-sional view of the county.

Each night as I loll on the settee in my dressing gown and slipper socks, I take stock of my quest to unpack Yorkshire and lay it out on the table to study its component parts. I have to admit I'm just as baffled now as I was when I started. I thought this job would be as simple as writing a Christmas Number One: two verses, some choruses, a few buzz-words like 'holly' and 'mistletoe' and maybe a chil-dren's choir who would appear on *Where Are They Now?*

shows on TV in decades to come. Well, I've got news for me: it's harder than I thought. I've never written a Christmas Number One, either. I've bought the Yorkshire kit and I've got the instructions and the glue but I can't quite seem to fit it together. Maybe I'm rushing the process. Perhaps I should be somebody who leans on his shovel rather than somebody who digs frantically and bursts a water main.

The name Horbury is intriguing, given in some sources as meaning 'filthy fortification', which probably refers to a mud-spattered building by the side of the River Calder rather than any more interesting derivations. Like many small towns and big villages in this part of the old West Riding, Horbury was a place of wool and cloth manufacturing and the noisy Luddites passed through in the early nineteenth century, shouting and breaking things as they went. As well as the softness of wool and the comfort of cloth there was a railway wagon makers and the aforementioned Slazenger's. In some ways, Horbury is a West Yorkshire everytown, 3D printed from a template. A mixed economy built around making and remaking and fixing; a place of self-sufficiency and hard work. A place where a bath was always well deserved, and the settee was always so beautifully low that it made you groan as you sank into it after a long day's graft.

But when I walked down the main street in a November dusk that felt darker than it actually was, I got an inkling of something magical about the place. The year felt that it was turning like a cup in a microwave and as I scribbled in the notebook I'd called Not Yorkshire Enough I started to think that maybe here, in these tight small town streets, I'd find the essence of the county I was seeking rather than in the wide and brightly lit avenues of the city.

Then, as I cursed myself for leaving my woolly hat on the worktop, I began to think a thought I'd formulated and discarded a few times as I jotted my notes in the light from closed charity shop windows and mobile phones with near-death batteries; maybe I'd chosen completely the wrong season to write this book. Autumn was falling from the year's tree and shivering into winter. My trip to Hull had shown me that there's not a lot of fun to be had wandering soggy streets in search of philosophical truth. Maybe I should hold the book back until the summer. Maybe it would be more fun to stroll down the sands at Bridlington with my trousers rolled up rather than running across them in a borrowed Rainmate begging for shelter from the Siberian gusts. Yorkshire winters are harsh, let's face it, making snowmen and snowwomen of us all as we stand at the bus-stop and glance pleadingly up at the town hall clock, willing the hands to drag the double-decker round the slippery bend.

For years, we in Yorkshire followed the predictions of an amateur weatherman Bill Foggitt whose folksy, lyrical and occasionally accurate forecasts on local TV brightened up the minutes between the football results and the adverts. He was known, only half-jokingly, as the Oracle of Thirsk, and his family had been collecting and disseminating and, possibly, inventing weather lore since the 1830s. He was good at Yorkshire winters, though, perhaps because omens show up better in the dark. Waxwings are the key: if you see what ornithologists call an 'irruption' of these birds migrating from their homes in Scandinavia to what wax-wings in waxwing language call God's Own County then the winter will be harsh as Izal toilet paper. When the moles of Thirsk burrowed up through the snow, Foggit's wisdom said that there was a thaw on the way.

'Moles know these things,' Bill might have said, tapping the side of his nose.

And perhaps, come to think of it, winter is the best time to gaze at this place and write about it. Somehow, indefinably, it feels like it's best to try and look at Yorkshire through a mist of chilled breath. This feels like a winter county rather than a summer one. It's more like Finland than LA. I'll be a mole burrowing and burrowing and then blinking my way through the metaphorical and real snow to the surface. Besides, in the summer I'm moving to Lancashire. I'm kidding.

Two teenage schoolkids get off a bus and I swear on the life of my mother's sensible shoes that they're talking about Jack Kerouac. They come to no conclusion, which is right and proper. In the florist's, a woman is carrying pots of extravagant flowers back into the shop because it was almost time to turn the sign round on the door, and across the road a man was doing the same with vegetables. It was almost like being in a little town in't Loire Valley.

I decided to apply the Pork Pie test, if I could find a butcher's that was still open. The Pork Pie test isn't too scientific, I have to admit, but my view is that a place that sells a proper pork pie is a place you would want to live and die in. You wouldn't want to die of pork pies, of course. But what a way to go.

I like, indeed I love, pork pies of the Yorkshire variety, where the pork isn't cured and the crusts are works of abstract art and the jelly is often still warm and just right for chin-dribbling and shirt-staining. They're food for the working man or woman to take to the mill or the pit or the field with the crust as a holding device and they're objects of culinary cultural identity, like empanadas or chapatis. By eating the pie, I'm reading a map and a history text and a commonplace book and several bound volumes of the local paper. It's as though I'm adding a pebble to a cairn or doing a selfie by a road sign. I have to confess that as a younger man I liked pork pies too much and this showed in my girth and my hanging garden of chins. It was just the way the pastry crumbled and mixed with the meat and the jelly in your mouth with a kind of saliva-driven alchemy. I couldn't resist them.

Recently, when it was too late to do so in any meaningful way, I felt a profound regret that I hadn't saved every small white bag from every butcher's I'd ever been to in search of pies. I could have stuck them in an album and leafed through its pages on pieless afternoons. My wife read Pork Pie as Perk Pie recently and that's what they are. Specially in Hull.

They're works of art, symphonies or epic piems, although after 18 in one sitting with brown sauce you do become a tiny bit bilious, it's true, and you have to retreat behind the *Barnsley Chronicle* until the waves pass. They're worth it though. They really are.

I once visited the Pork Pie Appreciation Society who meet every week in the Old Bridge Inn in Ripponden near

Halifax and read them a praise piem I'd written; I was pleased with the rhythm and the euphony of the piece and I delivered it as well as I could in the tight shiny room but I could see that they were looking straight past me and my words to a plate of pies on a table that were to form the basis of that evening's blind tasting. All my eye contact was lost to crusts; it was like being in a room full of celebrities and talking to someone who kept looking round the room for more interesting and famous and red-carpet-friendly people to engage with. It hurt just a little that an inanimate piece of snack food was more attractive than my deathless verse.

The blind tasting at the Pork Pie Appreciation Society is a magnificent sight to behold and should perhaps have been included in my chapter about Yorkshire sport. The pies are brought in, ceremoniously. In my imagination a choir is singing 'Ilkley Moor Baht 'At' in close and treacly harmony. The pies are gazed at like the knowledgeable crowd gaze at muscled humans at a bodybuilding contest or Turner Prize judges stare long and hard at installations that feature somebody up a ladder pretending to be an owl. Attention is paid to the pies; paid in full. A pie is raised, not to the lips but to the nose. The smell is noted. A pie is raised, not to the lips but the eye, as the dimensions and aesthetic quality are noted. The pie is nibbled with a certain aficionado's delicacy. The crust, the jelly, the meat; the *je ne sais quoi*, as they say in certain of the edgier parts of Ripponden. Recent comments on the blind tasting on the society's website include Howard's 'cathedral roof to it' and Kevin's 'big soft man's pie with lots of afterburn'.

There is no hint of irony in the room; it is checked at the door. They could be discussing wine or opera (it's a big soft man's opera with lots of afterburn) and it is beautiful and moving to my Not Yorkshire Enough soul that they are discussing pies with seriousness and depth.

In Yorkshire we like to be good at things, whether it's pork pies or long jumps, mitten-knitting or bingo. It's not just that we're competitive, as I hinted at in my sport chapter: it's that we like to do things well. And we like to do things right. And a perfect pork pie is just as good as a skilfully knitted pair of mittens. And a bad pork pie tastes like a pair of mittens. And we know the difference.

My mother used to buy huge pork pies for Sunday tea; they were the size of stabiliser wheels on a child's bike and she sliced them with care and fanned the slices out on a Coronation plate. She'd lived through the war and rationing and so, like lots of parents from that era, food meant love and abundance of food meant real and undying love. My dad worked in an office once he'd left the navy and my parents weren't poor and they liked to buy food. My mother's table would groan, literally because it too was from the war, under the pie and the flan and the sausage rolls and the sandwiches made on what she called dinner buns.

The rationing hung on in her head, though, because if you had a slice of pork pie, particularly when I was younger and the war was still closer to memory than history, she'd insist that you had it with a slice of bread and butter. White bread and butter, of course. Brown bread was for people who voted Liberal or put slices of orange into their dilute squash. There was something talismanic for me about those four slices of white bread and butter, a pale flag of an unknown country unfurled on the table. Even when I was at secondary school I'd sometimes come home in the winter and my mother would silently gesture at the table where the bread and butter waited and I'd eat it slowly as I reread *Of Mice and Men* ready for a mock exam. I jokingly asked Miss Clegg if you could take bread and butter into the exam for brain food and she gazed at me over her monumental bosom and her winged spectacles and told me to make sure I wrote in paragraphs.

Yorkshire food has a beautiful singularity that you can boil down, in musical terms, to *solo* and *duo*. The pork pie on its own: a statement of fact and possibility. The pork pie with the slice of bread and butter: a reference to a history struck with poverty. The pork pie with the archipelago of chutney colonising the edge of the plate: Sunday tea sophistication with a classic serial on the black-and-white TV in the corner of the room. The pork pie with the impressionistic smear of mustard colouring the ceramic surface: first tea with the nervous new girlfriend meeting the family in the overheated back room. Would you like some bread and butter with your pie?

Or then, as Sherlock Holmes might say, pie crumbs dotting his cape, there's the Fruit Cake and Cheese Mystery. There was always cheese on my mother's crowded tea table and it was there for one purpose only, to have with your Christmas cake. If you got yourself some cake and there was no cheese on your plate she'd lean over, give you a pointed look, and place cheese on top of it in an action reminiscent of a charity helicopter dropping supplies to starving people or a Lord Mayor laying a ceremonial brick on the wall of a new community centre. It had depth, in other words; it had meaning beyond the mere movement of the hands. There was no point protesting; you may as well have said that you wouldn't have milk in your tea. In fact, as a newly married man, I once said that I didn't want milk in my tea and she added cold water instead from the tap.

Visiting relatives in Scotland as a lad (I recall I was wearing green corduroy Tyrolean bib-shorts and carrying a Tarzan book) I asked my Uncle Jimmy if there was any cheese to go with the cake and he looked at me like the beadle looked at Oliver when he asked for more. Then began to laugh and he laughed so much that he almost choked on his black bun and had to slurp Irn-Bru as my cousin Stuart slapped him on the back. No one really knows why Yorkshire people like cheese with their fruit cake and although the practice was once more widespread throughout the north and the northern diaspora it's now shrunk to the three Ridings. We're either hanging on to a tradition or anticipating the zeitgeist. It is lovely, mind you. As John Peel once said about an album by Bridget St John, it's like renting a cottage by the sea.

There are so many things to say about Yorkshire food and so many ways to say them. As Yorkshire people, we are defined by our food and our relationship to it. We like a full plate, a full plate that is piled so high it could feature a cable car and which gradually, like the cable car, empties with the smacking of lips and groans of satisfaction. Like my mother's bread and butter with pork pies and, now I come to think of it, apples cut into quarters with slices of bread and butter, our interface with food is born from poverty or memories of poverty. We have names for it that are short and brisk because we want to get on with eating it: snap, scran, chow.

There are rules and conventions for Yorkshire food that should be pinned up like planning permission notices on the back of every kitchen door in the three Ridings: Parkin is always on its own on the plate and is never eaten before bonfire night because if it is the bad luck will land on you and a jumping cracker will probably get stuck in your turn ups, setting them alight. Ham always tastes best at funerals. The best pop is the Dandelion & Burdock that was delivered on the back of a clattering lorry by Hey! Pop of Pontefract every Sunday morning in bottles the size of small children. It's a scone not a skon. A Barnsley chop is more lamb than there is on a lamb. A dripping sandwich is as much a visual experience as a culinary one. Parsnips are always best if they're brought in from the allotment with ancient muck on. You can only ever say lunch if you say it with fistfuls of air-quotes. You drink tea with your dinner, not after. Any tea drunk in Yorkshire is Yorkshire Tea, no matter where it's from. A Fat Rascal is a scone with attitude. The best Yorkshire Mixtures are the ones that look like fish but don't taste like fish. Curd Tart edges close to culinary perfection and it never lies to your tongue. The Bistort Pie is only eaten at the Lancashire end of Yorkshire; the name of the pie describes the shape of your face if you're unfortunate to taste one. A breadcake is not a teacake and a teacake is not a breadcake. Supper is something you have on a plate balanced on a stool while you watch telly and the supper is often chips and gravy and the programme is often a rerun of *Voyage to the Bottom of the Sea* on a channel right at the haunted end of the EPG. The full Yorkshire Breakfast is poverty, despair and defiance. Tripe goes very well with cowheel and in the sentence the tripe always goes first; no one has ever said cowheel and tripe. Dinner is something you have at dinnertime, obviously. You can only ever say baguette if you say it with fistfuls of air-quotes. Henderson's Relish goes with absolutely everything and not just food; it goes with weeping at a film, cleaning out the hamster and gazing at the constellations in the clear, clear sky. Herbal tea is referred to as That Herbal Tea or That Theer Herbal Tea or That Theer Semmas Herbal Tea or That Theer Tha Knows Semmas Herbal Tea. Cheese with apple pie is almost as acceptable as cheese with fruit cake. Tap water is Council Pop. If you ask what's for tea you get told, 'A cup of hot nowt' or 'Three runs round't table' or 'Lob Skoosh'. When you have fish and chips you have bits with them. When you ask for two portions of fish and chips to take away you just say, 'Twice. Oppen.' The best gravy is as thick as treacle. Meat is meyt unless it's meeat. If the meat is lettuce it's Rabbit Meyt or Rabbit Meeat. A Chorley Cake is an object of loud hooting derision.

These are irrefutable peer-reviewed Yorkshire food facts. Or they are wobbly Yorkshire food legends. Or they are resonant Yorkshire food stories. You decide. Do you want this bread and butter while you're thinking?

Then, in a chapter about food in a book about Yorkshire, there's no way you can avoid the gravy-filled elephant in the parlour, the Yorkshire Pudding. I've capitalised it, of course, but maybe not as much as I should have. THE YORKSHIRE PUDDING. That's better, that's much better. The Yorkshire Pudding is as real and as fake as 'Ilkley Moor Baht 'At'. It's the flat cap and muffler of local cuisine, both a cliché and the truth that launched the cliché hiding inside each other: batter-spattered Russian dolls.

I still serve Yorkshires as a first course on a Sunday and as I serve them wearing my World Curry Festival pinny I say, in a Yorkshire accent that's only a slight exaggeration of my normal tones, 'There'll not be many round here having this!', and my family laugh dutifully and perhaps a little too loudly. Maybe it's because I'm Not Yorkshire Enough that I believe in the symbolism of the Yorkshire Pudding a bit too much; it represents continuity and history. It speaks eloquently of times of poverty in the early years of the Industrial Revolution when you chomped a Yorkshire Pudding as big as a footstool to fill you up because the Sunday roast was only as big as a vole if you had one at all. It's an unbroken link to a past you can hardly imagine but which hangs on like a museum audio-visual tour.

The first written recipe for the pudding was by Hannah Glasse in 1747 and she seasoned the batter with ginger and grated nutmeg, which would give it more piquant flavour than mine. Mind you, I once dropped a satsuma in my batter but I fished it out pretty quickly and I don't think anybody noticed. Glasse also gave the dish its name; before she intervened it was called a Dripping Pudding, although that suggests fattiness and the true Yorkshire can almost fly unaided through the kitchen steam. In his masterly study of Yorkshire food, the writer Peter Brears declares that the classic pudding has 'a high crisp rim and a deeply rippled centre', very much like Yorkshire itself. In 2008 the Royal Society of Chemistry declared that a Yorkshire Pudding didn't deserve the name unless it was at least four inches tall.

None of the above strictures and precedents apply to my puddings; they're sometimes as flat as a postcard and sometimes as chewy as Bazooka Joe and that is why, in my mind, they are elusive and almost alive; they are the fingerprints of the White Rose culinary world and they should always be unique. If a Yorkshire Pudding was a form of music I think it should be free improvised jazz rather than a strict and pattern-heavy Strathspey.

And, of course, you never wash the tins. You never, ever wash the tins. You can leave them out in the sweet Yorkshire rain, of course, but that's a different matter. My lard-fossilled pudding tins are the equivalent of those ancient fires that never went out, that burned for generations in smoky hovels with a constantly refilling stew-pot balanced on them. When my family moved from one part of Darfield to another when I was a teenager, somehow my mother's favourite Yorkshire Pudding tins went missing somewhere on the short trip; they were there and then they weren't, and my mother said that her puddings were never the same again. For years I thought I might find the tins in a ditch or a car-boot sale, to name two ends of the reclaiming spectrum, but I never did.

And she was right: the puddings never were the same, even if we ate them with bread and butter. They were better. The old tins were filthy.

The main ingredient for the Yorkshire Pudding, I think, is experience. Experience, flour, milk, eggs, water, more or less in that order. Line up the ingredients like soldiers going to war. Except the water, of course, that waits in the tap like Special Forces. Tip some flour into the bowl; don't bother measuring the amount because your Yorkshire ancestors are in the kitchen and they'll adjust your hand and the bag as it tips as your Scottish ancestors look on, aghast. Crack the eggs and try and get them to crack in a Yorkshire accent; it hardly ever works but when it does it's magical and somehow it adds to the puddings. Pour the milk in. Pour the water in. Bend over and turn the oven up high; higher than high. It has to be as hot as the hell of the Industrial Revolution.

Now whisk the mixture with an old fork that belonged to your mam and that she didn't lose in the house move. Never use a whisk because a fork is the tool of choice; using a whisk would make the mixture too fluffy, too, well, whisked. The older the fork the better: next time you're at a car boot sale in Yorkshire buy a fork because the chances are it'll have mixed enough pudding batter to float a boat. Your Yorkshire wrist is strong through years of whisking and bending over to peel stuck pound coins from the damp ground. Make that fork dance and sing and tumble and pose. Leave the mixture to mature and take in the Yorkshire history around it through a form of calligraphic action, osmosis and reverse sweating.

Turn the oven up some more; risk conflagration. Risk the Great Fire of Darfield like you do every week. Put blobs of lard into the old tins and slip them into the oven with a satisfying clanging noise. Let the lard heat up. Almost leave the lard too long, almost until it catches fire. Get the tins out. The kitchen is sweating and your glasses have steamed up. Pour the mixture into the tins and listen to the satisfying sizzle that's calling to you down the centuries that people have made Yorkshire Puddings. Slam them in the oven and watch them rise. The pudding seems to hold all our Yorkshire hopes and dreams as it rises and rises. Midas has touched the batter. That's Frank Midas from Kippax.

Just as the real Yorkshire Pudding is a thing of wonder, the fake Yorkshire Pudding is an appalling waste of time and space, a lookalike that looks nothing like. The true citizen of Yorkshire never eats a Yorkshire Pudding in a pub or a café because these will almost certainly be frozen imitations or simulacra from a packet; the tyke can always tell because they taste like old toupees or beer mats. No wrist action will have been expended on these aberrations. They will sit limply in the mouth like guests who won't go home from a wake.

Once, though, just once, a fake pudding built a beautiful Yorkshire myth that resonated like a dinner gong in a Scarborough guesthouse. A Yorkshire Pudding company once sponsored a Yorkshire Pudding Boat Race that I was involved with in a small venue in the village of Brawby near Malton in the north of the county. The venue was called the Shed and it was a marvellous example of wilful and glorious Yorkshire eccentricity under the leadership of sculptor and enthusiast Simon Thackray.

The Shed at that time was really just a village hall in a place that was so small it was hardly on the map; he called it the Shed because he stuck his old shed door, decorated with a round piece of metal he'd found in a stream, at the back of the hall and the ordinary space became an extraordinary space. He began by promoting gigs, putting folk singers and avant garde jazz into that intimate arena and then his ideas began to expand. He liked the idea of taking radical performance ideas to a place that was inherently conservative with a small C and a big C and an enormous C that took up three fields. I tell the story of the Yorkshire Pudding Boat Race because it seems germane to my investigation of what makes this place tick.

One afternoon, not long after the start of the new millennium, I was sitting in Simon's house having a cup of tea when he left the room and came back in with a Barbie doll. She was wearing a severe and modest bathing costume and sitting in a Yorkshire Pudding of the packet variety. A tiny outboard motor from a toy boat was fastened to the back with gaffer tape.

'Come and have a look at this!' he said, and he took me into his bathroom where the bath was almost overflowing; he lunged forward and turned the taps off, then placed the Barbie in the water. He turned on the outboard motor and she sailed in her pudding craft towards the plug. He turned her round and she buzzed back.

'Why doesn't the pudding sink?' I asked, innocently.

'Yacht varnish,' he replied, his eyes sparkling. Possibly through proximity to yacht varnish. I smiled, perhaps a little too indulgently.

He spoke loudly, projecting his voice above the humming of the motor and the whirring of the bathroom's extractor fan.

'I've got a plan,' he said.

That didn't surprise me. Simon Thackray is in a long tradition of enthused Yorkshire inventors.

'We're going to have a Yorkshire Pudding Boat Race,' he said.

Barbie was bobbing against the side of the bath; he reached over and turned her round and she buzzed away through the water on her endless journey.

'With her?' I asked. Simon shook his head and gestured at me to follow him out of the bathroom and we went outside to the lean-to in his garden where he constructed things. Something lay under a blanket. It was like a moment in a Yorkshire Frankenstein film. Music should have swelled, filling the room. Thunder should have clapped somewhere over Castle Howard way. As an artist, Simon likes to sculpt moments from time as he was keeping one hanging now.

He paused for just a little too long by the thing under the blanket and something occurred to me that's obsessed me ever since: how do Yorkshire people think? Is there a specific Yorkshire philosophy, not just of the 'hear all, see all, say nowt' variety but of a turn of mind, a way of using language to get at and define the truth? A sort of logical positivism that always queried the price of an idea?

He whipped the blanket away to reveal a Yorkshire Pudding the size of a coracle.

'What do you reckon?' he said, his eyes gleaming.

'You're going to stick a Barbie doll in that?' I asked, my voice doing an involuntary Antipodean upswing at the end.

He literally and symbolically threw Barbie aside; she lay spread-eagled on the floor like an extra at the start of a six-part murder mystery on Sky Atlantic.

'Kids,' he said, dramatically. 'We're going to put kids in them and they're going to row round Bob's Pond. And you're going to recite poetry and we'll have live music.' He leaned over the coracle. 'It really is Yorkshire Pudding mix.' His voice had dropped to an inclusive whisper. 'But it'll float. I've got five more on the go.'

'Yacht varnish?' I asked.

'Chicken wire!' he replied, and then, in a sudden gear change from the specific to the general, 'People will talk about this for years.'

Simon had had the idea several years before, sitting in a pub and, in his words, 'seeing the waitresses float by with trays of beer'. This could just be a silly idea but I think that somehow, in these floating puddings, there's the kernel of Yorkshire that I'm trying to get to. Lots of things are here, almost everything that I've been thinking and writing about already: the man with the plan, the eccentric with the vision, the single-mindedness, and the Yorkshire Pudding as foodstuff and symbol and more.

Simon had a manic genius for publicity but this time he surpassed himself; because the idea was simple and beautiful, newspapers, radio and television went wild, and the race was featured on German television and armed forces radio, each outlet no doubt providing a different spin on what was, in the end, a very simple and very Yorkshire event. Some people even complained about the ticket price, which made it perfect. I found myself being interviewed about it on local radio and comparing it to a Tristan Tzara Dadaist happening, and in many ways it was.

On the day itself a large crowd gathered round Bob's Pond at the back of Simon's house. I stood with my verses. Snake Davis stood there with his saxophone, looking happy and bemused at the same time. Snake is one of the best purveyors of cool soul-based saxophone in the country and also, as it happens, the best accompanist to a Yorkshire Pudding Boat Race you could ever want; he turned that muddy patch halfway to the middle of nowhere into a romantically lit club on the Lower East Side where they didn't – but should – serve Yorkshire Puddings.

Health and safety concerns meant that the Malton Sub-Aqua Club had to be on hand in case any of the young rowers fell out of the puddings and got into difficulties. An early idea had been to fill Bob's Pond with gravy and I, for one, was glad that notion never got further than the planning stage. The members of the Sub-Aqua Club were keen to take their duties seriously and Simon had them standing in the pond in full diving gear. The pond was only about 18 inches deep and the puddings wove between them like they were lighthouses. The race became a regular event in the world's calendar of eccentricities and featured in all sorts of guides that told you what to do off the beaten track in the UK.

In 2001, at the height of the foot-and-mouth outbreak that locked much of the country down, the race was run using Barbie dolls, small puddings and outboard motors in a row of household baths, but the Malton Sub-Aqua Club were still there, stoically enjoying the joke, sitting beside the baths on high stools of the sort cabaret artists sing from.

Simon went on to organise many more weirdly Yorkshire-ish events, like getting a free-improv trombone player to busk the chip-van queue as it parked in the village greens of Ryedale and placing the saxophonist the late Lol Coxhill in a skip and touring him about on the back of a lorry because someone had said his playing was rubbish. I myself, in a knitted Elvis wig, took busloads of people around Malton and Pickering claiming that Presley was from the area and visiting fictional (although real if you were on the bus) places from his childhood and early life. It was on these tours that I discovered that any Elvis Presley song can be sung to the tune of 'Ilkley Moor Baht 'At'. Try it: it works. We handed song sheets out. Well, bless my soul what's wrong with me? I am caught in a trap (in a trap). Maybe that's a clue to Yorkshire thought processes: every-thing has to fit our templates, even if we have to corset-squeeze it.

People still talk about the Yorkshire Pudding Boat Race in Ryedale and it has become, like Up Helly Aa in Shetland, one of those traditions that people think is much older than it actually is. One day I want to be sitting on a bench in Slingsby as a man next to me fills me in on the story of the race, which began in 1738 when someone dropped their Yorkshire Pudding in the river Rye and a child jumped in to save it and ended up floating in it all the way to York.

The puddings are almost ready in my inferno of a kitchen. My pinny is beginning to smoulder. It's so hot that even Mr Lowe next door is sweating in his chair. It's time to get the puddings out of the oven. This is a *reveal* of the sort that happens in detective stories. How will they have turned out? Will they have risen the regulation four inches? Will their centre be deeply rippled? I take them out of the oven, hissing, 'Bloody Hell,' as the heat rattles my face. I place the puddings carefully on the big white plates. Two each, like twin suns in a white sky. Add the thick gravy that hesitates its way out of the jug. There you have Yorkshire represented in miniature. Time to eat. The first course: the puddings. The second course: the meat and veg. The third course: the crumble. The sneaky mid-afternoon visit to the kitchen: the pork pie. Maybe with a slice of bread and butter.

At the far end of Horbury High Street, I came across Charlesworth's Butchers, their window still lit, still gloriously meat-full. I went in and the door-bell clanged like a butcher's bell should. There were pork pies in abundance like an edible terracotta army and there was something unusual about them: they were oval. Most pork pies are round. I bought one pie.

'I see it's oval,' I said to the woman behind the counter.

'Is it? I've never noticed before,' she said.

I took the pie out of the white paper bag and examined it. It looked oval to me; maybe geometry is different in this part of Yorkshire. I held it up to her.

'Oval,' I said, firmly.

She took my round pound coin and rattled it into the till. The pie cost 90p. That's the kind of price a Yorkshireman wants to pay for his pie. Just under a pound. That's what they should say on the label, 'Just under a pound', an imprecise maths that lifts the tyke heart.

I once paid £3.65 for a pork pie in Aldeburgh in Suffolk and I was profoundly tempted to buy it and leave it on the counter in protest with a £1 tip. I didn't, though. I bought it and grumbled as I ate it because I'm from Yorkshire. I got a receipt: that's the south for you. It was a lovely pie, too, but I didn't want to admit it: when I held it up to my ear before I ate it I could hear the sound of Peter Pears singing a Benjamin Britten song. Doesn't everybody hold pork pies up to their ears before they eat them? If you don't, you should: you can hear the flavour settling.

There is a widespread myth that people from Yorkshire are tight, that the two words they will say most often in a shop are 'How much?' and that they'll dart to the pavement to retrieve glinting pennies. I admit I'm guilty of the latter. I don't think we're tight but I think we're careful. We live in a county that for many years didn't pay its workers their due, where phalanxes of miners and steelworkers and textile workers were at the whim of employers who could lay them off at a moment's notice so money had to be saved in banks and socks and drawers and envelopes. Now, no matter how badly off we are, we're much wealthier than our grandparents and their grandparents but there's still an all-pervading feeling that the really bad times might return when we're not looking and cut holes in the bottoms of our purses. That's why, in my Yorkshire/Scottish heart, I really resented paying £3.65 for the Suffolk pie; it was the extra 5p that almost tipped me into saying, 'How much?' I think I may have mouthed it.

I stepped out into the cold Horbury evening. Although it was only the day before Armistice Day, it felt oddly Christmassy; I hadn't seen any Christmas decorations yet in the shops or pubs but I felt like I was in one of the final scenes of *A Christmas Carol* and Scrooge had sent me to Charlesworth's for a turkey. I took the pie from the paper bag again and gazed at it lovingly.

A bus passed and someone gazed at me through the thick glass of the bus window in a pair of thick glasses, quadruple-glazed. I like to think they were envious because they were going home to beans on toast. I bit into the pie and crumbs fell to the ground. At that moment I was a happy, happy man. Yorkshire was enfolding me in its gloaming. I turned and walked back up the street chewing and, despite myself and the mouthful of pie, wanting to whistle 'God Rest Ye Merry, Gentlemen'. I stopped wishing that I'd decided to write this book in summer.

People who knew Horbury had told me it retained a village feel and that's true and perhaps it's another truth about Yorkshire that I can put in my pocket: if you're not in a town in Yorkshire, you're in a village. I know that has all the profundity of a bowl of semolina but I think that if I was in other counties there would be more individualism, less collectivism. Yorkshire people seem to thrive by being next door or, at the most, two doors down; solipsism wasn't invented here, even if cats' eyes were. I like the fact that I can hear my old next-door neighbour Mr Lowe's radio through the wall; I like the fact that he likes Radio 4 and Radio 3 so I sometimes hear me through the wall, as though I'm calling to myself from another planet. It's not a myth that we used to leave our doors open and nip into other people's houses. It happened frequently, and not just with people we knew.

Once, late in the evening just before a family trip to Weston-super-Mare in the summer of 1968, a man walked into the kitchen as my dad and I were watching Alfred Hitchcock's *Lifeboat* in the back room. My mother was standing in the kitchen baking scones to take away with us because of her belief that Somerset scones would probably taste like stiletto-heeled shoes. The man, in a long mac and a flat cap, had an Alsatian dog on a length of washing line.

'Excuse me, missis,' he said to my mother in the voice of an extra from a film of a John Braine book, 'have you got any water for my dog? We're walking to Rotherham.'

My dad and me wandered into the kitchen, leaving the lifeboat sailing to nowhere in the empty room. I seem to recall that we didn't seem concerned; we didn't immediately rush to ring the police. Not that we had a telephone. We'd have had to write to the police.

The dog did indeed look parched, its face pinched and dusty and somehow sucked in on itself, as though it was going to Rotherham to escape demolition. Looking back on this incident now, it seems to come from a time so strange and so far away: the unlocked door, the mam in a pinny, the black-and-white television, the cap, the dog, the acceptance that someone would, if you asked, give you water.

My mam turned the tap on and filled a bowl and the dog lapped rhythmically. The man had taken his cap off and his hair was sparse grey scrub. He looked down on his luck and his odour was wrestling with the smell of baking.

'We're just watching a Hitchcock film,' my dad said, by way of ice-breaking small talk.

'I liked *Psycho*,' the man said, 'but our Geoffrey didn't. He went in the other room and put his wireless on. To Luxembourg.'

The silence after that remark was vivid and charged with a timeless electricity until in the other room the music swelled with the waves. The dog finished drinking.

'Right then, I'll get off to Rotherham,' the man said.

Looking back on the incident now, after decades, I've come to the conclusion that he was a genuine tramp, a Gentleman of the Road, who cadged kindnesses from strangers and vicars and slept in graveyards or bus shelters or disused cricket pavilions.

My mam, rubbing her hands on her floury pinny, opened a tin and gave him a slice of malt loaf. He tore it in half and chucked some to the dog. He walked out of the house, nodding at Mr White next door who was putting glowing ashes in his bin. My dad and I watched as he clicked the gate and walked off towards Wombwell and, eventually, Rotherham.

My mother went back to her baking and my dad and I went back to the settee and Hitchcock.

'He's very unusual,' my dad said, and I thought he was talking about the tramp, 'he always makes a guest appearance in his films and you have to look very closely or you might miss him.'

It was 1968; across Europe, revolution was in the air and students were chucking things at coppers in riot gear. In America, hippies were walking the same streets as Vietnam veterans. In Darfield, nothing was changing and it felt like nothing would ever change. Because I was 12 and starting to grow up and fancy Emma Peel in *The Avengers* I wanted things to change. I felt like I was making a guest appearance in my own life and if you didn't look very closely you'd miss me. Another idea to hang this book on.

When we went to Weston-super-Mare, to show my true revolutionary spirit, I wrote a play called *The Diamond Studded Triceratops* in a reporter's notebook with a spiral binding and I performed it in the residents' lounge to a pair of elderly twins and a large family from Solihull. Revolution felt a long way away. Further than Solihull.

There's a Carnegie Library in Horbury, named after that great Scottish-American philanthropist who wanted a beautiful and spacious place for everybody to read books in, and there's a small church called St John's where the curate, Sabine Baring-Gould, wrote 'Onward Christian Soldiers' in 1865 for the procession up Quarry Hill.

However, if Horbury has a crowning architectural glory that lifts it beyond a village into something approaching the sublime, it's the Church of St Peter, a gorgeous Georgian building built over a period of four years from 1790 by one of the most distinguished Horburians (if that's what they're called) of all time, the architect and former Lord Mayor of York, John Carr. The *Leeds Intelligencer* newspaper reported in June of 1794 that the church was 'allowed to be the handsomest building of its size in the country. The spire is truly elegant, and the body of the church is rendered perfectly commodious.'

It seems to me that John Carr wasn't a 'how much?' merchant; he wanted the best and he didn't mind paying for it, shelling out £8,000 of his own money which compares to the £9,228 paid to build the nearby St John the Baptist Church in Wakefield, raised from a number of different sources. In one sense, Carr is just a version of those other Yorkshiremen I've already come across on my travels, Fitzwilliam and Ferens, who to a greater or lesser extent wanted to shape the county in their image and to leave behind a legacy: a great church, a vast house or a public art gallery. I don't know if this is a particularly Yorkshire phenomenon but these coin-rich lads were definitely prepared to put their walls where their mouths were, and they shaped the place I live in today. They knew it, too, which is what bothers me a little. Mind you, my Uncle Charlie and his son Little Charlie made sure they drew their initials in the cement when they built their new garage in the back garden of 34 North Street in 1963, and great men weren't their thing, Little Charlie constantly reminding me that Winston Churchill once said the miners were earthworms.

I try to sing 'I have got a pork pie/it is very nice' to the tune of 'Onward Christian Soldiers' as I walk back down the main street and I think I almost succeeded. The lady in the florist has more or less finished putting her plants away; I linger for a moment by her fragrant window and then wander into the Rickaro bookshop next door. It says a lot for a place when they can sustain an independent bookshop, and Rickaro has been on the main street in Horbury for 14 years.

Inside, the owner, Richard Knowles, was in the back room trying to sort out a failed bulb. Richard doesn't only sell new books, he has an amazing collection of dialect publications and when I remembered he was in Horbury I decided to have a look. He emerged into the shop and started talking about a customer they'd had earlier in the day.

He pointed to a space by the counter that represented the customer. 'He kept talking to the dog, and I could tell the dog didn't like it. He kept saying, "It's all right, I used to work at Whipsnade zoo with lions and elephants and snakes."' Richard kept looking at the dogless emptiness. 'She kept growling at him and he kept saying, "I've worked in a zoo, I've worked in a zoo …"'

Rickaro hasn't always been a bookshop, Richard tells me as he shows me round; he bought it from a couple who kept it as an antique shop, and before that it was a baker's. He said that a customer had come in once and said that, during the war when her husband was away at sea, she'd brought loads of apples in from her trees and persuaded the baker to make a cake for the homecoming hero, a gesture that you guess might not happen today.

'I can't get over the Zoo Bloke,' he says, giving the customer a name that lifts him from reality to the Land of Anecdote.

A woman sitting by the till says, 'What are we going to do about all that erotica in those cardboard boxes?' just as the woman from the flower shop comes in. She and Richard go in the back to look at the failed lightbulb but I can't get the erotica out of my head.

'I can't get it in, it's too dark,' says Richard. The double-entendre Luddites would have a field day in there, breaking up all kinds of language machinery with their huge hammers. He meant a light bulb, of course. Of course he did. I meant proper hammers, too. Proper big ones.

Rickaro Books have shelves and shelves of second-hand dialect books including lots of copies of the wonderful *Saunterer's Satchel and West Riding Almanac* which were a kind of precursor of this book and which pulse with the kind of information and jokes and wise old sayings that would certainly, if I could learn them off by heart, make me Yorkshire Enough before I'd properly digested my pork pie.

I'm in the shop on 10 November and the entry for that day reads 'Plevna Captured, 1879', and I'm sure it wasn't referring to the shanty town beside Little Houghton built to house the people who were sinking Dearne Valley drift mine but to the Russo-Turkish war. I've been wrestling with the concept of how to write dialect on the page for this book but the *Saunterer* has no such worries; his 'A Midneet Mystery' releases crowds of apostrophes that flock around the page like homing pigeons: 'Ah wur dahn at Leeds t'other week an' bein' rather dry after lewkin' rahnd t'tarn I happened to pop intuv an aleharse nut fur fro t'stayshun where there were bahn ter be a raffle fer a cuckoo clock.'

Read it aloud; it's mouth music or t'scat.

The great Leeds poet, Tony Harrison, wrote that 'we're the ones Shakespeare gives the comedy parts to', and that's part of the problem. I find the Yorkshire dialect dignified, euphonic, almost operatic, but some people think we sound like the living embodiment of stuffy mufflers with half-eaten chip sandwiches in our heavy-woollen gobs. Here, perhaps, is the true core of Yorkshire: a linguistic locus that the county spread out from; an archery target with Darfield as the bull's eye. I wonder if I can ever see this county properly, dispassionately, objectively, as though from a great height. I'm not sure that I can. I keep returning to what Seamus Heaney called the Omphalos; the centre, the navel.

Outside the shop, it's pitch dark now, but it feels like, to quote the *Saunterer* in his poem, 'nowt o'clock'; time to go home. As if I'd ever been away. Jesus maybe Horbury; oh, go on then: Jesus yes Horbury.

INTERLUDE: THE CAT AND THE MAN AND THE MAN AND THE CAT

BACK IN THE house, I take stock of what I'm finding out about Yorkshire on my perambulations and I'm pleased to say that, despite the rain and the cold and my winter worries, it's adding up to quite a bit. Everywhere wants to be in the county, no matter how far from the centre they are; it's a place built on graft and philanthropy; its language is richer than I thought it could possibly be; it's cold and wet. The latter epiphany is entirely based on the time of year. It never rains in summer. Yorkshire is at its best in autumn and winter; snow makes the fields glow with a purity that you can't define, and the post-industrial ruins look better when leaves float around them poetically. These out-of-the-way places, these *edgelands* to borrow a phrase coined by a pair of poets, are where the truth is to be found, I think.

The phone rings. It's Iain the Artist, wanting a trip down Cat Hill for what we both call 'research', and when we say the word we do the air-speech marks in our separate houses at opposite ends of the village. Iain Nicholls appeared in Darfield ten years ago, riding a bike with such huge wheels

I could hardly see the bus shelter behind them. He shouted across the road to me as I wandered lonely as a man carrying a bag of bread rolls, 'Are you Ian McMillan?' How did he know? It must have been the bread rolls.

Iain had been making a living as an artist in London and had come home to Darfield to help look after his dad, who'd had a stroke. Like me, he'd been born in Darfield but unlike me he'd moved away so when he returned he saw us through a visitor's eyes and I envied him. I always wanted to look at this place like an anthropologist would but I never can because I know things: for example, I know where Colin Lillee used to stand to sell the *Green 'Un* and I don't have to find it out through field research: on the corner of North Street and Morrison Road and next to Edgar Wroe's ironmonger's in Wombwell. His glasses were as thick as marmalade and his cap fitted his head so well that I guessed he might have gone to bed in it and when he took it off there's be a ring round his head like a cycle track. He'd stand and shout, '*Green 'Un*!' and people would rush out and buy the paper to find how many Barnsley had lost by.

There was a lad at Low Valley whose mother sent him to elocution lessons in the hope that she could educate him out of Yorkshire's restricting girdle into pastures new and more relaxed and for a couple of weeks he stood by the Post Office with a pile of paper the colour of nausea shouting, '*Green One! Green One!*' No one bought one and he went to work for the milkman.

Iain gave up the bright lights of London for the orange streetlights of Darfield and, in a way, this means that unlike me he's Quite Yorkshire Enough because he took the Yorkshire coat off, slipped it into a wardrobe and then put it back on because he wanted to, not because he felt he needed to. I'm thinking more and more that wanting to be Yorkshire means that, no matter how hard I try, I might never be Yorkshire Enough. To stay is a second prize, an honourable mention. To go and come back seems to elevate you to a podium. I'm thinking too hard and too vaguely, as usual. Self-knowledge excludes me; I'm cast out of the garden of Yorkshire. Cast way out.

Because of a shared love of muttering about culture in cafés, Iain and I formed an easy friendship, the man of words and the man of paint, and we bonded over a desire to get to the bottom of the enigma wrapped in a mystery that is Cat Hill.

Cat Hill is, like the Owl in the Tower and the Valley Ghooast, a legend that resonates far beyond this tight valley and this old Salt route to the north. The story goes that, in the fourteenth century, a knight called Sir Percival Cresacre was returning from the crusades, making his way by Conisbrough Castle and along the route of the rivers Dearne and Don when he got set on by a wild cat, which clawed at his throat. He slashed at the cat with his heavy sword, injuring it but not fatally. The cat and him played a game of Cat and Percy all across the woods that were like the woods those old Romano-British-Yorkshire people had settled near Wombwell until they stumbled into Darfield and specifically to the small and insignificant hill that runs down from the main A635 to where the railway used to cross the flatlands that are now a bird reserve and where my father-in-law and I went coal-picking in the 1984 strike.

A column of coppers in vans trundled past and I could hear their truncheons rattling against the sides of their southern accents. I looked at my father-in-law and he said, 'Keep picking. I can't run and tha can't feyt.' They passed us by.

Back in the 1970s, a flamingo floated down to where the bird reserve now is like a sweet wrapper in a light breeze, having been blown off its migratory course. Thousands of people turned out to see it, to catch a glimpse of this most un-Yorkshire of visitors. A crew came from local TV to film it and I remember the bathos (although I didn't call it that at the time. I called it Too Daft To Laugh At) of watching the pink flamingo on our small black-and-white TV when we could more or less see it from the back bedroom window and cheering when we caught a glimpse of Eddie Lang from the top street at the edge of the screen.

The cat and Percival fought like picket and bobby all the way down the hill and then, inexplicably, turned left towards the neighbouring village of Barnburgh, about four miles across the fields where, after more scratching and slashing, they rolled cartoon-like to the steps of St Peter's Church where the cat leaped one last time at Percival's bull-neck and Percival's sword cut through the air like a breadknife. The man, so the story goes, fell dying on top of the cat, crushing the ninth and last life out of it. At this point in the tale, if you're being told it in Barnburgh, the teller will gesture at what appears to be a smudge of mud on the step, or perhaps the shadow of a smudge that was once mud, and say, in a creaky voice like a Yorkshire Vincent Price (Vincent How Much?), 'And yer can still see blood on't step …' If you're cruel, you'll lean towards the step and say, 'It looks like Henderson's Relish to me,' but you won't because Yorkshire people aren't like that. It's a tale that's full of pleasing ambiguity about the way that conflict will always lead to mutual destruction, about the way that claws are mightier than steel and when the steel is gone the claws will remain.

Iain and I meet by the old florist's and walk down the hill by Middlewood Hall and past the river to the round-about where Cat Hill slopes off unconvincingly. The roundabout, in the way that roundabouts are these days, is named, in letters as big as a baby, CATHILL ROUNDABOUT, which in my opinion is like calling a freeway in New York STATUEOFLIBERTY FREEWAY. It's Cat Hill, not Cathill.

The roundabouts on the new roads that criss-cross this part of Yorkshire are all named after things and places from the past, which gives them a kind of epic, mythic quality, especially because they're round. Go to South Elmsall from Grimethorpe and you negotiate Beamshaw roundabout, named after the Beamshaw Seam at Houghton Main, and Ferrymoor roundabout, named after the Ferrymoor Seam and Ferrymoor Riddings Pit, and the Hague Hall roundabout, named after the hall built by a pit owner, which in a piece of delicious justice, is reputed to have fallen down because of mining subsidence. If that's true, it's beautiful.

The section of road with the Cathill roundabout on it is called the Dearne Valley Parkway and it links the M1 to the A1; it's been one of the engines driving the regeneration of this area since heavy industry collapsed round here. It didn't fall, of course; it was pushed. Oddly, we still call it the 'new road', despite the fact the first part of it opened in 1992, which tells you something about Yorkshire years, which are like dog years but more sentimental and self-regarding. The new road was a council and government initiative to link us to civilisation and now it can speed people to the call centres that have replaced the pits; they're a form of civilisation, of course. With headphones. Just before the new road you turn right onto the old, old road that is Cat Hill.

It's only just a hill, to be honest. It's a wrinkle in the landscape's rug. It wouldn't be many contour lines on a map. Hotel stairs are harder to walk up. We walk down it and Iain points out puddles and discarded bricks and a lost sock, raking them all with his artist's eyes and storing them for later. He deals in image and colour which seems to me to be a more profound currency than language but which would be out of place in a book made of words.

'There are tarmac shapes on the pavement in Darfield that remind me of the birth of abstract expressionism,' he said to me once as I ate a toasted teacake in the café. You see, I couldn't get away with that because I've never moved.

The old Darfield station, hurled on a decaying scrapheap by Dr Beeching in June 1963, would be somewhere over to the right and I picture the goat being delivered, the man from the Probus taking it to the accordion player.

One of my earliest memories, one of those memories that is so early you think it must be a false one constructed from anecdote and overhearings and newsreel footage, is of me and my mother catching a train from the station to visit my dad on his last ship, the *Ark Royal*, which was docked in Plymouth; he left the navy in 1958 so I would have been two years old and maybe I can't really remember it. Maybe I'm recalling a photo and a train ticket kept in an old biscuit tin. I'm sure I remember the steam, though. I remember a man in a cap opening a door for me and my mother. I remember sitting and looking out into the dark at the north sliding by.

By the ruins of the old railway bridge we strike right into the woods where the line used to be; there are tin and plastic scatterings that suggest nocturnal gatherings and there's a balloon hanging from a tree in a way that seems deliberate and shamanistic. I feel like I'm back in those other woods with John Tanner near that ill-defined circle and I feel the timelessness of ritual here, the way that woods will always make the Yorkshireman want to pull something into a circle and light a fire and tell stories and sing songs. The watercooler moment began here, in the cold air.

Further into the woods, there seems to be evidence of houses for railway workers and, remarkably, we can see fragments of ghost gardens laid out for pleasure and produce; we can make out lines where vegetables may have been planted, and flowerbeds seen as though through layers of tracing paper. We stand and listen and of course we can't hear voices or see a flamingo or spot a transit van full of strike bobbies going by, but we pretend we can. That's the visceral hold this place has on you. Maybe that's why he came back and why I've never left. I bend down and pick up a discarded penny, then I hurl it far into the trees in a symbolic gesture. Symbolic of what, I'm not sure. I can't be a real Yorkshireman, sending brass curling and twisting into the air. A real Yorkshireman would put it in his pocket.

Iain points to the remains of a wall that looks as though it's been in a fight. A huge slug that could almost be the tongue from a pair of trainers is making its way down a brick towards what I once called a piece of 'dog piano' because the person I was with, a vicar's daughter, didn't like me saying 'dog poo' or anything less decorous. It's a scene that fills me with fascination and disgust as the slug slides closer to the piano.

'Looks like a blind date,' I say, 'and they're meeting for the first time.'

We turn and walk back to Cat Hill as it starts to rain November rain.

The school bus to Wath Grammar School used to bring us this way when this was a proper road, and sometimes we had to wait for ages as a coal train passed, clanking endlessly, wagon after wagon full of the stuff that gave this place a reason for being. Jock Coughtrie would take advantage of the pause to finish his history homework, balancing his exercise book on his knee. He was called Jock because he was from Scotland and lived, with a handful of Scottish families, in a couple of streets in Darfield. They'd arrived from Ayrshire in the mid-1960s, and an NCB recruiting agent from Darfield had driven round the pit villages on his motorbike convincing them that South Yorkshire was the land of milk, honey and coal. He told them they would have a job for life and they believed him, chugging down the country in Fords and Vauxhalls like the Joads in *The Grapes of Wrath*. An account in the *Glasgow Herald* from June 1963 talks dispassionately about a hundred miners from Barony Pit applying for transfers to Yorkshire, meeting Yorkshire NCB representatives, even though Gavin Stocks from the local branch of the NUM appealed to the men to stand firm. I guess one of those representatives might have been Johnny Williamson, his motorbike parked outside the office, his crash helmet on a peg. He would be pointing at a map spread out on a table. Wombwell would have seemed like an exotic Shangri-La.

So much of the South Yorkshire Coalfield was worked by people from outside the region, all of them, like me, Not Yorkshire Enough. The population of Darfield increased hugely as the pits were sunk, leaping from 591 in 1853 to 2616 in 1881, three decades where people walked over the Pennines from Lancashire or down from Scotland or up from Staffordshire. In hard and unforgiving times in the rural economy, families would simply drop their wide forks on the ground and walk to the nearest pit, presenting themselves for work.

In Royston, one of Barnsley's many satellite villages, there was a mass influx from the Black Country to work at Monckton Colliery in the late nineteenth century and Kate Burland from Sheffield University has made a study of the way that their accents have pervaded and survived in Royston's tight streets. Try going into Royston and asking for a kipper tie and you're almost bound to get asked if you want milk and sugar with it. Parts of the village are still known as 'Little Staffs' and residents are sometimes called 'Staffs'. No academic has yet recorded whether the citizens of Royston prefer Staffordshire Terriers to Yorkshire Terriers but it will be only a matter of time before there's a chapter in a book or a peer-reviewed journal about it.

Oddly, although a number of other villages had significant numbers of incomers who would have shaken and stirred the local locutions, Royston is the only one that's well known for its metalinguistic features, as they say in the club on a Friday night. It may be, as Kate points out, that the language flux is due to the proximity of the village to the border of South and West Yorkshire, although surely these are artificial boundaries? Where's the bloke from the Isle of Coll when you need him? Probably still lying on a gravestone under a Hebridean sky singing 'Holy Wullie's Prayer'.

The last coal wagon would pass and the bus would jerk into motion; the sudden movement would make Jock splash a long thin blue line all the way across his hastily constructed essay on the Etruscans. Mr Billington would mark him down for that. The Scottish miners and their descendants hang on in Darfield and other ex-pit villages; the newsagent gets a couple of copies of the *Sunday Post* so that Oor Wullie and the Broons can cheer up the sons and daughters of exile with their Ibsen-esque goings on and one or two of them are rumoured to sit on buckets rather than chairs in the sun on July afternoons. My dad didn't mix with these latecoming Scots in any kind of diaspora-club that might have met at the library on a Thursday evening to read Walter Scott and Neil M. Gunn together before eating shortbread, but he remained as Scottish as ever, all the way through his long life, most of which was either spent on a ship or in the dry dock of Darfield. He kept his gentle lowlands accent intact, he supported Scotland when they played England at rugby or football, and he liked Soor Plooms. Somehow it always felt like he was a visitor to Yorkshire, brought here by the happy accident of love, correspondence and war, on a long shore leave that eventually he would sail away from.

Mr Coward the milkman, in a gesture of cross-border solidarity, always gave my dad any Scottish pound notes that turned up in his change. He would knock on the glass door on a Thursday evening to collect his money, his shape silhouetted and held in light, his flat cap glowing like a halo. 'I've got one for thi, Mac,' he would say as my dad paid him, and my dad would wearily accept the Royal Linen Bank quid and put it in an old cigar box that he brought back from Cuba, because he knew he could never spend it. And of course Mr Coward's philanthropy was woven with economic nous; nobody else would take the money, not even the other more worldly Scottish pitmen on Upperwood Road.

It's obvious to me that my dad's outsiderness shaped my feeling of always being at the wrong, if more interesting, side of the street. I've always thought that I'm only visiting, and that must come from my dad, standing in the kitchen drying the pots in a Loch Lomond pinny and singing Moira Anderson songs in his tenor voice that could break your heart at fifty paces. The Yorkshire accent remained a source of almost anthropological delight to him; my brother once tumbled out of bed and said 'Ah fell art!' which my dad quoted for years as an example of Daft Darfield Speak. I always think I sound Yorkshire but in the past people who weren't listening properly have said that there's a hint of the Scot in my voice, as though my dad is speaking in my mouth through thick layers of muslin or, more accurately, thick layers of that material they make kilts out of. I like being dual heritage and bilingual. I like the fact that I can call a pitstack a bing and my snap a piece without the use of a phrasebook. I can look both ways at once, which always helps when you're crossing a border road.

The late 1960s and early 1970s were a time of great expansion in the South Yorkshire Coalfield and there was a sense that we actually were living somewhere important. I recall an advert from the *Barnsley Chronicle* that showed a man in a suit with a bowler hat, carrying a briefcase, heading to Barnsley with determination in his eyes and a grin on his bag daft southern face. The slogan said: 'Barnsley: The Natural Centre of Attraction', and I imagined people with their sleeves rolled up and their brows furrowed taking days if not weeks to come up with those six words in that order. There would have been a moment of existential angst just before the poised felt tip darted at the flipchart page.

We had NCB recruiting films at Low Valley Junior School and because there was no big area of white space to show them in, we had to watch them in the boys' cloakroom. Mr

Challenger lugged the enormous projector into the tight space, the veins on his neck straining, and took the reels of film out of the brown envelope that had been delivered that morning.

'Sit quietly while I set this thing up,' he barked and we sat quietly on the benches that were normally full of going-home excitement or pre-PE nerves because we might not get picked or we might get picked.

After a while the West Riding County Council projector began to whirr wheezily and the film flickered into black-and-white life and we settled down to watch. Because there was no screen we ended up seeing the film on the back of macs and gaberdines and balaclavas, which meant that heads would sprout pegs and scarves would dangle from coal trucks.

A posh voice spoke over the gleaming torsos of men hewing a narrow seam: 'The nation needs coal and the nation needs miners,' it said as music rose to a crescendo of strings and brass. It was like a socialist realist epic, which of course in some ways is exactly what it was because the NCB was a cradle-to-grave organisation where the bosses would continually remind you of the slogan of nationalisation: 'We are the Masters Now.'

In a stroke of supreme irony photographs depicting nationalisation hang in the café of the Morrison's super-market at Cortonwood, which was built on the site of Cortonwood Colliery, the announced closure of which led to the 1984 Strike.

All this was in a future that we couldn't guess at, as the cloakroom gradually became very warm and increasingly smoky and it soon occurred to even the slowest of us that the projector was on fire. Mr Challenger, who had probably been dreaming of holidays on the Isle of Wight, seemed startled and flapped his arms as though being a bird, like we had to be in Music and Movement, might help douse the flames. The film started going backwards very quickly and the miners ran out of the pit and returned to their houses, hanging their caps back up at the bottom of the stairs as the commentary Mickey-Moused its way back into the speaker's mouth. The projector blew up, quietly and feebly. It could have been a cheap indoor firework or a sneeze. There was an exhausted silence. Mr Challenger put his arms away and led us back to the classroom, leaving smoke hanging in the air.

A week later Iain comes to my house with a painting of the dog piano and the slug.

'It's called True Love,' he says. Somehow, in his surreal and visual way, he understands this place more than I do.

THE NORTH: I'M JUST AFTER A BALE OF HAY

BECAUSE OF MY peripatetic word-driven lifestyle, touring the country spouting jewelled verse to small-but-keen audiences ('We've moved you from the big auditorium to the studio space because we thought the sense of intimacy would suit your style'), I wake up in lots of different hotel rooms and as soon as my eyes clang open I glance to my left. The old cheap alarm clock that I take everywhere not only tells me the time but somehow, in a mysterious way, informs me exactly where I am.

I've thought a lot about this as I gaze at the bland, generic art on hotel room walls and wait for the slow kettle to boil and I think it's simply because, as I put the clock on the bedside when I arrive in the room, I take note of my surroundings, so the clock performs the function of memory, with fingers and hands and a face. When I look at it a small bell rings in my memory and I remember where I was when I went to bed.

This morning is different. This morning it's balaclava-back-to-front dark and I have no idea at all which city, town, village or hamlet I'm in. This has never happened to me before as an adult and it's destabilising and worrying; I think to myself that perhaps this is what death is like and I check that I'm wearing pants. Phew: I am. This book is making me think hard about place in a good way but maybe my mind, like the engines on the Starship Enterprise, can't take any more and it's snapped. Place has lost all meaning. I may as well go and live on an uninhabited island, or in Colne.

As a child I once woke up in borrowed pyjamas in my Auntie Mary and Uncle Jack's house in Sheffield. I'd slept hunched over and twisted like a discarded skipping rope; somehow my left arm had snaked round my neck so it refused to come to life to welcome the day like the rest of me did. It lay on the sheet like somebody else's hake. The morning was shining through the thin curtains and I imagined Mary and Jack sitting in the 'sun loggia', which is what they called their conservatory, him reading the *Trout and Salmon* and her knitting a set of bootees for 'the poor children who lived cheek by jowl' as she called them. I only imagined them doing that because that's what they did in the evenings when we visited. For me as a child, evenings and mornings were cut from the same cloth as far as adult activities were concerned, it was just that the light outside was different.

Somehow, though, as an adult in this dark room decades away from the ambience of a Hillsborough 'sun loggia' and as my mind clears of the dreams it was having, I start to realise that I'm in Yorkshire. It's as though the clock is going T' T' T' T' rather than tick tock. Maybe the lack of light is somehow a Yorkshire lack of light; perhaps the traffic is rumbling and the birds are singing in Yorkshire accents. I stumble out of bed and catch a glimpse of myself in the mirror: a slow trembling avalanche with a scribble of stubble designed by unpaid interns. The year seems to be running away from me as though it's on wheels and I'm stumbling to keep up. I'm only a little further forward in my quest to find the beating heart of this county and I don't really know why. My optimism of a few days ago has floated away as though it's been vaped into the air. To be honest, everywhere I look I see versions of myself and that's not enough variety to base a county around, even though, let's face it, a lot of Yorkshiremen, Yorkshirewomen, Yorkshire dogs and the occasional piece of Yorkshire furniture do look quite a lot like me.

I put a shirt on and open the curtains. My mother used to call larger people 'stiffish' and the man emptying barrels of beer into a pub cellar looks stiffish in this muted late-autumn light. Now I remember: a day of hard travelling on trains full of regret and lateness and a taxi ride with a driver who used to be an ex-copper and who liked doing semi-acoustic music with his mate round the pubs brought me here. The Village Inn, Brompton. Not far from Northallerton and a stone's throw from the Yorkshire Dales. I'm on the scent of a version of the Real Yorkshire.

I get dressed and go for breakfast; the black pudding is tempting and I'm not disappointed but then a strange thing happens, a moment that seems to brim with omens that spread over the day and soak it in, if not foreboding, then significance.

On the windowsill of the hotel's breakfast room, there's a plant in a terracotta pot; I'm not good with plant names but I can tell you that it looked pretty and that perhaps its name would have reflected and enhanced its prettiness. As I chew my toast and contemplate a world where all the questions in PMQs would be about free black pudding for Yorkshiremen, the plant pot suddenly rolls off the sill and smashes into smithereens and larger jagged shards you'd have to call smithers. There is a silence you could have poured sauce on.

A man from the group of four who are sitting at the next table, who all individually studied the menu and then, one by one, asked for a Full English, takes out a large camera and it looks as though he's going to photograph the mess, possibly for a truly niche Yorkshire calendar. He just looks at the back of it and I realise he's looking at the snaps he snapped yesterday. He shows it to the rest of his party: 'That's us at the abbey. That's us near the abbey. That's us walking up the steps to the abbey. That's us eating fish and chips near the abbey.' They must have been to Whitby. They're having the full Yorkshire experience along with their full breakfast and, unlike me, they've got Yorkshire nailed and kept for posterity.

I, as ever, try to be too clever. I say to the waitress, 'That's a big sprinkling of condiments on the floor.' What Yorkshireman would say something daft like that? One who's Not Yorkshire Enough, that's who.

'It's not salt it's dirt,' she says, and sweeps it up into a green dustpan. The cameraman says nothing.

Why would a plant pot suddenly fall off a sill? We aren't too far from the A1 with its columns of wagons and caravans of caravans thundering north and south, but then again we aren't really that close. It would take a lot of shuddering by a lot of traffic to shake a pot from a sill. Maybe something has shifted, slightly, in the year. Perhaps my examinations of the roots of Yorkshireness are causing some kind of tear in the often-darned fabric of the universe. Maybe the year really is fraying at the edges, daring me to draw conclusions from everything I see before it fades away into next year. Odd things are happening, that's for sure. They'll all add up to something in the end.

I get up to leave; my plan is to go to Leyburn and Settle, places that tourists flock to when they want to experience Proper Yorkshire; I might see the Whitby-appreciators there, taking pictures they can talk about later to each other. They'll say to their mates at the bridge club (because there are four of them and they wear cardigans I imagine they're in a bridge club) they've Done Yorkshire, and I can say that Yorkshire's Doing Me.

Maybe the pot-shattering really was trying to tell me something. Maybe this book will be broken if I don't try and change its direction and the way it's shaping up. Perhaps a plan could be to stay here for a while, rent a room in the pub for several weeks and try to come to terms with the place and try to draw conclusions about it and if I can't draw them, write them. Through a long stay of temporary residence I could enlighten myself on what Yorkshire is through osmosis and steeping.

I could become known as The Man in the Room. The Man in the Room with the Notebook. The Man in the Room with the Grey Quiff and the Notebook.

'He comes downstairs every now and then, you know; he goes out for a walk and you can see him scribbling things down. They say he's writing a book. They say he's writing a book about what Yorkshire is. They say we're going to be in the book, we're all going to be in the book and when the book comes out they'll read about us and they'll know what Yorkshire is. Let's go and tell him a few things because we know what Yorkshire is …' I could live in that room for months like the great wordsmith Jonathan Raban would. When he tired of being a travel writer he simply moved to America and took root. I should do that. I could do that.

The nearest I ever got to that state of 'here I am and here I stay' nirvana was when I spent a week in a cabin in Maine, at the edge of a tiny village called Georgetown, in a chilly late November. I was making a radio programme about the Round the Bend café on the crossroads, simply sitting there with my recorder, listening as the fishermen and the old timers sat and chewed the fat and ate the most amazing breakfasts I've ever had. The café opened at four in the morning so I'd get up at 3am and wander down through the insect-noisy dark. The café then shut at nine in the morning and I'd pack up my microphone and walk back to the cabin in the bird-noisy sun. I sat in the cabin and pretended I lived there. I put my boots on and went for a walk and a man in a hat said, 'I wouldn't go in them woods. They're shooting in there,' so I walked back to the cabin rather too quickly and sat there all day watching TV and dreaming about being back in Yorkshire before going to bed at seven in the evening and sleeping badly.

In the café one morning, a man with a voice that creaked like a hinge said, 'You sound Welsh,' and I said that I was from Yorkshire and he said, 'I've heard of that place. Do you know Norman?', like Americans are supposed to do.

To my eternal shame, I pretended I knew Norman. I do know a Norman who I see at the football but I don't think that was the Norman he meant.

'Yes, I know Norman,' I replied.

'Norman from Yorkshire?' the man said.

'Yep, Norman from Yorkshire.'

The man mused: 'Met the guy once in Bangor, Maine. He was staying in the same motel, he was just on a tour around New England, said he'd always wanted to go to Maine. We sat by the pool and we jawed a little. Then we kept in touch a bit, cards at Christmas, that kind of thing. Ain't that a coincidence? How do you know him?'

I should have confessed there and then that I was fibbing but I was already far too enmeshed in the Net of Lies.

'I knew his sister,' I said. 'We used to work together.'

He looked at me curiously, as though I'd just attempted to tell his fortune by reading tea-leaves and failed badly.

'His sister? Did she get over the operation?'

I was in far too deep. I pretended I had to go and I went. I sat in the cabin looking out of the window; maybe who I was would never leave me. I'm a Yorkshireman who makes things up, and I daren't venture into the woods because of the creatures and the hunters there. I've never felt more like I was living in a folk tale.

I knew I couldn't stay in Brompton-on-Swale because I'd end up inventing things, making up a history for myself and the place. This is meant to be a factual book, after all.

I've got to go. I'm Settle Committed and Leyburn Hungry. Brompton makes me nervous, anyway: I woke up there and I didn't know where I was. Even in my pants. Writers should always know where they are, I reckon.

It's Friday so it's market day in Leyburn at the top end of Wensleydale by the River Ure. Leyburn is a good example of that kind of Yorkshire I mentioned earlier; the kind that people go to, the kind that people from the south of England would visit and say to each other in pubs in Benfleet and St Albans, 'Oh yes, we like Yorkshire. You can't guarantee the weather, of course, but if it's the weather you want you can always go abroad. And the locals are always very friendly. If you can understand a word they say.' There will be a pause in the conversation and the kettle will boil and the Yorkshire Tea will be infused. Humorous banter will ensue in baroque-mock-faux Yorkshire accents. The words 'flat' and 'cap' may be uttered in the aforementioned accents. Don't tell the people of Benfleet or St Albans this, but it never tastes the same once it crosses the Yorkshire border. It tastes brackish and unhealthy. That's the tea and the accent.

The last time I came to Leyburn, I visited the Elite Cinema, and it's my mission on this trip to go again, mainly because I like the name: it seems to be a Yorkshire kind of name, because we feel that we're superior, even when we're watching a bad print of *Carry On Up the Khyber* with a melting Mivvi in our dripping fists. The Elite opened in 1928 and had a beautiful auditorium that held, according to its website, 173 people. I did a poetry reading there sometime in the 1990s and since then it's become an emblem for me of the kind of entertainment a small town can provide. There weren't 173 people there, by the way, but there wasn't a smaller space to move the event to.

I'm unusual in that wherever I am I always assess the space for its potential as a gallery or performance space. That bus shelter? Great for huge impressionistic pictures of Malham Tarn. That quiet room in that café? Turn it into a theatre showing scenes from Yorkshire history. That clearing in the woods? A site-specific interactive sculpture. I have this shimmering and untested idea that maybe I can stage a dramatised extract from this book at the Elite with a scratch cast of local people. Maybe that bit where Michael Parkinson walks into the West End Club in Cudworth, with a local woman in a bespoke grey wig playing the part of the TV host.

I have a memory of the cinema being at the end of the hill with the market on it, and I stroll amongst the stalls. Leyburn is one of those places that's built around the beating heart of its market and on this Friday it's thronged with people. There's plenty of space, though, so the throng never becomes a jostle. I almost buy a spectacular tree of sprouts but I don't because if I carried them around with me people might think I was performing a one-man show about the Fertile Earth. Be good to do it in that bus shelter, though, or that clearing in the woods.

A woman goes up to a stall that's selling, amongst other country-based goods, bales of hay.

'I'm just after a bale of hay,' she says, laughing, as though she knows the word 'just' is always a lie, and that before the end of the morning she'll end up with a forest of sprouts and a companion set.

Of course I could ask somebody for directions to the Elite ('Which way is the Elite, sir?' 'Just follow the road south, young feller') but, because I'm from Yorkshire and I'm a man, that would be a laughably comprehensive admission of defeat that would haunt me for years. I'll find my destination by dead reckoning. I have a sudden sharp-as-a-fork vision that the cinema is in completely the other direction so I walk uphill. Drizzle is sketching on my glasses, giving Leyburn a post-impressionistic air. I wipe them with an old monogrammed hanky of my dad's that I seem to have ended up with. There's a ceremonial sword of his somewhere, from his navy days. I haven't got it on me, obviously. It would be useless for spectacle-cleaning.

There's a sign: The Shawl. It can't be the case that so little happens round here that they have to indicate pieces of clothing for you to go and marvel at.

'Mam, I'm bored. I've seen the Shawl! Do I have to go and look at it again?'

'Shurrup and come and look at this cummerbund!'

And of course the Shawl has a deeper historical and cultural significance, as an interpretive board informs me, breathlessly (or perhaps it's just that the letters are fading). The Shawl is a stretch of land overlooking the river, named after the item of clothing that Mary, Queen of Scots, was meant to have dropped as she fled from nearby Castle Bolton where she'd been imprisoned; she knew the area well and dodged the guards as they ran after her, presum- ably shouting, 'Your Majesty! Stop! Stop now, Your

Majesty!', using a mixture of aggression and obsequiousness, their voices alternately loud and soft, wheedling and commanding.

The story goes that as she ran the royal frame and possibly the royal legs got entangled in some bushes and she left her shawl behind. Think of a regal equivalent of those carrier bags you see entangled in branches like they've grown there. The leaving of the shawl may well be true although Mary, Queen of Scots has visited so many places and escaped from a number of them and left items of clothing in quite a few; her life could be measured out in dropped stitches of fallen cloth. The fallen shawl led the half-bowing, half-charging guards to the conclusion that they were on the right track and they eventually cornered and nabbed her in a series of choreographed movements near the appropriately named Queen's Gap, unless it was named after the event and not before.

The Shawl is an escarpment stretching up towards a playing field where swings hang in the misty absence of breeze. A man walks by with his dog carrying a bag of puppy piano, swapping it from hand-to-hand as though he's about to hurl it somewhere shouting 'Yeeeeha'; he sees me and gazes at his feet sheepishly. I imagine Mary running up this slope with the sweating guards in pursuit; I imagine her standing, like I'm doing, awestruck by the view, not just by the majesty of it (sorry, Mary) but by the sheer Yorkshireness of it: the roads, the barns, the houses, the crows rising from trees like tea-leaves stirred in a cup. I could be wrong, of course, and that's becoming a bit of a refrain for this book: the things that I perceive as being ur-Yorkshire, of shining in a Yorkshire way when I hold them up to the light, are maybe not that much different to anywhere else. I could be in Staffordshire here, where the moorlands begin to melt into Congleton; I could be somewhere on the edge of Whitehaven in Cumbria; I could be in Devon, looking down at a place where Cream Tea is a Household God. But I'm not. I'm in Yorkshire. Obvious. But why?

'Morning,' I say to the man with the dog.

'Aye,' he says, a syllable that speaks hardback volumes. The Yorkshire 'aye' means, 'Yes, I agree with you,' or 'I am content with the universe and my station in it,' or 'Yes, the world is going to Hell but at least we're in Yorkshire,' or 'I could tell you a thing or two, kid, but I won't this time. Maybe next time.' Or 'What you said, repeated back to you but with my own idiosyncratic linguistic fingerprint.'

The tiny sack of piano hangs as limp as the swings. I could say 'Bit misty' but I'd only get another 'Aye' back, and this one would mean slightly different things that I couldn't really interpret because I'm from a different part of Yorkshire. It would be like trying to second-guess an Inuit describing slush.

He wanders off. You don't often see people in Yorkshire loping, because you'd never lope to the pit or the mill, you'd trudge or shuffle, but this bloke loped. I carry on up the Shawl towards the top.

There are lovely detached houses by the side of the grass that are of the sort I covet. They look like you could live simple lives in them, simple Yorkshire lives in rooms that hadn't been changed for years. Room with high ceilings and old-fashioned light fittings. Rooms with calendars on the wall from years ago, left there because the picture was nice and with TVs that still show programmes in black and white. Rooms that J.B. Priestley could wander into and sit down in and go unnoticed and undisturbed, taking notes for his *English Journey*. Priestley is one of the great chroniclers of this county, forming an unlikely trio with Ted Hughes and Emily Brontë as a writer who has imprinted a certain vision of Yorkshire on the collective mind. I like to imagine them meeting at a weekly writing workshop and responding differently to the homework which was to describe Yorkshire in 50 words; no more, no less, in verse or descriptive prose' Priestley would have been the most practical, I think, Hughes the most lyrical, and Brontë would have somehow managed to squeeze a bit of plot into her 50 words. They'd all have featured rain.

I linger outside one house by the side of the Shawl for perhaps a bit too long. The mist begins to deepen and thicken. Its swirling becomes a bit more laboured and grinding. It feels heavy, wet-flannelish. I hear a distant sound that could be the loping bloke frisbeeing the doggie bag into a hedge of the sort Mary, Queen of Scots got shawltangled in.

In the front room of the house there's a Yorkshireman who could be me in 20 years. He's got grey hair like mine but his is a little wispy, a non-quiff. He's wearing a baggy jumper that could almost have knitted itself. There's a mug of tea on the chair arm and a picture on the wall that could be an Ashley Jackson landscape of the glowering and romantic moors over Holmfirth way. That man is me. He really is, he's a projection of me, with one difference: he definitely looks Yorkshire Enough. He's reading the *Yorkshire Post* for a start. Of course he is. The *Yorkshire Post* is the White Rose *Le Figaro*, a journal of record for the Ridings. He turns the page, looking for even more local news to chew on.

It's a broadsheet and I can see that the man is struggling with its dimensions; he could be adjusting rigging on a barque or folding the sheets ready to put away in the tallboy. It's as though he's doing his origami homework at the last minute. I write for the *Yorkshire Post* but that shouldn't stop me saying that it's a great paper. It's like this book in that it filters everything through the prism of Yorkshire. 'Yorkshire's National Newspaper', its masthead trumpets, but somehow you know that the news from Gilling East will be given just as much weight as the G20. It's like the apocryphal fantasy headline from the *Western Mail* that reads NUCLEAR APOCALYPSE: BOVEY TRACEY MAN INJURED.

He's turning the pages slowly, slowly and they still create a breeze that agitates his wisps. He's doing that flap/snap manoeuvre you have to do with big newspapers to try and get them to turn properly and not crumple up and they almost never do as they're told. I'm staring too hard at him in the mist; this won't do. He might see me. He might raise his fist and shout, 'Gerrof and gerron yer own part!', like Mrs Froggatt used to do. I turn and walk back down the Shawl, not a sentence you often get to write.

So the Elite Cinema isn't this way. Back in the market, I see the hay woman again, carrying the hay. The market is busy and, like I always do, I end up by a stall selling what can only be described, even in Yorkshire, as lingerie.

This always used to happen to me when I was a pre-adolescent man-child being dragged reluctantly round Barnsley's thronging market by my mam. My voice was starting to crack if not break and an absurdly long hair had sprouted from my chest overnight. We'd dance a stately purchasing polka around the fruit and veg and the stall that sold net curtains and the tripe-dresser and I'd be struggling with heavy bags of carrots and shoe polish. My mam would bump into somebody like Muriel who used to do her hair, or Mrs Yelland who taught me at school, and they'd stand and kall.

Kalling is what lesser civilisations might call gossiping or chinwagging or gassing. It's a choral and ritualised series of stories and responses to stories with its own strict and unbreakable oral rules: no one must start a tale until another tale has finished; laughter is only a good response towards the end of the kalling exchange; gestures, when used, must be used sparingly and without the huge movements employed by Les Dawson and Roy Barraclough in their Cissie and Ada routines; names should be employed sparingly, partly because everybody knows who you mean. In other words, to say 'Frank' is only acceptable once, but you can say, 'him from the top street who ran off with her from Worksop that kept a poodle parlour' as many times as you like.

As my mother and her co-kaller kalled to an Olympic standard, I would put the heavy bags down and rest my arms and I'd lean against a stall only to realise to my horror it was one selling scraps of lace and industrial-strength restraining devices that would restrict the growth of a new town if you pulled them tight enough. I'd glow red as a beef tomato and my mind would be drawn to those pages in my mother's catalogue that featured young women with conical breasts and Wonder Woman thighs staring into the middle distance, as though they were deciding whether or not it was warm enough to walk to West Melton without a scarf. Or, indeed, without a dress. Visions of Emma Peel from *The Avengers* or, worse, all the girls in our class and all the female teachers at school wearing the garments flooded my head unstoppably. My voice cracked some more and the hair on my chest appeared to stir slightly under my white vest.

I'd lurch forward to try and escape just as a man in a cap was holding up a bra and saying, 'Have you got three of these in bottle green for a big woman?' I'd pick up the bags and almost spontaneously combust. I'd stand by my mother and her mate as the kalling subsided to a halt. They'd go their separate ways and I'd follow, several steps behind to hide my frightening erection. It was the three green bras that finally broke me.

That was the past. In the present I slope away from the lace and wander across the road to a café where I ascertain from a group of three women at a table who were, indeed, kalling, that the Elite Cinema had closed a few years before and was being converted into flats. I feel a deep sadness and think about the Darfield Empire in the late 1950s. Yorkshire was once full of these palaces of delight, but so was everywhere.

For a number of days a Scottish £5 note has been weighing heavy in my man-purse like a bundle of roubles or zlotys. For some fiscally obscure reason, it's hard to spend Scottish money in South Yorkshire; indeed there used to be a sign in a butcher's on the High Street in Barnsley that read, presumably in a broad local accent, NO 50 OR SCOTCH NOTES, and you could tell them until you were puce that the Clydesdale Bank tenner you had in your hand was legal tender but they still wouldn't have it and you'd have to go home hamless. At least you weren't buying lingerie.

'Will we take a cheque for these novelty Days of the Week G-strings, Dennis? He's asking if he can leave a deposit on these pants?'

I dig the McFiver out and say to the lady in the café: 'Do you take these?' She looks at it.

'I know some places don't,' she says, popping it in the till, 'but we do. Because we're closer to Scotland.'

That's a robust Yorkshire, it seems to me. A Yorkshire that isn't afraid of dilution by Celts. Or, in the other direction, people from Lancashire. Or, in the other direction, people from the sea. Perhaps that's another Yorkshire lesson learned, here in the café entrance next to a till that's just eaten the money: this is a confident county, a place that is self-aware enough to withstand the battering of cliché and misunderstanding, that isn't fragile in any way. Yorkshire, and the idea of Yorkshire (which are perhaps two separate things although maybe not), is not a precious ornament that might smash if you drop it so you have to handle it with care. It's something you can kick around the room and throw against the wall and get a herd of cattle to stampede across and it won't break. It might crack a little, like my voice did around the swaying suspenders, but it won't break. We can take your Scottish money and your other dialects and your other languages and your different foods and your odd ways of describing teacakes and we won't be dissipated even if we're diluted. Like the hole in the middle of a half-sucked mint, Yorkshire will still be there, in all its multilingual glory. The North Yorkshire O will always shine like a full moon, sounding more like an A; 'I'm on the bus to Yark' somebody from Slingsby will say to someone on the other end of a mobile phone, sounding almost like a Viking would have if they'd had a pay-as-you-go. West Yorkshire people will throw the letter T away as soon as they can after starting a sentence so that (pardon my apostrophes) they've 'Go'a go to Ba'ley from Bra'fud.' And South Yorkshire language glories in the idea that the thing being said is either of no consequence at all or of the greatest consequence ever.

The 'no consequence' trope is illustrated by the expansion of the phrase 'Or summat'. A man from Barnsley will say, when he goes to the newsagent, 'I'm going for a paper or summat,' and this means that the buying of a paper is the most trivial thing in the world and he's only going to buy it because he has nothing better to do. Then the phrase will become 'I'm going for a paper or summat like that' and, in the filigreed world of Yorkshire semiotics that doesn't mean that he's going for a paper or something that's a bit like a paper, it means that the action of going for the paper is of even less moment than we suspected.

Later, the phrase will become 'I'm going for a paper or summat daft like that' which makes the action of going for the paper the most ridiculous thing the man has ever attempted. At the other end of the scale is the hyperbole of 'Tha what?' which doesn't mean 'pardon?' it means 'I can tell you that the thing we're talking about is on a colossal, not to say epic, scale.' So you say to somebody from Darfield, 'That was a good goal at Oakwell on Saturday, wasn't it?' and they'll reply, 'Tha what?', which mixes rhetoric and exaggeration and which contains the hidden phrase, 'it was the best goal you'll ever see there!' – the unsaid words rattling behind like carriages on a train.

And now, of course, the Yorkshire language is being transformed and enlivened by recent arrivals from all over Europe, carrying on the enriching process begun by those who came here from Asia and Africa. When I drop my grandson off at his school in Grimethorpe, I marvel at the way the parents can speak English as well as words I don't understand but which sound like a stream going over pebbles but in the classroom the children can speak pure Grimey as well as English and words I don't understand. Tha what? (in the celebratory sense of the phrase).

Time to go to Settle, one of the few places in the UK named after a piece of furniture; another one is Chesterfield, of course. Settle is another part of the great archipelago of tourist towns that are scattered over this part of Yorkshire but the reason I love going to Settle is that I can travel there on the Settle-Carlisle railway. I know I said that the Barnsley-Huddersfield line is the best railway journey in the world but this one is not too far behind. From Leeds you go through Shipley, Bingley, Keighley and Skipton, and then through Gargrave, Hellifield and Long Preston to Settle and at each stop, at each view, at each moment when the train lingers at a signal and then moves on, you thank goodness for the people who fought to keep the line open when all around them lines and stations were folding their wings forever. Building of the line began in 1869 and lasted seven years; it was created to cater for the growing Anglo-Scottish market as the railways shrunk the country and redefined time, and it was the last main-line railway in the country constructed almost entirely by hand, which is an amazing feat to contemplate when you think about the twin hammer blows of weather and landscape that would have pounded the bodies of the workers. Towards the end of the 1960s, however, the line was hanging by a thread and many of the smaller local stations were closed by the start of the new decade.

British Rail seemed to be keen to close the line but eventually, following a number of charter trains for walkers that were run by Dales Rail along the line which led to the reopening of some of the smaller stations, the whole line was saved from closure in 1989, a triumph of persistence and public opinion.

Once you arrive in Settle, it's hard to remember that you're not really that far from Bradford and Skipton; it feels remote, feels almost like an isolated island in a choppy sea of rough hills, and yet you could catch the train home and you'll be scuttling through Leeds station in just over an hour. When you tell people you're going to Settle people tap the sides of their nose or wink and say, 'Watch out for the naked man!' as though you're going to the Garden of Eden. The Naked Man Café is one of Settle's main attractions; it's a listed building that was once a private house where, presumably and only on suitable occasions at certain times of day, men were naked. Now it's a café and the sign, with a naked man who resembles the kind of key you might get in a downmarket hotel, dominates the High Street. The story is that it's called the Naked Man because someone was once buried under there, naked, and that's as plausible a reason as any.

I'd recommend visitors to Settle to tear themselves away from the Naked Man's buns and visit the Victoria Hall, England's oldest surviving music hall, in the heart of the town. Daniel Defoe said of Settle that it was 'the capital of an isolated little kingdom of its own surrounded by barren hills' and as I stand on the stage of the hall, feeling that I can almost lean over and touch the audience (although I wouldn't do that, I'm not that breed of flat cap rapper), I feel like I'm in the pocket-sized royal palace of the 'isolated little kingdom'. I stay in a hotel on the main street and I sit by a fire and watch people checking in and I get a snapshot of the kind of people who visit this end of the county. They're mainly people my age, grey-haired and leisure-suited. Their luggage matches and their walking shoes are new, perhaps bought as retirement presents; there's a young couple who can't wait to check in. He pats her bum with a kind of Morse code that everybody in the bar can read. There's a man checking in on his own and I guess that his rucksack, and probably his head, are full of railway timetables and facts. Like a version of that old Paul Simon song, they've all come to look for Yorkshire.

I guess that my idea of finding a venue everywhere in Yorkshire, a place to perform, to hang art, to show films, is exemplified in places like the Victoria Hall or the carriages of the Settle-Carlisle but then, as I think about it more and more, much of this part of Yorkshire is a permanent venue, three shows daily, Sundays and Bank Holidays a speciality. They never close even when they're closed, these venues: when every shop and café and pub is shut you'll still come across somebody wandering down a darkened street near a caravan park, walking a yapping dog and just taking in the view.

'It's gorgeous, isn't it?' they'll say as the tiny bells in the tiny church strike midnight and the light from the stars is symphonic and you realise that this person is taking his dog round an exhibition, a piece of art that's simultaneously ancient and modern. A display called Yorkshire. Or Yorkshire Through The Ages. Or Yorkshire Ancient and Modern. Or Yorkshire Perspectives. The chap walks past and him and his dog are not from these parts and you realise you're not just somebody on the street, you're an attendant in the National Gallery of Yorkshire. The visitor is the curator, deciding what to see, what to write home about, what to buy and move around the country. He might leave something, a few select words in a visitors' book, but essentially this is a buyer's market, and Yorkshire is the bargain.

I was once sitting at a table outside a pub in Settle when a child approached me. He looked about nine years old although his face was that of a wise old philosopher who was just on the brink of coming up with a new theory of Mind. 'Buy us a pint!' he said, and I laughed and offered him a crisp. He became more aggressive. 'Will yer buy us a pint?' he snarled. He showed me a purse. 'I'll pay yer!' A similar thing happened to me years before in the Leopard, a pub in Doncaster by the railway station. I sat in the dark interior nursing a beer before my bus was due and a gaggle of eight or nine lads of junior school age came in and sat with me at the table. The landlord shouted 'Hey, get out!' and the leader of the boys, who could almost have been the kid from Settle's brother, said 'He's me dad!' and the others, in a Spartacus moment, shouted 'He's my dad! He's my dad!' I supped up and left and they ran out after me then scattered across the streets. I must have the face of a bloke who will buy drinks for anybody. The Settle beer-beggar persisted. 'Go on, mister! It's only one pint! I'll give yer't money!' 'You're not old enough,' I said with an air of finality. He looked at me with pity and said 'I'm 38' and then I knew, if I didn't know already, that I was in Yorkshire, and his confidence and bluster and persistence told me a lot about why they kept the Settle-Carlisle railway open. He didn't scatter at a raised voice like my Doncaster family did; he just carried on asking until I drank up and left.

I find myself in the offices of the Settle-Carlisle railway development company and I'm left in charge as the people who are really in charge have to go out for a while. I do what I always do when I'm in charge; I gaze out of the window. Life in Settle is wandering by at, I have to say, a settled pace. A woman in late middle age walks past and suddenly and unexpectedly upends a bottle of pop and drinks deeply from it as though the street is a desert and she's found a stream in spate, and I'm instantly transported back to The Day Auntie Drank the Bleach. Sometime in the summer of 1965 I was at my auntie's at 34 North Street for tea, which consisted, for me anyway, of a bowl of baked beans with brown sauce on and some bread and butter. In the way that irony always butters life's bread she'd lectured me earlier about not drinking straight from the bottle and then went into her little kitchen and had a big glug of what she innocently thought was lemonade. I know that you're not supposed to store bleach in a lemonade bottle and I guess Auntie knew it as well, but that hadn't stopped her and Uncle Charlie deciding to do it. Maybe the bleach bottle had fallen off the shelf and smashed.

I heard Auntie gasping for breath and choking, and ran into the kitchen to see what was happening. Auntie's face had turned the colour of self-raising flour and her eyes were like those of a lemur. Then, because she was Auntie and she was a strong Yorkshire woman, she started buttering more bread even though her mouth and throat were combusting. My life has been shaped by strong women, from my mam who brought up my brother (and, for the first two years of my life, me) and looked after her ailing mother while my dad was away in the Navy, to teachers like Mrs Hudson with her vivid red lipstick and Mrs Hinchliffe who sang in a piercing chapel contralto all the way through assembly and made sure your punctuation could do all the heavy lifting in a sentence, no matter how long it was. On many evenings during my childhood, as my dad tied fishing flies in the conservatory and me and my brother watched TV, my mam would go two doors down the street and sit with Miss Hirst, an elderly lady who was reputed to be a hundred years old. I resented this a bit, and I remember asking her what they talked about and before she could answer my dad shouted, his voice muffled and transformed by the feathers in his mouth, 'Women's things!', and my mam tutted and went out of the door. I guess I'm just reinforcing a stereotype here, a seaside postcard of the daft-as-a-brush Yorkshire Bloke and the Steely Yorkshire Woman, the brains behind the outfit, the person who keeps everything together as the man flails and hops from one ridiculous escapade to another like a glove puppet where the hand has been withdrawn.

I love voting; I love that almost sacred, almost holy moment in the booth with the stubby pencil and the string and the paper on which your X could help to make huge changes possible, and I owe that love of exercising my democratic right to my mam and, indirectly, to Miss Hirst. One night my mam came back from her house and I asked her what they'd been talking about. 'Voting,' my mother replied, and she told me about Miss Hirst's excitement when women got to be allowed to vote after the First World War, about how she would get dressed up to walk down to the polling station because to be able to vote was a wonderful thing. Auntie agreed: 'Keep 'em art!' was all she'd say, and of course she meant the Conservatives. That was obvious in North Street. And East Street and West Street too. And South Street.

She was still coughing and still buttering bread. My Uncle Charlie came in from the garden and pinched a slice. 'She's drunk some bleach,' I said. He looked at her with a kind of opaque pity fringed with genuine concern and then slapped her on the back as though the bleach was a coin he could dislodge. It was a true Yorkshire moment, it seems to me: a cliché of the rock-hard woman carrying on buttering the bread because the family had to eat and the silly bloke stepping in off the street to help himself to the bounty. Like all clichés, it's a palimpsest of truths layered on top of each other, but it's still a bit of a crudely drawn cartoon. Later, when Auntie was lying on the settee moaning feebly, Uncle Charlie asked her if she wanted to go to the hospital but she shook her head and tried to speak. Her voice was a rasping Tom Waits whisper; we had to loom over her to hear what she was saying. 'It's okay,' she croaked, 'it was diluted.'

I catch the first train back from the isolated little kingdom to Leeds on a Saturday just to check the commutable possibilities of Settle, and it's raining so much I think I'm back in Hull. The streets seem to made from old blotting paper and the sky, as well as being dark, is black, if that's possible: the colour of night and the colour of the rain overlaying each other above my dripping head.

At the time of the first train the shelter and the ticket office aren't open so I find myself huddling in a doorway at the side of the station, the lintel showering me with drips; lit cigs and glowing smartphones show my fellow passengers squeezed into tight spaces like me, illuminated like images on a medieval manuscript. Every so often I glance at the electronic departure board because, although I never want a train to be cancelled or late, I particularly don't want this particular train to be cancelled or late. It isn't. It arrives on time and its imminence is signalled by a mass difting of cigs and a turning off of mobiles. There's nothing better than the sight of a train's lights approaching on the gleaming rails through the enveloping gloom.

I get on and sit behind a bloke who has one of those odd old/young faces. He could be a wrinkled tomato or an experienced infant. He could be that lad who tried to get me to buy him a pint, decades on. He's got two teenagers with him, one of whom is probably his son, and the other one who is the son's mate. They look tired, like lads that age often do, peppering the carriage with jaw-cracking yawns, and the dad is the opposite: he's full of beans and he's like me in that he likes to talk all the time about what he's doing, about what he's just done, and about what he's about to do. Other people in the carriage avert their faces, hide behind printed or electronic reading matter, or feign sleep. I gaze.

After a few minutes, I ascertain that they're off to London to watch a rugby match and I can see that this trip is designed by the chatty chap as a kind of Yorkshire initiation ceremony, a visit to That London to show the lads that Yorkshire is better in every possible way than any capital city could ever be through a series of beery escapades. He is so, so excited. If he was a pond he would ripple.

People often think that we in Yorkshire say 'That London' as a joke, and I've known media types to say it ironically to show how far they'd come from the grimy streets of their birth. People believe that nobody would ever say it without irony. Klaxon: we say it. Without irony.

In Barnsley we tell the legendary tale of the school trip that went to That London and one of two brothers got separated from the crocodile. He didn't panic but walked straight up to the nearest policeman and said, 'Heyop; has tha seen our big 'un?' The copper asked him what their big 'un looked like and the schoolboy replied, 'He looks like me without a cap on.'

The man is trying to nudge some ideas from the lads as to what they should do when they get there. They're going to be in the big city nice and early, he says, and there'll be hours before kick-off so they may as well take advantage.

'The Tower of London,' he says. 'You'd like the Tower of London. Lots of history there and you can nip in and see the Crown Jewels.' I can tell he hasn't been to London for a while.

I want to lean over and tell him its official name is the Tower of That London but I don't. When I took my kids to the Tower years ago my son, then aged about nine, kept saying that he wanted to go to the Bloody Tower just because he liked saying the word Bloody without being told off. Imagine him emphasising the L in Bloody; it becomes the BLoody Tower.

'We'll go to the BLoody Tower first,' he said, 'and then when we've been to the BLoody Tower we'll go to the other bits but I've looked at a map and you have to go past the BLoody Tower to get to the rest of it.'

The lads snooze whilst pretending to listen. 'Then when we've been to't Tower of London we can walk down to

Oxford Street and do some shopping, get your mam a souvenir, and then we can walk down and check into't hotel and then get down to't match.'

I think he's being wildly optimistic in terms of time and space but I daren't say. London isn't Middleham, though. I should have said that I preferred the Bastard Tower but I BLoody didn't.

One of the lads says, 'Where is the hotel anyway?' and the man shakes his head, looking slightly worried.

'I can't remember. I'll have to ring your mam. She'll not be up yet. She booked it. It'll be fine. It'll be fine.'

The cheerful guard comes round and checks the tickets. 'Have a good day in London, lads!' he says to them. Damn! He didn't say That London. Perhaps in the comfort of this book he can; it's my view of Yorkshire, after all.

'Have a good day in That London, lads!' the guard says. That's better.

The man with the young/old face warms to what seems to be his favourite subject: debauchery lessons for the Yorkshire Young.

'We'll have to find plenty of time for beer,' he says. He rattles a carrier bag. 'I've got some cans,' he says, 'just to start us off. Real ale or as real as you can get in cans: Timothy Taylor's, Theakston's. Proper Yorkshire brews. We'll probably crack them open after Peterborough, that's best. That's best all round. So it's essential that before we get to Peterborough you have a bacon sarnie to line the stomach. You might not feel like one but it's for the best because later on you're going to get terribly bladdered.'

I don't want to give the impression that this bloke is some kind of hooligan looking forward to a weekend of liquid mayhem in That London. He's telling the boys in his charge all this in a spirit of earnest endeavour. He's passing something on. He has tablets of wisdom and he's disseminating. He wants them to do well in the world and in his view to approach Yorkshire manhood you must, as a long-distance lorry driver called Adrian from Leeds once said to me when I hitched a lift up the M1, not drink beer but wallow in it.

One of the boys is now completely asleep, snoring gently.

'Then when we've been shopping and that and the Tower, we'll check in and have some more beers in the hotel bar and maybe summat else to eat and then we'll go to the match and have some more beer. Now,' he nudges the sleeping lad who must be his son, 'I heard you come in last night and you were staggering and that because you'd had a few and I heard you pissing like a hoss but do you know what you didn't do? Eh? Do you know what you didn't do? You didn't have a glass of water. I blame myself because I knew you were going out but I'd had a few real ales and I wasn't thinking straight and I should have put a glass of water beside your bed. So tonight when we get in we'll have had a lot of beer and some real ale and maybe some shorts if we're bloody desperate so it's essential, are you listening to me? It's essential that you put a glass of water beside your bed. Two glasses if you like, because they only give you bloody dinky ones in them hotels.'

Both the boys are fast asleep now, mouths open cavernously. The train is filling up with shoppers. The woman who's been knitting since Skipton is knitting faster than anyone has ever knitted. I bet she has to have a glass of water beside the bed to dip her needles in. The man pulls his mobile out of his pocket and rings a number, slowly, his lips moving. Needles click, lads snore, a baby cries, the train rattles.

The man looks at his phone impatiently. He puts it away. He gets it out again and presses the redial button with a broad thumb. He speaks slowly and carefully, leaving a message.

'Can.you.just.tell.me.where.our.hotel.is?Ta.' One of the lads wakes himself up with the noise of his snoring.

SLEEPLESSNESS AS A CONDITION OF YORKSHIRENESS

I T'S 2AM IN late December and I'm awake; an owl woke me up, hooting eerily from the cemetery, and now I'm lying waiting for the next hoot. Sometimes there's thick silence for several minutes and I think the owl must have drifted off to the fields to hunt voles, in defiance of the hunting ban. Then it hoots again, plaintively, a kind of stuttering sob that breaks your heart. And those of several voles and a newt. They say that if you hear an owl hooting you're actually hearing two owls hooting, one to the other in a kind of antiphonal mating ritual, but this just sounds like one. Or one and an impersonator. My mind won't let me rest; it seems to be playing ideas in my head at the speed of a very fast bebop trumpet solo.

I blame the owl for all this but I've been restless for days. It's this book, I think, and the huge task of it. Yorkshire is such an enormous ocean and my net is so tiny and so full of holes. Extra ones, of course, not the ones that make it a net. I chuck the net over the side, hoping to catch ideas and conclusions and revelations and it comes back full but it misses so much. I'm also sleepless because since I've been to Settle

I've been thinking about Daniel Defoe and George Orwell. I'm also sleepless because I've been thinking about sleeplessness and that would keep anybody awake. My dad, during his long Navy career, was often on the four-hour watch, which meant that he always woke up four hours after he went to bed. I'm my daddy's boy. Gags like Sleepless in Settle come to mind and are instantly dismissed. *Hoot.*

Daniel Defoe, in his *Tour Thro' the Whole Island of Great Britain*, came to Yorkshire in the 1720s and wrote about it vividly and entertainingly as he helped to invent the theory and the practice of English prose as he went along. The book is in the form of letters and you get the sense he must have been running for the last post when he described Barnsley.

> … passing a town called Black Barnsley, eminent still for the working in iron and steel: and indeed the very town looks as black and smoaky as if they were all smiths that lived in it; though it is not, I suppose, called Black Barnsley on that account, but for the black hue and colour of the moors, which, being covered in heath (or heather as 'tis called in that country) look all black, like Bagshot Heath near Windsor …

I've been to Bagshot Heath and I've never thought it looked like Barnsley before but I'm pleased that the thought has been planted. I always feel disappointed for my town when I see that Defoe has skirted over it like this, although I'm in love with his long and particularly un-Yorkshireish sentences. He wasn't taciturn, that's true. I know that Barnsley isn't Yorkshire, of course, but it's the middle of the night and my net is small and the water is vast. *Hoot*.

George Orwell came to Barnsley and lived there while he was writing *The Road to Wigan Pier* in 1936. His description of the working conditions down Grimethorpe Pit would keep anybody awake.

> The place where the fillers were working was fearful beyond description. The only thing one could say was that, as conditions underground go, it was not particularly hot. But as the seam of coal is only a yard high or a bit more, the men can only kneel or crawl to their work, never stand up. The effort of constantly shovelling coal over your left shoulder and flinging it a yard or two beyond, while in a kneeling position, must be very great even to men who are used to it. Added to this there are clouds of coal dust which are flying down your throat all the time and which make it difficult to see any distance ... they work bent over, naked except for their boots.

The sentences are shorter than Defoe's and less discursive and inclined to kalling but they still say the same thing: Barnsley is mucky. There should be ways for me to describe it that clean it up and there will be ways for me to hurl myself out of this part of the county and explain the rest of the White Rose to myself and then to everyone else. Just not now. It's too early or it's too late. *Hoot*.

I get out of bed and go downstairs slowly and carefully so as not to wake anybody up. It's been snowing and outside the streetlights are turning the snow orange. I sit at the table and glance at my open journal, the one I've been scribbling ideas for this book in. The sentences are scattered and half-formed, and trying to decipher my handwriting becomes a form of redrafting. It turns out, as I try to get the kettle to boil quietly through the power of thought, that I've been using the notebook to ask myself the big questions I want this book to answer. What is Yorkshire For? What Does Yorkshire Mean? Are There Therefore Layers of Yorkshire Meaning That We Simply Don't Understand? Can You Have a Yorkshire of The Mind That Floats Alongside The Real Yorkshire? I read them and think of Defoe who skirted this part of the county like I'm skirting other parts and I think of Orwell who lived here to let the place soak in. There are also single words floating in the clear soup of the white page: Narrative. Alternative. Unity. Layers. All these words suggest themes for me to expand on.

Then, there's a note upside down at the bottom of the page that really tickles my fancy as the night seems to shift and late becomes early: Yorkshire as Pub Name. I suppose it's at the top of the page if it's upside down.

Now there's an idea. Now there's an organising device. Now there's something that might give the book a shape that can help it to wrestle the idea of Yorkshireness to the ground until it taps out. I sit at the desk and scribble. Then I get the notebook and scribble in that. I'll wash my hands later. I could imagine a pub called the Yorkshire Arms that would be a metaphor for everything about the county. The beer would be cheap, of course, and the crisps would be parkin flavoured; the bar staff would wear flat caps that were slightly too large and waistcoats that were slightly too small. That would just be window-dressing.

The real purpose of the pub, at least in this discourse, would be to highlight the social, cultural and class differences that Yorkshire is drenched in. In the tap room, those workers that Orwell described would hunch round tables glugging ale. Their voices would be a bit like mine but they would be louder because of the noisy conditions they worked in, and occasionally one of them would stand up and sing a revolutionary song about 'Utopia Just Around the Corner' or, more likely, an old music-hall ditty about a 'Girl Down Our Way'. They might both have the same tune. Accents and dialects would battle for supremacy and it would feel like something profound was about to be said, like that moment when an orchestra is tuning up. Someone would be reading a strident political pamphlet and a lesser writer than me would have him wipe his sweaty brow with it after finishing a page. Women would be smoking pipes. A glass would fall to the ground and shatter and there would be a moment of tense silence. Beards would be long and moustaches spectacular. Someone in a corner would be talking excitedly about *Homer's Odyssey*. A fight would break out as a consequence of the dropped glass and faces would be slapped and arses kicked and ale would fly and people would shout 'GEEOR NAR' and 'STOPPIT JUST STOPPIT NAR' and 'OY MARRA NAY NAR' and 'JUST SIT DARN AN SHURRUP AND SUP YOUR ALE NAR' and you wouldn't really know if they were talking or shouting or indeed singing.

In the lounge, the landowners and the mill owners and the factory gaffers would be sitting at slightly larger tables sipping halves and glasses of sherry and talking about horseracing and the price of lace. Their voices would be a little bit like mine; they would sound like me as though through a sieve. The room would be quieter and the people in it would be making an attempt to speak, not only in sentences, but in proverb-like word-clusters that showed just how clever they were. They would be making education audible, celebrating their newly acquired literacy with long words that they may or may not have been using properly. One would be ostentatiously reading a newspaper to show how far away from the people in the other room he was. A lesser writer than me would have him reading it upside down. The people in the lounge would occasionally glance at the noise coming from the tap room and tut and make their eyebrows dance. Someone would stand up and sing a few verses from a hymn or a gentle folk-influenced song that featured shepherds and moons. An argument would break out, quietly at first. Hissing sibilants would rise in the smoky air: '*Sir. My good sir. Simply an untenable state of affairs. Unacceptable.*' A hand would be raised. A soft cheek would be struck softly. People would say, '*Oh stop. Do stop. Do stop now.*' '*Sir, no fisticuffs or kerfuffle; you are not like Faust selling his spirit to the gods, sir.*' A cravat would be tugged at and tugged at until it became dangerously tight. Someone else would be reading Dickens' *All the Year Round*. A lesser writer than me would describe his lips moving in an exaggerated and comedic fashion. The voices would be raised a tiny little bit and you wouldn't know if they were talking or shouting or, indeed, singing.

Maybe that's too simplistic, but perhaps it's a good model to work from. Rates of literacy for men and, to a lesser extent, women, grew in the nineteenth century and the people in the lounge might have been disturbed to know that for the people in the tap room the idea of reading, any kind of reading, was good for soul as well as the mind. And it can't be far, especially at this time of night, to make a leap from these autodidacts and self-made men to the West Riding and Sir Alec Clegg.

I sit at the table and continue to write and the pub sign of the Yorkshire Arms swings in the breeze as I type. Pub names can tell you so much. I think I've hit a rich seam here: I might have to work bent over, naked except for my boots. Pub names can resonate with meaning and a kind of found poetry. At secondary school in the French class we had to write about what we'd done the night before and one girl meant to put that she'd spent the night in the Gardener's Arms but she actually put, in a Lawrentian way, that she'd spent the night in the arms of the gardener.

As a young married couple, my wife and I lived not far from Low Valley Juniors near the place where the River Dove divided Darfield from Wombwell. Our nearest pub was the Bricklayer's Arms, which was known locally as The Drop, because you had to mind the gap as you went in because of the huge step. Unofficial language was taking over from official language. Many years later the pub bit the bullet and renamed itself The Drop but that felt like a step too far because once signage is involved a word stops being colloquial. Ask those who live at the Top of Dodworth Bottoms.

We were sitting in The Drop in the very early 1980s when a man came in with things to sell.

'He's here!' somebody shouted. 'The spiv!'

And indeed he did look a bit like Private Walker in *Dad's Army*.

'What's tha got for us?' a faceworker from Darfield Main shouted, his eyes rimmed with the coal-dust mascara the pit painted on and which was almost impossible to wash out.

The man put two bags on a table. He opened one bag and pulled something out, something that almost wriggled as though it was alive.

'Pit socks!' he shouted.

A man replied 'Pit socks?' and it felt like I was in the rehearsal of a contemporary opera. The man opened the other bag and blades flashed in the lights of the fruit machine.

'Bacon scissors!' he shouted, triumphantly. There was a silence you could have cut with a pair of bacon scissors.

I'd never heard of bacon scissors before although Delia Smith (who wasn't often in The Drop) once wrote that her grandmother called kitchen scissors 'bacon scissors', and she should know.

There was general bemusement at the idea of the scissors but people fell on the thick white pit socks like they were going out of fashion, although of course they'd never been in fashion. They'd be good to wear in a narrow seam though, and they'd stop you cutting your feet. I didn't work down the pit so, in an extravagant beer-fuelled gesture, I bought a pair of bacon scissors while my wife was in the toilet and presented them to her when she returned as though they were something precious, as though she was a Lady Mayor about to cut the ribbon on a new playground paid for out of the public purse.

She was sceptical. 'We don't need any bacon scissors,' she said, as though they were the most ridiculous thing in the world. I offered to buy her some pit socks to wear as bed socks but she declined.

Later that night, a little drunk in the kitchen, I ostenta-tiously cut the rind off some bacon with the scissors and made myself a bacon sandwich. My wife had gone to bed and I kept shouting upstairs, 'By, this bacon's well cut!', until I fell asleep on the settee, dribbling.

Geoff Hattersley, a marvellous writer from Wombwell, once wrote a poem that ended with a man running through Low Valley with a pair of scissors sticking out of his back, and I often wondered if they were bacon scissors and if that would have made a difference to the poem.

Pub names are like tree rings in Yorkshire or anywhere that's gone through post-industrialisation; they're diaries and ledgers and they have a narrative arc. Another local pub, one of a cluster built to serve the thirsty clacks of the three shifts at Darfield Main, was the Miner's Arms, a safe and self-explanatory name until it changed hands some-time after the strike, when there weren't many miners around anymore, and it became the Viking Bar. Its USP was what the management claimed was a full-sized Viking longboat in place of a bar and the rumour was that the staff would be dressed as Vikings, although this never happened, much to the disappointment of some of the young lads who clustered round the pool table. It felt odd and disconcerting to stand with a pint and a bag of dry roasted nuts at the side of a ship, as though you'd fallen overboard earlier. After a few years the Vikings left town and the pub was renamed again, this time as Thawley's, which is reputed to be haunted, possibly by a Viking or a lost pit-socks-and-bacon-scissors salesman. I could find no reason why it was called Thawley's and I suspect that the American landlord got the name by sticking his finger into a phone book. It was a relief in a way: it could have been called the A1Ace Arms. A pub is an envelope, its name is the map, and the new names are the postmarks that take you very specifically through time. Now, Thawley's is boarded up and is rumoured to be about to become a convenience store, which is what a pub is in a way, a convenience store of memories woven into pit socks.

Our other pub of choice, a hundred yards from the Miner's/Viking/Thawley's namechanging vortex was the New Station Inn, named after Wombwell's second station, Wombwell Central, which closed in 1959 when it ceased to be the new station. There were thousands of keyrings hanging from the ceiling and banknotes of different countries pinned to a space above the bar so that when you walked in, and often when you walked out, it appeared that you were entering a still photograph of a museum that was turning and turning in a hurricane. The landlord had a very high voice and he always greeted you like a long lost friend even if you'd just been in that dinnertime. He could have been a counter-tenor in his spare time at the Wombwell

Amateur Operatics and I believe somebody once suggested that to him and he barred them and sent them to the Viking Bar.

In 1979 I innocently had my stag night there which amazes younger people when I tell them. They prefer Lodz or Riga. I vaguely remember me and the lads sitting at a table surrounded by a mountain of crisp bags singing Bob Seger songs. I vaguely remember us buying a bottle of whisky from behind the bar and drinking it as we staggered across Hope Street towards Darfield Main. I'm embarrassed to recall that I began to hammer a metal dustbin with a stick as I sang 'Take It Easy' by The Eagles until a window was flung open and a man shouted, 'Will yer shurrup! Am on days!'

I laughed and replied that I was the knocker-up and he shouted, 'I'll knock thee up when I get hod of thi booans!', and we ran through the darkened streets like only a stag party can run: discursively, letting the incident spill into anecdote as we went.

Then for no reason that anybody could fathom the New Station changed its name in the late 1980s to The Wat Tyler Inn. Tyler was that famous radical who led the Peasants' Revolt in 1381, marching from Canterbury to London to make his point. As far as I know, he never visited Wombwell; perhaps, like Percival Cresacre, he may have been blown off course a little but not by that much.

When it opened as the Wat Tyler, the pub sign stuck out into the road so much that passing buses and trucks clipped it endlessly, making it swing until it was removed and fastened to the wall like a mural. The Wat Tyler eventually became the Low Valley Arms and then it closed completely. As I write this, it's still shut and a board outside is announced planning permission for a small development of town houses. When things look up, of course, they'll be built. New Station Road will lead to Wat Tyler Close and you'll turn left into Low Valley Road. Except then the address will be Low Valley Road, Low Valley. Like New York: so good they named it twice. The pub is being demolished and you can see Yorkshire light through the remains of its walls.

It's almost morning now and the owl has gone to bed. I stand by the window gazing out into the street I've lived on for more than 30 years on the feet I've stood on for nearly 60 years. On the main road a lorry passes noisily, perhaps on its way to the ASOS warehouse down by where Grimethorpe Pit used to be, where the ceilings are higher and the work is hard in a very different way. Change, that's what this county is about. Stasis, that's what this county is about. Time for bed. *Hoot.*

THE YEAR TURNS LIKE A PIT WHEEL

NEW YEAR'S EVE. One year is about to click into another with a sound that can be heard for miles. Or maybe that's just the fireworks echoing across the valley, waking the ghost of Sir Percival Cresacre and almost reanimating the cat that chased him through the woods. This could be classed as Yorkshire dourness but I normally go to bed early on New Year's Eve, even earlier than normal, at about half past nine. I don't like new years: I like the old year, the year that's as comfortable as a cardigan, the year I know like the back of my hand. And yes, I know all years were new once but I think a condition of Yorkshireness is nostalgia for the very recent past, the past that hasn't cooled yet. The Germans call it Ostalgie and I know what they mean. I lie there listening to classical music on the radio and thinking about time and the way it speeds up the older you get until it appears to have caught the bus you were running for. Indeed it seems to be driving the bus away from you as quickly as possible.

I try and devise a system of Yorkshire time, where each minute is worth two ordinary minutes. That'll slow it down to a walking pace and give it time to look round.

I think all this is also partly a reaction to my mother and dad, who always stayed up to see the New Year in, even though by half-past eleven my dad was yawning like Pavarotti with the sound down and my mother was fussing that nobody would come to the door shouting, 'Old Year Out, New Year In,' and was endlessly rearranging buns and mince pies on her best cake stand, shuffling and cutting the pack, dealing each layer a hand. My parents made a lot of the New Year because my dad was Scottish and for him it was as big a deal as Christmas, if not bigger. He took great delight in calling it Hogmanay: I rarely heard him exaggerate his accent, but when he said Hogmanay he sounded like Janet, Dr Finlay's housekeeper.

Recent research, however, has shown that the word Hogmanay was actually used for the first time on these islands in Methley, not far from Leeds, in 1444 by the master of Sir Robert Waterton's Household, Richard Whitwood, who referred to it in the household accounts in the original sense of the word as meaning a gift; indeed children would shout the word on the streets at that time as they went in search of presents. In vain, probably, if they were in Yorkshire. Unless you count a clip round the ear as the gift that keeps on giving.

An etymologist, writing in the *Scotsman*, the tartan equivalent of the *Yorkshire Post* but with fewer Rugby League match reports, said:

The Yorkshire citation does raise the question of whether the word came to Scotland as a result of the Auld Alliance and the country's links with France, or whether it is something that existed earlier, in English. I wouldn't say the definite point of origination of (the word) Hogmanay was Yorkshire, but I think we're probably still looking at British influence at the Northern British Isles sometime in the Middle Ages.

Yeah, yeah, Mr Etymologist. Hogmanay is from Yorkshire and you know it. It's just another aspect of civilisation that Yorkshire has given to the world.

Back at my childhood New Year's Eve, people normally came in small loud groups, giddy with beer, and my mother would give them a glass of sherry and a slice of cake. My dad would have nodded off on the settee so for a moment, when he woke up with the snort of an interrupted snore, he'd think we were being burgled by a glee club. In the background Andy Stewart would carry on singing and the accordion notes would skirl around the room and land on the canary's cage.

One year, probably because of the howling gale outside, nobody came and so about 20 minutes into January, my brother John had to go out in his paisley (more Scottish influence) pyjamas and dressing gown, knock on the door, and then be readmitted into the room to be the first foot. He solemnly gave my mother a lump of coal, which she dropped into the coal bucket with a noise that was slightly different to last year's.

'What do you wish for the New Year?' my dad asked, ritually, and my brother replied, with a glint in his eye, 'Home rule for Scotland,' knowing that my dad wasn't a fan of that particular branch of politics. This was the late

1960s when the idea of an independent Scotland was as likely as Leek in Staffordshire becoming a sovereign nation, and my brother's remarks and my dad's silence brought the party to an awkward premature end with my dad washing up at the sink singing 'The Mucking of Geordie's Byre' and my brother and I going to bed as my mother put the uneaten buns back in a tin.

That was then, of course. And this is now. In 2014 Scotland came within a caber toss of voting for independence, and as I'm writing this book I seem to feel the seismic shifts of a United Kingdom starting to, well, ununite. It's like being on a flag-festooned bouncy castle that's either slowly deflating or is pumped too full and is about to spring a sudden and fateful leak and go whizzing all over the north of England at the speed of an inter-city train. And maybe because it's late and maybe it's because my grandson has come to stay and he's asleep upstairs and I'm getting sentimental and a little weepy about the idea of him being the future, I'm starting to ask myself about the idea of Home Rule For Yorkshire. Yes, I know: once that would have been like talking about the Kingdom of Macclesfield but now it's starting to make sense. Or 'sense', if you like. What a glorious thing it would be, or what a terrible thing it would be. I just can't decide.

The idea of the separate Land of the White Rose has been around for a long time. In a 1968 *Spectator* article by John Rowan Wilson, a man who mainly put together *Reader's Digest* condensed books and so was used to shaping reality to his own ends, wrote in a piece called 'Home Rule For Yorkshire':

If the Yorkshireman has not yet fully awakened to the possibilities of an independence movement, it is not because of any lack of confidence in his ability to make it on his own. He believes implicitly in the racial superiority of Yorkshiremen. This doctrine is passed down from father to son. As soon as Yorkshire boys can understand connected sentences, they are regaled with stories and legends of a self-glorifying nature. They are told Yorkshire jokes and taken to see Yorkshire comedians at the pantomime. They are taken to cricket matches and bribed with ice-cream and chewing gum while they are indoctrinated with the details of the religious ceremony taking place in front of them.

I know he's being tongue-in-cheek, but I can't argue with a lot of that. It makes sense to me. I was taken as a child to see the great Yorkshireman David Whitfield at a pantomime in Leeds with the Sunday school, and I remember that he tried to pick on Miss Tunstall and get her to come out of the audience and onto the stage. He might as well have tried to get the Queen to peel off a first class stamp and take part in the slosh scene.

Later in the article, Wilson gives as good an argument for us as a self-ruling gang as I've ever read. Or ever read in the *Spectator*, anyway:

And yet ... there is something about the people you find nowhere else. Proud but self-mocking, stoical, independent; they are, in the fashionable phrase, alienated, but in a rather grand sort of way. And the voices.

Who would not trade the strangulated courtesy of the
Old Etonian for the harsh, contemptuous bark of
Cleckeckmondshedge, or for the ferocious baying
insults of Allerton Bywater?

Putting aside the fact that I've been to Allerton Bywater
and have never been bayed at there, ferociously or not, I
think Wilson is on to something there, particularly with
that wonderful sentence, 'Proud but self-mocking, stoical,
independent, they are, the fashionable phrase, alienated,
but in a grand sort of way.'

Yes! In a grand sort of way. In a champion sort of way.
In a gradely sort of way.

Independence is in the air at the moment; like smoke,
like spores. The Yorkshire Devolution Movement's website
tries to be cool and objective, but you can still feel their
hackles rising at the perceived injustices meted out on us
alienated Yorkshire folk by the rest of the galaxy. In the
section 'Why a Directly Elected Assembly?' they talk about
the equipment on the county's railways:

87 per cent of northern rolling stock was built in the
1980s whereas 64 per cent of southern rolling stock is
built after 2000. This is another example of the north,
especially Yorkshire, being given the short straw. A
Yorkshire Parliament would better prioritise transport.

That's telling them, and it's true about the rolling stock.
Ours doesn't so much roll as hobble, pausing for breath. I
like the idea of being given a short straw rather than having

to draw one, too. It makes our downtrodden state feel inevitable and pre-ordained.

The answer to the FAQ 'But isn't Yorkshire too small?' is breathtaking in its beauty and matter-of-factness. It's blunt, to put it mildly:

> Yorkshire has a population of 5.3 million which is larger than Scotland and a GDP double that of Wales but the powers of neither. Furthermore, Yorkshire has a larger population than that of eight European countries.

I love that 'furthermore', echoing like an ungloved fist on a table at a public meeting in a church hall as the zumba class pounds away upstairs.

A newly formed political party called Yorkshire First is to put up a number of candidates at the general election, including a former Golcar Councillor and champion of local transport, Paul Salveson, whose aspirations include 'halting the brain drain of young people to London'. I'm all for that. I expect, though, that there'll be a lot of the condescension Leeds Metropolitan University got in 2007 when it set up the School of Northern Studies. Northern, mind, not just Yorkshire, but we seemed to get the sneery end of the stick, particularly in the press. The headline in the *Metro*, the free newspaper picked up all over the country, spoke volumes – EEH BAH GUM UNIVERSITY OFFERS NORTHERN STUDIES – and the first paragraph read, 'University students wanting to learn about coal-mining, Rugby League and brass bands can now enrol on a degree about life up north, it was revealed today.' You can hear the strangulated courtesy of Eton sizzling like Yorkshire Pudding batter in a hot oven.

Mind you, some commentators go further, fragmenting the new republic before the paint is dry on the commemorative mugs. Angus Young in the *Hull Daily Mail* wrote in 2014: 'Perhaps it's time to draw a line in the sand and declare our independence from Yorkshire once and for all.' The sub-heading to the piece goes further: 'In a fictionalised account of East Yorkshire's War of Independence, Mel Gibson could play a simple farmer from Burstwick who rises up against the West Yorkshire mafia.'

He can't mean me. I'm South Yorkshire. For years I was a proud member of the Socialist Republic of South Yorkshire and now I'm just from South Yorkshire. I think that people picking this book up in a second-hand bookshop in years to come will see it as a prophetic tome about Yorkshire becoming an independent state which will certainly happen sometime soon. In my lifetime anyway, I hope. I'll be the honorary life president, of course, like a benign version of a dictator. Simon Thackray would be Minister of Culture, and we'd all go to parliament in Giant Yorkshire Puddings. The parliament would move around, rather like the presidency of the EU; six months in Leeds, six months in Harrogate, three years in Barnsley, six months in Bradford, six months in Hull, three years in Barnsley. And the real head of state would rotate too; every year we'd elect a strong Yorkshirewoman from the crowd, a version of my auntie, someone who could metaphorically drink bleach and butter the bread of policies and decisions. Remember: this is where the seeds of that New Utopia were sown.

It's late on New Year's Eve now and you can tell that I'm half asleep on the settee; I'm having a part-dream, part-fantasy about me becoming honorary life president of an independent Yorkshire.

I'm being carried shoulder-high by a cheering crowd towards a kind of altar draped with a huge flag that depicts a white rose on a blue background. Because the flag is so big the rose looks like a small island on a flat calm sunlit sea. The crowd's cheers coalesce into a chant, rhythmic and all-enveloping: 'Yorkshire Enough! Yorkshire Enough! He's Ian McMillan and he's Yorkshire Enough!' Freddie Trueman is standing in front of the altar with an orb that looks from here like a giant Yorkshire Pudding. Behind him, in the harsh light of miners' lamps, my mother's lost pudding tins glow. Freddie greets me with a Yorkshire noise that's indecipherable to the rest of the world but which speaks volumes to me about history, and opposition to the mainstream, and Yorkshireness. He passes me the pudding orb and leans forward and he's about to say something even more profound and/or indecipherable, I can tell. The chanting of the crowd is getting louder and louder. They seem to be talking in staccato bursts and one or two are popping celebratory balloons with my head on. Huge balloons. They seem to be exploding.

I wake up lolling on the settee like a Rubens' nude with a dressing gown on. It's midnight and there are fireworks going off everywhere outside. Happy New Year, I say to myself and to the receding figures in my dream. So am I Yorkshire Enough now? Is the fact that I'm uncovering the complexities of the county making me more authentic, more tyke?

If writing this book is teaching me anything it's that Yorkshire is a many-layered place. It's not something you can spend a few minutes or a few hours manipulating before you come up with a definite answer. It's not a Rubik's Cube. It's not a jigsaw. It's not a paint-by-numbers image that gradually reveals itself as you dab.

SHEFFIELD: A CITY BUILT ON HILLS

YEARS AGO SOMEBODY from Sheffield City Council reminded me that when you came out of the station there used to be two signs, both pointing in different directions, but both pointing to the city centre, and that was Sheffield's problem: it didn't know where it was and where it was going. Perhaps this was because it was so busy churning out world-class steel that it didn't have to worry about visitors; they'd find their own way about by the noise of ingot-on-ingot action and the afternoon light glinting on glasses of Wards and Stones fine ales. That's all changed now, of course: when you stroll from platform 1, you realise that you're at a Visitor Destination. You walk out by a series of fountains and water features, past a gleaming metal and water sculpture that looks like a blade and is designed to guide you smoothly up towards the hill that leads towards the Crucible and the aforementioned city centre.

On the day I cross the road, everybody else who crosses it with me seems to be a student, and there's no doubt about it, Sheffield is a great city of learning with thousands of undergraduates at two universities, pushing past the middle-aged, grey-haired man on the crossing because they've got to go to lectures or to the pub or to the future.

It's true that people come to Sheffield as students and they stay forever; for years they carry on looking like students and then, over a long weekend in autumn, they start to look like their parents but they still pretend they're young and they walk in the hills and gaze down at the city and say, to each other or to anybody else who happens to be passing, 'We like Sheffield because it's just a big village. And it's a great place for walking because the countryside's just on your doorstep,' to which I often want to reply, 'It's okay, I'll scrape it off.'

Yorkshire as Visitor Destination is something that's troubling me throughout the writing of this book and it's something I've not quite fathomed yet, and maybe I won't. I don't think this is really a guidebook, though. Unless it's a guidebook to the Yorkshire of the Mind. Or unless it's a guidebook to me. Maybe they're both the same thing.

Walking, though: walking. Today I'm checking out the way people move because I want to discern whether there's a Yorkshire walk that's different and distinctive to any other kind of walk, and the only way I can do this is to make my way out of the city centre to the suburbs because around here there aren't that many Yorkshire folks walking the Yorkshire walk as well as talking the Yorkshire talk in the civic space between the station and the Howard Hotel. There are folks from the Home Counties and the Midlands and the South West. There are Chinese students and an American couple with a guidebook. Maybe they're looking for Norman. I catch a Lancashire accent bleating in the air, and two Scottish girls are chatting as they cross. Hope they haven't brought their funny money with them.

I walk past the Showroom Cinema, where my wife and I love to go and watch subtitled films where nothing happens for hours and people sit in rooms talking in low voices and looking out of the window until a person in stockings limps in and begins to recite Rimbaud as outside a biplane is being built on a lawn to the sound of jagged ocarina music. That's my kind of film. Once the first five minutes of the film were shown upside down and it didn't matter. I once went there for dinner and asked what the soup du jour was; the lad went into the kitchen and came back and said, triumphantly, 'It's soup of the day.' Ocarina music should have played, then faded.

I'm interested in the idea of a Yorkshire walk because I've identified walks from other parts of the country and they seem to define a place as much as an accent can, and so the walk will be useful in my quest. Also, it's not raining, which helps: in the rain everybody runs and keeps their head down and so all the differences in gait are soaked away and ironed out. The Liverpool walk is springy and welcoming, like the accent; and like the accent it seems to go up at the end, lifting its foot into the Scouse air before planting it on the ground on the way to the Pier Head. The Manchester walk is a physical representation of the Manc accent, the slow Liam Gallagher drawl reflected in the take-your-time lean-forward that's halfway between a trudge and a lope down Portland Street towards Piccadilly. In literary terms, it's a trope. People in East Anglia walk slowly; that may be a cliché and I hope it's not an insult. It's just a fact, insult's more methodical twin.

In Beccles once I genuinely thought I was having some kind of stroke, or rather an anti-stroke, because I seemed to be walking much faster than anybody else on the street even though I didn't feel like I was. The other pedestrians appeared to have been wheelclamped. I was trying not to walk quickly because I didn't need to be anywhere in a great hurry; as far as I was concerned I was just wandering down the street looking in shop windows and grimacing or winking at my reflection. Doesn't everybody do that? To the locals I was a combination of Billy Whizz and Alf Tupper. I slowed my walk down to a parody of a walk, and I still appeared to be running. Sorry, East Anglia, but that's true.

So given all these examples of walking dialects and how they differ from county to county, region to region, is there a Yorkshire walk and how does that help somebody like me to define us?

Well, let me stick my neck out here and say that much of Yorkshire is hilly and so the Yorkshire ambulation is one that naturally flows upwards. I know there are flat areas of Yorkshire but that's a bit like saying there are warm areas of Baffin Island. It's true, but in such a small way as to hardly disturb the surface tension of truth. I bet that if I was to examine, under laboratory conditions, the legs of Yorkshire people, I'd find that their calves were more developed than those of Suffolk people, and that their thighs were more tree trunk-like because of all the years they'd had to power up the hill to catch the work bus as it came round the corner by the garages. I would never walk up to anybody on the street, of course, and say, 'Can I examine your legs for signs of Yorkshireness?' but at times I must admit I'm ever so slightly tempted. This development of the legs wouldn't happen overnight or if it did you might have to seek medical advice. The Yorkshire leg, born out of the Yorkshire walk, would be something that would take generations to develop, like the loss of the third eye at the back of your head, just above the rim of your flat cap.

During my childhood there was a Darfield walk, which the old miners used to practise, which mainly consisted of standing still for quite a while, so technically it probably wasn't a walk at all. You'd see a bloke in a cap set off down the street very slowly, coming down his path and opening and closing the gate with care. He would be wearing sensible braces and his trousers would be Cowell-high. His lungs would be shattered into porridge by years of working at the coal face but he still liked to get out for some fresh air and to get some sun on his neck. You could hear him wheezing from Ashby-de-la-Zouch. He'd go a few yards and then, like a toy with a failing battery, would grind to a halt. If there was a wall nearby, he'd lean on it. He might have a stick, he might not. If there was a fence he'd put his hand on it to steady himself and the world. An old miner who lived near us would always pause for air beside a care home that they'd built in a former hairdresser's and after a few seconds a woman in a dressing gown would appear at the door and shout at the man, 'Help! I am being kept here against my will! Could you please contact the relevant authorities!'

The man would sigh and walk on.

The wheezing would grow louder and louder and would mutate into a liquid cough that wracked the man's whole body as though he was a fragile canoe in a storm and would seem to almost make the earth under his feet shudder a little. Passers-by who didn't know him might think he was dying. His mates, sometimes passing him, sometimes stranded like him, a bit further down the wall, would say, 'All right, George? Coughing better!' or, 'It's not the cough that carries you off, it's the coffin they carry you off in!' or, 'They told us it weren't a dusty pit, didn't they?'

Sometimes, to pile irony on pathos until the day almost snapped under the strain, the old gentleman would come to a halt by a little mountain of Home Coal, delivered by a wagon and left in the street for somebody, probably a miner when he'd come home from the pit, to shovel into the cellar. Home Coal was one of the few perks of working down the pit and I wish I'd had the foresight to photograph the piles of it on the side of the road, the HomeCoalScape, before the whole tradition came to an end. At the time you thought it would last forever.

At Low Valley School in 1964, we had to do a piece of imaginative writing with the title 'Darfield in the Year 2000' and I wrote that we would all be wearing silver suits and we would have our dinner in tablet form and we would go to the pit on an electric monorail because, in my unformed brain, the pit would always be there. Always. Mrs Robinson gave me a star and said my work 'showed imagination' and said I should show it to Mr Owen in his office at the top of the stairs. It must have slipped Mrs Robinson's mind that I had a pot on my leg after I'd broken it joyfully kicking a lump of snow which turned out to be covering a huge slab of concrete. I limped out of the room and took ages to climb the stairs, my pot clicking under the strain. I was like one of those miners would be, decades hence, pausing for breath and gazing grimly at the distance I had to cover. Mr Owen was pleased with the work, though. He said it showed imagination. I could have told him that. It was a long, slow way down the stairs and I missed playtime.

The old miner would hold on until he'd stopped coughing and he had enough breath to continue and would then go a few more yards until his breathing became too ragged again and he had to spit voluminously. As a pretentious sixth-former, I suggested to my mates that a miner's favourite Dickens novel was *Great Expectorations* and of course none of them laughed because of course it wasn't funny. This Darfield walk has died out with the pitmen, so it's become that odd phenomenon A Relic Walk, like the lost Fop-Jitter of Regency Bath.

I'm going to test out my theory of the Yorkshire walk being an uphill struggle so I'm going to walk up, out of Sheffield city centre towards Sharrow Vale Road and beyond. I'll put my thighs to some kind of rigorous test. I'll give my calves some humpty. The pain may well be localised but fierce, like the pain of losing a village cricket match at the final ball.

Sheffield is a city clinging to hills and sloshing with water; local legend has it that, like Rome, it was built on seven hills although I have to say, even though you'd expect me to say it, that people say that about Barnsley too. Perhaps if I combed the country I'd find plenty of places that lay claim to the 'built on seven hills' legend in the same way that Paul Simon is claimed to have written 'Homeward Bound' on the platform of any station in the country. We all know it was Thirsk. Or Seamer. Or Bolton upon Dearne. Somewhere in Yorkshire, certainly. I know this because he'd just finished rearranging 'Scarborough Fair'.

It hurts me (just here, if I'm being honest) to say that the seven hills theory is probably more factually correct about Sheffield. Barnsley is more likely to be built on seven muckstacks by seven sets of pitwheels. George Orwell has sometimes been said to have been the originator of the idea; in *The Road to Wigan Pier* he writes of Sheffield, 'the town is very hilly, said to have been built on seven hills, like Rome, and everywhere streets of mean little houses blackened by smoke run up at sharp angles, paved with cobbles which are purposely set unevenly to give horses, etc, a grip.'

Trust an Eton man to remark on the mean little houses, I thought to myself as I set off out of the station, wondering what the etceteras were that were able to get a grip alongside the horses. Squirrels, maybe? Postmen? People who'd had one too many and were westering home for their dinner and a zizz on the settee?

As I walk, someone sees me and shouts, 'The Bard of Barnsley!' and his mate says, loud enough for me to hear,

'I call him The Twat of Barnsley.' Ah, the glory of the plain-speaking Yorkshire folk emerging from their mean little houses and getting a grip on the cobbles.

Some authorities contend that the way to identify the hills is to mark the rivers, and the rivers and streams are named as the Don, the Sheaf, the Loxley, the Rivelin, and Porter Brook, Meers Brook and Owler Brook and from there, as they contend, the hills are identifiable as Dykes Hall Road, Stannington Road, Redmires Road, Ringinglow Road, Derbyshire Lane, City Road, Barnsley Road and Jenkin Road. The author of the web page about the Seven Hills of Sheffield then concludes by saying, 'At no point can I identify seven hills within Sheffield's boundaries.' Ah well: print the legend.

Sheffield is an ancient settlement and, like much of Yorkshire, grew hugely at the time of the industrial revolution. Those hunter-gatherers who hunted and gathered in Wombwell Woods wandered here too; indeed at Creswell Crags (across the border in Derbyshire and therefore of no interest to us whatsoever whether in this book or beyond into the wider world, whether now or in the future or the past and I wish I'd never mentioned it and I want you to erase it from your memory) there's evidence of some of the earliest settlements in Europe, cave-dwellers who paved the way for the Iron Age people who fortified Sheffield, using the seven or eight hills to build their forts on. People still think of steel when they think of Sheffield; in Chaucer's *Canterbury Tales*, the Miller in 'The Reeve's Tale' has a Sheffield knife; steelmaking took time to become established, with only two furnaces shown in the city in an eighteenth-century illustration. New methods of creating crucible steel, steel plate and stainless steel meant that by the twentieth century the city industry employed thousands and thousands of people working day and night.

As a young man, I remember the way that the steelworks lit up the night sky when we went to visit Uncle Jack in Hillsborough, and the backbreaking, dangerous work created a particular type of person who valued sweat and hard graft although if you wanted to tell steelworkers that you valued their skill and craftsmanship you'd have to speak up because so many of them lost their hearing in the constant barrage of noise in the works. Local legend tells us that the cinemas in Attercliffe, which was almost a separate town at the edge of Sheffield, had to have the sound turned up because the audience were half-deaf and if it wasn't, they'd think they were watching a silent film. Attercliffe is another Yorkshire place that first popped up in the *Domesday Book*, where it's Ateclive, or 'at the cliff', although, with typical Sheffield exaggeration, the cliff is actually a small escarpment that can't be seen anymore.

I'm not going to Attercliffe today, though; I'm testing out the hills. I turn left by the Showroom and walk towards Bramall Lane, the home of Sheffield United. At the moment there are no hills to speak of. Occasionally there is a slight lift in the pavement but nothing to make me change my gait. A man answers a mobile phone in the sweetest Sheffield accent: 'Nar den, Fatha!' He's walking quickly with his head down slightly. Perhaps he's a Sheffield Wednesday fan who doesn't want to be seen too near the home of the Old Enemy. I turn left and right, enjoying the sensation of being slightly lost in a city I know fairly well. Where a road should be, according to the map on my phone, there's a supermarket and I stride by a puzzle of trolleys to find a back street. A man without a Sheffield accent talks into a phone: 'Yes, I'll remember the rocket.' Ah, Sheffield; you city that thinks it's a village. They come here as sociology students and they stay forever.

Now, at last, I'm walking uphill, towards Sharrow Vale Road. At the other side of the road a young woman is pushing a buggy and we could almost be in a race except that I'm letting her win. I am, really. She has a determined look on her face as though by gazing at the top of the hill she is somehow almost already at the top of the hill. The Yorkshire uphill walk seems to be second nature to her, and I reckon she must have been brought up round here, always having to go up the hill to the shops, to school, to go and play with her mates and with that kind of child-hood a hill is simply a more interesting plain.

Her mobile rings with a raucous ringtone that doesn't wake the baby up. She answers, laughing, in an East European language that I don't recognise. So much for my theory that she's a Sheffield girl born and bred. She must come from a hilly place, though, because now she's pushing faster and talking at the same time, her phone cradled in her neck. She's the opposite of the old miner paused by the wall. I give up pretending that we're in a race. I'm breath-ing slightly heavily.

If there are ancillaries to the Yorkshire walk they include the heavy breath, the mopping of the damp brow with the hanky, and the saying of 'By ...' either singly, in twos or as a combination of all three: breathe/mop/'By ...' I convince myself that this is nothing like the Scouse or Manc or East Anglia walks: it's more purposeful, less playful. It's a walk that insists that where there's muck there is indeed brass.

There are odd little bits of Sheffield that really are like a village and Porter Brook is one of them; the Porter Brook slithers down the hill towards the railway station where it meets the River Sheaf that bubbles away under that part of the city. It's called Porter Brook because the water used to be the colour of porter when it ran over iron-ore deposits on its way from the high hills of its source. The area I know as Porter Brook has got a bookshop and a proper fishmonger's and at least one proper butcher, just right for the city village. I go into Roney's Butchers, a Sheffield landmark since 1935, and for a moment consider repeating the Pork Pie test but then plump for its more exotic cousin, the Sausage Sandwich test, although I could have gone for the variation that is the Bacon Sarnie test. It's a butter question, I think.

If you have butter on your bacon sandwich then you are not from South Yorkshire. Having butter on your bacon sarnie is like putting yoghurt on your custard; it's just too much of a good thing. It's also like having a Yorkshire Pudding at the side of your plate with your Sunday dinner rather than as a separate course. It just doesn't ring true. The sausage sandwich should be butterless, too, just to help you enjoy the flavour of the sausage more.

The man in front of me at Roney's is ordering a sausage sandwich and the man behind the counter asks a question which firmly places us in the north.

'Do you want flat or link sausage?'

Ah, the flat sausage: he has flat sausage and I do too. Now, I know the flat, or Lorne, sausage isn't a particularly Yorkshire phenomenon, but if I can have one in the county, I always do because, to my poetic and allusive way of thinking, it's almost like eating a flat cap between two slices of bread. I've often thought of getting in touch with some razor-quiffed PR and marketing types and suggesting the Flat Bap or the Flat Cap Bap: the edible flat cap.

As I wait for the man to be served, I imagine the marketing campaign. In a TV advert a stout-thewed Yorkshireman is working down a mine. It's a suspiciously well-lit and clean mine but this is TV. He sits down and gives the camera a stare that manages to be both honest and ironic at the same time. It's to do with the motion of the eyebrows. I hope they cast an authentic Yorkshire actor for the part; the provenance of the dulcets can be crucial in selling a new concept like this. Can I apologise in advance for the extended family of apostrophes we're about to encounter?

He speaks.

'Heyop. When tha darn't pit an' it's snap time tha wants ter be reminded of 't rest o'thi life artside t'pit. And that's why I like these ...'

The camera swoops down on a Flat Cap Bap being prised from a snap tin. In the background a brass band is playing a specially commissioned piece of music called 'In F Flat'. The man lifts the Flat Cap Bap to his anticipatory lips and begins to chew orgasmically.

A voiceover, sounding like the actor's dad, says, 'T' Flat Cap Bap. A true taste of Yorkshire.' The brass music rises to a crescendo. Perhaps a male voice choir sings. Exiles in places like the Isle of Wight and Truro begin to weep with a kind of overwhelming Yorkshire hiraeth and rush out to buy dozens of boxes to lay down for winter.

It's my turn to get served. I almost ask for a Flat Cap Bap but I don't. We're in Yorkshire so art can't really follow life. The flat sausage is really nice, though, tastes like Yorkshire, somehow, and I file away my marketing idea for when times get really hard. I buy a bottle of Henderson's Relish, too, to make me seem more authentic. I'll blob a few drops on the sausage when I get out onto the street and people on passing buses will raise their thumbs at me because I am one of them, I am on their wavelength and we share a past. The bottle is a baton and I have just won a kind of Yorkshire relay.

Henderson's Relish, or Hendo's to the initiated, is the nearest thing Sheffield has to a truly regional dish, if relish can be considered a dish and if you don't count the hot pork sandwich with stuffing. Think of it as the equivalent of Irn-Bru or the liquor they put on pie and mash in the East End. It was first made by Henry Henderson at the end of the nineteenth century and it's still made just a few hundred yards from the original manufacturers in an unprepossessing factory in the shadow of high rises and within the sound of passing trams near a roundabout by the university. Maybe it's the Henderson's in the air that makes the students do so well? I'll get one of them to do a PhD on that. Over the last few years

Henderson's has become an unofficial brand of Sheffieldness, with famous fans like Sean Bean, Richard Hawley and the Arctic Monkeys, and you can buy pinnies and T-shirts with the bottle on.

Trendy cafés will put it on their tables and people with more money than sense will ask disdainful waiters in posh southern restaurants if they've got any, then pretend to get cross when they haven't. I guess places often need a bit of cultural shorthand for purposes of definition. How Sheffield are you? Henderson's. That's okay then. I shouldn't really like it, being from Barnsley, but I quite like the tanginess of it on a pork pie or the hint of it in some tatie hash. A precise description of the taste is hard, and I have to define it through other senses: it tastes like that moment when you just come into a warm house after a long walk in the hills. Your glasses steam up and you take your balaclava off and your head is simultaneously warm and cold. That's the taste of Henderson's.

Across the road from Roney's I notice another shop that I recognise from somewhere: it's called GoalSoul and it's selling the kind of obscure football magazines and memorabilia that I like. I go in and the bell dings; they should have a referee's whistle. The manager is called Christian Bustamente and we bond over memories of old football magazines like the wonderfully erudite *Perfect Pitch*, which aimed to be the *London Review of Books* of the beautiful game and we discuss why the Sheffield Wednesday fanzine was called *War of the Monster Trucks*: the answer, of course, is that ITV once cut to an edition of the aforementioned Monster Truck-based televisual entertainment just at a crucial point in a Wednesday game.

Then it occurs to me where I've come across the shop before: it opened a few years ago as a shop for the world's oldest football club, Sheffield FC, which was founded in 1857 and has been credited with devising the rules of the game and as such attracts fans from all over the world who want to come to the source of everything that's happened since. The club celebrated its 150th anniversary in 2007 with a game at their Coach and Horses ground in Dronfield against Inter Milan, with a young Mario Balotelli savouring the atmosphere and perhaps chewing on a flat sausage sandwich with a splash of Hendo's. These are challenging economic times, even in a part of Sheffield with a fishmonger's.

Even as a Barnsley man, I can't help but feel my chest swell with pride at the fact that the game that's played most in this planet originated in Sheffield. In fact three games that are played all over the world originated in Yorkshire: football, the aforementioned Rugby League and Knurr and Spell.

The more I think about it, the more I'm becoming convinced that this county really is at the heart of so much that we think of as British. Maybe we really should aim for independence. The more I think about it, maybe we're not just a bag of disparate city-states, perhaps we are all Yorkshire under the skin. Maybe Dewsbury isn't that different to Thorne, after all.

I buy some football magazines and begin the long trudge down the hill. My calves and thighs exude Yorkshireness.

My brow exudes sweat and Henderson's. My mind swims with definitions and uncertainty. Maybe none of us are Yorkshire Enough. Or maybe we all are. A bus passes and for a moment I wish I'd caught it into town.

POEM CYCLE: AS DEEP AS ENGLAND

WHEN I REALLY think about it, two writers define Yorkshire for me: Barry Hines and Ted Hughes. Emily Brontë and Winifred Holtby and J.B. Priestley are there too, shaping the place I'm in and the man I am, but if I'm being honest I just see them as support acts. The two H's are the headliners, doing their stuff in the bright lights, making us laugh and making us cry. Barry Hines, from Hoyland near Barnsley, is mainly known for his novel *A Kestrel for a Knave*, published in 1968. It's a parable about a local boy, Billy Casper, who rears a kestrel and trains it, until it's killed by his brother, Jud. The kestrel is a metaphor for freedom, of course, the kind of freedom that a lad like Casper would never have felt in Barnsley in the mid-1960s. Billy, like so many of his peers, would have had no choice of career. He had to go down the pit and his kestrel gave him a glimpse of something unknowable, unattainable.

Yorkshire people in general and Barnsley people in particular take the book, and more so the 1969 film, *Kes*, to their heart. A skinny Dai Bradley as Billy, hanging from the goalposts in a football match he doesn't want to be in, pins down a certain kind of Barnsleyness in the same way that Henderson's Relish exemplifies a sort of Sheffieldness.

I wrote the introduction to a new edition of the book and I put that, if you come from Barnsley, '*A Kestrel for a Knave* is your defining myth, your *Domesday Book*, your almanac and your pocket diary. It's your *Moby Dick*, your *Great Gatsby*, your *War and Peace*, your *David Copperfield* and your *Things Fall Apart*.'

I believed those words when I wrote them and I believe them now. Hines celebrated an uncelebrated place and made poetry from a kind of speech that's considered rough or, worse, inarticulate and inferior, and I personally would give him a Nobel Prize in Literature if I had a spare one in my pocket.

I once went with him to the street in Hoyland where he grew up. He stood and looked at his old house and an elderly man, in the traditional Yorkshire male summer costume that's still worn by many around these parts, walked by and said, to the ground and his feet as much as to Barry, 'Don't worry. We know who you are.' Barry turned to me and said, 'See: what did I tell you? They're not bothered!' He hadn't told me anything, actually. But then, as I intimated in the introduction to the new edition of his book, he's told me everything.

Everybody in Barnsley, even if they weren't born when the film was made, says they were in the film. When you meet people from Barnsley on holiday, and they find out you're from the same town, they say, 'Do you remember that assembly scene in *Kes*? That's me, second from the left at the back with the glasses on.' If everybody who'd said they were in the film were actually in the film it would have been a *Ben Hur*-style epic that you'd have had to show on a wide screen to squeeze everybody in.

As I hinted, though, there are two dazzling literary suns in the sky of my Yorkshire, and that's why I'm standing outside a furniture shop in Mexborough with a man who used to teach my kids at school. I still want to call the man with the beard and the flat cap Mr Ely, but he insists that I call him Steve, which I more or less manage to do. As we stand and talk, two boys with their baseball caps on back to front stare at us like we're in a museum. This could be because we're chaps of a certain age looking up at a blue plaque on the wall of a furniture shop with a certain excitement and we're both clutching books. They're the ones in a museum, of course: the museum of youth, where everything is old straightaway and entry really costs you. Baseball caps back to front, boys? Come on: this is Mexborough in the second decade of the twenty-first century!

Over the past few years, Steve Ely has become known as a poet, curating Yorkshire's close and distant pasts from the miners' strike to Richard Rolle the Hermit of Hampole in long verse sequences that shimmer with dialect and hint at lost Middle-Englishes that, if we listened hard enough, we'd still hear in the chip shop queue, and we'd still understand. He's like Barnsley's historian, John Tanner, in that he seems to see links between everything he encounters and he also seems to be able to link the *then* to the *now* in ways that I find almost impossible. People like Steve Ely seem capable of holding the whole

history of Yorkshire in their heads; they seem to understand it in a way that I can't.

I was first introduced to Ted Hughes's work by my
teacher Mr Brown (I can't bring myself to call him Rob) in
his green corduroy suit with the big pockets stuffed with
poetry books. He passed me Hughes's violent and visceral
poetry collection, *Crow*, and said, in his voice of cultured
gravel, 'Here's a book of jokes by a comedian from round
here. I think you'll enjoy them.' I was hooked.

Later he told me that they were poems not jokes and
I was hooked again and placed them in the keepnet. I
absorbed Hughes's biography, and like a lot of people I
skipped over the South Yorkshire section of it like it didn't
matter because how could you have a writer that good
who lived in a place like this? Surely great writers, great
artists, came from that place beyond even the 70 bus route
that went from Sheffield to Upton? Yes: they came from
that place called Elsewhere. Mr Brown had excited my
attention with the idea of a local poet but then I was
drawn into the legend of Brooding Hughes the West
Yorkshire Poet of Mystery. As far as I was concerned he
was born in Mytholmroyd near Hebden Bridge in West
Yorkshire, where he spent the first few years of his life,
and he went to Cambridge where he met Sylvia Plath. Oh,
and there was a bit in Mexborough in the middle. But
Mexborough was my back yard, and Hebden Bridge was
the other side of the world. At that age, significantly for
my life in general and for this book in particular, I saw
any other part of Yorkshire as more interesting than the
view from my window.

Steve is here to take me on a tour of Hughes's Mexborough and South Yorkshire haunts to convince me of the weight and influence that this end of the county had on him and I'm going along with this because I'm still, despite myself and all the things I've written so far, seeing the other parts of the county as the more authentic ones. Maybe I'm too familiar with this end of the map, or maybe I believe that the rest of Yorkshire is the Yorkshire Enough part. I'm like those tourists I've been mocking, wanting to rush up to the Dales rather than hanging round the scrapyards of Rotherham where dull and decayed things will probably fail to catch my eye. The lads in the baseball caps wander away; the winter sun is bright in my eyes and it's reflecting from the shop windows and so for a moment, because their baseball caps are on the wrong way round, it looks as though they're walking backwards out of sight.

My main question about Ted Hughes's family is why they moved here from Mytholmroyd? It's still Yorkshire, but it's a very different Yorkshire. The answer's simple, Steve tells me.

'Ted Hughes's dad couldn't get work in the mills so they looked around for a little business. They travelled all over South and West Yorkshire looking for a shop to buy and they ended up here at 75 Main Street in September 1938.'

My heart thumps with What Ifs. 'So Ted Hughes could have ended up in Darfield? His dad could have had the paper shop near the Post Office where Tony Wistow used to refer to the *London Times* to distinguish it from the *South Yorkshire Times*?' Steve nods. It's a distinct possibility. Suddenly my interest is piqued; Ted Hughes, the Poet

Laureate, could have lived down our street! This is more like it; he could have had his View of a Pig down at Craven's Farm! Steve carries on explaining.

'Mexborough suited them because it was a little town with the usual shops, Woolworth's, Boots, that kind of thing. It had a train station so that people would pop in to buy their papers on the way, and although there were no pits in the town it was surrounded by them and the miners would be able to come for papers and sweets and cigarettes and tobacco.' The teacher in him is still there; he's burning with what another Barnsley poet, Donald Davie, called 'articulate energy' as he does his best to train a torch on a hidden segment of Hughes's life.

We move closer to what used to be the paper shop; now it's full of settees and chairs, some of them displayed and lit at odd angles, to help them sell. Like many furniture shop windows, it's like looking into a dream of a strange distorted front room that you think you remember from childhood. I assume we're going to go in but Steve stops me.

'I want to end up here,' he says. 'I want to take you to some other important places first. Let's make this the climax of our journey.' It's not often people say that about furniture shops.

I'm a guinea-pig, I can tell. I'm one of the first in a number of people that Steve wants to take on his pilgrimage around Hughes. He envisages bus trips and study tours; weekends full of Hughes-ophiles chugging across the valley. He's another example of the phenomenon I'm coming across time and time again; the person who wants to explain Yorkshire, to put it on a plate so that the visitor can eat it, and that suits me. I need this place explaining to me; cut the bits up once they're on my plate if you like, then I can digest them more easily. This book is another tangible version of this impulse, of course. Maybe I'm hoping for residential *Neither Nowt Nor Summat* week-ends in posh off-season seaside hotels with a keynote speech from me and guest appearances by Ian Beesley and John Tanner and Iain Nicholls and those orange blokes from the edge of Lancashire. Actors between sitcoms and pantos will play the part of people like Ferens and Earl Fitzwilliam and there'll be a diorama of the Newcomen beam engine working for the first time. It'll become quite an industry, explaining Yorkshire to itself and the world for fun and profit.

We pile quickly into Steve's car, poetry big-game hunters on safari. His car is actually a small green truck that used to belong to the Scottish Forestry Commission; there's a cage in the back for his dog because Steve, like Ted Hughes and like lots of the men in Yorkshire, like lots of the people in Barry Hines's books, are men who feel naked without a dog pulling them along. I'm relieved that there's no dog there because of my allergy, and somehow to my poet's mind, and perhaps to Steve's too, the empty cage is a symbol of all the ancient Yorkshire knowledge that will escape if you don't try and keep hold of it. Yes, I know: I've been thinking about this book too much.

Steve says, 'We're going to Roche Abbey because that's where I think the "pool as deep as England" is.' The pool he's referring to is in Hughes's poem 'Pike':

A pond I fished, fifty yards across
whose lilies and muscular tench
had outlasted every visible stone
of the monastery that planted them -
stilled legendary depth:
it was as deep as England.

I write down 'pool as deep as England', cross out 'England' and put 'Yorkshire'.

We drive back from Mexborough into Barnburgh, nodding to Barnburgh Church and the bloodstained step and the wild cat and Sir Percival Cresacre, also celebrated by Hughes in his poem 'Esther's Tomcat', and through the village of High Melton, where I once took part in a terribly unsuccessful charity balloon release. I only mention this because this helium-filled failure has haunted me for many years, sometimes even invading my dreams. It feels like a metaphor for high-minded endeavour that goes comedically wrong and somehow this feels like a very Yorkshire thing. It seems that there's something built into parts of the Yorkshire psyche that warns us against reaching too far or we might fall off the ladder. Or, worse, we might hold on to a balloon hoping to float away and remain anchored to the grass.

The charity balloon release story has the simplicity of a child's picture book. I was invited to release some balloons from a net in the grounds of High Melton College for charity. The event was to follow the usual balloon-release narrative. Each balloon had been bought for a pound and had a label on it with the name and address of the purchaser. The balloon that went furthest would win a cash prize and there were tales of balloons from other local releases ending up in Hemel Hempstead or Bergen. Ah, the inevitability of this story of good-hearted Yorkshire folk, winding to its conclusion as though driven by a machine!

The charity balloon release was part of a music and drama festival, where young people would recite learned-by-heart verses and sometimes passages of prose off by heart; I never found out if any of them were by Barry Hines or Ted Hughes, although it would have been almost too fitting if they were.

I was led to a vast outside area where willing volunteers were struggling to keep what looked like thousands of balloons inside the net, as though the balloons were fish and the volunteers were trawlermen. At times the balloons threatened to lift the volunteers into the air and fly them around. The man from the local paper was meant to be coming to take a picture of me releasing the balloons but he was late, probably held up at a chip shop fire that simply wouldn't die down or the handover of a giant cheque.

The release was happening during a break in the pro-ceedings and the organisers were keen to get back to the reciting. The net full of air bucked like a ram. The local paper man was nowhere to be seen. I was given a pair of scissors.

'Sheffield steel!' the woman said as he handed them over.

I approached the net. Ah, the way narrative moves along predictable tramlines!

I snipped the net. The wind dropped like a vest from a washing line. The balloons hovered. A few fell straight to the grass as though wounded, as though wanting to take cover. A volunteer shouted urgently, 'I'm sure they had enough helium in them!', and I wanted her voice to be high as a result of helium-inhalation. One or two balloons, then a few more, began to rise into the sky hesitantly, as though piloted by Orville and Wilbur Wright. More balloons flew, many balloons sat on the grass like special balloons you might buy for a picnic. A balloon got snagged in a tree and popped. A balloon got snagged in a tree and didn't pop. A single balloon, probably the winner, flew over the main hall of the college. The local paper photographer's car chugged up the drive and we all waved him in like he was landing on an airfield in the desert.

Steve Ely drives through High Melton and on to Sprotbrough, all the time letting gobbets of ancient and modern Yorkshire history float around the car in a speech balloon release of his own. He points to an innocuous-looking bungalow.

'They do say Hengist from Hengist and Horsa is buried in the back garden there.' He points at Sprotbrough Church. 'There's a connection between that church and Douglas Bader but I can't quite remember what it is.'

I'm agape but there's no time to ask questions because we've got to get to Roche Abbey. Huge clouds are being thrown across the sky and the sun is fighting a losing battle to define the light. The van is buffeted by the wind and sways a little from side-to-side. I wish, again, that I'd undertaken this quest in summer, or at least in spring. I've kept my woolly hat on and it's clamped tightly to my head, embracing my quiff.

We trundle past the Queen's Hotel in Maltby where, in 1982, I saw a troupe of Morris Men perform an anti-nuclear Morris dance in the upstairs room. It was bizarre and arresting at the same time. They danced an ordinary Morris dance accompanied by an accordion until the lights went out suddenly and there was a tinny but startling explosion delivered from a tape recorder; when the lights came on the dancers were bruised and battered, with filthy faces and ragged hankies. They did a dance to fierce drum-beats and wild violins; it was at a time of great nuclear tension and Barry Hines's other masterpiece *Threads*, about the effects of nuclear war on South Yorkshire, had recently gripped the nation. It could have been absurd but it wasn't. Sadly, as the dance faded into silence, you could hear Slade on the jukebox in the tap room, and the hint of an argument and raised voices, but nobody seemed to mind.

Maltby is another example of a mining town that has fallen on hard times; I know that the huge Monster Truck of capitalism lumbers on, and doesn't care what it squashes with its huge tyres, and I know that there are Maltbys all over the world, but it does seem to me that there are a huge number of these kinds of places in Yorkshire, and if I really am seeking to define this place, then *absence* is a word I should use.

We approach Roche Abbey down a track that could have been on the moon but with a lot more gravity of the sticky, cloying kind. The abbey is ruined now, but building was begun in 1147 on the north side of the stream known locally as Maltby Beck. What's left of the abbey is still surrounded by woods, and so as you trudge to it through the mud you can half-believe the legend that Robin Hood took communion here. The dissolution ordered by Henry VIII was the start of Roche Abbey's decline and, like so many great houses and ecclesiastical buildings that fell into disuse, it was helped on its way to becoming a ruin by the local people, who took away anything they could find because that's what local people always do. A contemporary account by a local priest, Michael Sherbrook, is vivid and noisy and full of destruction:

> It would have pitied any heart to see the tearing up of the lead, the plucking up of the boards and the throwing down of the rafters. The seats were like the seats in minsters, they were burned and the lead melted, although there was plenty of weed nearby, for the abbey stood among the woods and the rocks of stone. Pewter vessels were stolen away and hidden in the rocks, and it seemed that every person was intent upon filching and spoiling what he could.

The half-shattered walls are impressive in the rain, and Steve and I grind to a halt as the sun gives up the battle with the clouds.

'This is my favourite place,' says Steve simply. He puts his cap on like he's going into battle with a past that's reluctant to give up its secrets, particularly its Ted Hughes secrets. A man walks by and nods to Steve and raises his stick in salute.

'I know him,' Steve says. Well, we are in Yorkshire.

As ever in this part of the world, there's a landowner involved, and a big house. No matter how I try, I can't escape one or the other. In 1775, the Earl of Scarborough employed the great sculptor of landscape, Capability Brown, to reshape the area around the ruined abbey as a kind of picturesque addendum to Sandbeck Hall, Scarborough's South Yorkshire seat. It's said that Brown reinvented the landscape with little regard to history, knocking buildings down and constructing huge earth structures, covering much of the ruined abbey and leaving only two towers as romantic features in the landscape. In the 1920s, much of the work was undone and Roche Abbey, in the words of a local account, was 'reborn out of the ground'. The more I wander around this county, writing this book, the more I feel that it has been shaped by a few men with a few ideas and bags of money that weighed them down as they walked. So they got other people to carry them. But they didn't allow them to have any.

Steve and I get out of the car and walk by the abbey into the woods at the back.

Steve catches up with the man and says, 'Where's your dog?'

It's true that the man is walking as though there's something vital missing; his stick is in one hand but the other hand seems bereft, waving in the empty air.

'Lost the use of his back legs,' the man says, his words louder than they should have been in a brief respite from the rain. 'Took him to the vets and said, "Is there owt you can do?" And the vet said, "No, I'm sorry, pal, there's nowt to be done." So we had to let him go.'

The stick-man is doing that Yorkshire thing of making everyone in a piece of reported speech sound like they come from Round Here. He and Steve are walking one behind the other and the conversation feels like a radio play coming through two speakers mounted on walls in different parts of a room.

'Get another,' says Steve. 'I'm telling you. Get another. You need a dog. When you don't feel like walking, you need a dog. Without a dog you'll just end up in that chair.'

The man shakes his head. 'Anyway, what brings you here?' he asks, his stick indicating both of us.

'Ted Hughes,' Steve replies, and the man nods, as though we're talking about somebody who wandered off to get some chips and mushy peas one chilly Friday teatime in the mid-1940s and never came home.

Steve explains about Hughes and the pike and the pool as deep as England.

'It's this one down here,' says the man, pointing with his stick in the local way (straight forward, with a slight tilt, a bit like our walk) at a gleam of water behind some bushes. He turns again, stick still pointing, and I resist the urge to duck because I feel that somehow it would have insulted him.

'But has tha ever seen Lord Scarborough's private booat house?'

The way he says booat for boat makes my heart swell with a pride that's too obscure to notate. Steve, who's combed this soggy ground for years in search of stories, hasn't, and I certainly haven't, so we follow the man's mud-caked boots and his jutting stick which aims, unerring as a compass point, to the left.

'Tha'd better tap the Tappin' Tree,' he says, in the matter-of-fact way that South Yorkshire people approach the supernatural and the unknowable. He points out a tall tree with a ragged trunk. 'Just tap it an' mek a wish,' he says, 'but keep it to thissen.'

I gaze at the tree and there's evidence all over it of people patting or scratching it. It looks a bit like a tree that some huge wild creature has rubbed itself against and indeed the Wild Creature of Superstition has been here, many times. I tap the tree and make an obscure wish about wanting to be More Yorkshire, about wishing I could become Yorkshire Enough to make a pattern of this elusive place. I realise that much of this book has been formulated in woods on damp days, and that much of it is about wishing. After we've all made a silent wish the man leads us through increasingly wet grass and then points again.

'Theer,' he says with his stick. I can't see anything that I haven't seen before. The pool is to the right, still and timeless.

Steve says, 'Yes, I can see it. There it is.' He's pointing now, too. I still can't make out a boat house. They're speaking boat house and I can't translate.

I know what my problem is; it's part of the reason why I'm nowhere near Yorkshire Enough. I'm expecting to see a boat house, a fully functional little shed of a place with a smart roof and a wooden door and maybe, just maybe, the hint of an old boat inside, bobbing on the water. I'm struggling, as I've been struggling for ages, to look beyond the present to the past. The Boat House is a tiny indentation, a few fallen pieces of stone, an almost-rectangle of water.

Steve and the man stand by it, and I can tell they're imagining Lord Scarborough and some family members and maybe an important man from the city up for the shooting being helped into the boat in the boat house by servants who talk a bit like us. Steve nods at some wet scrubland next to the water.

'I bet there would have been picnic tables there,' he says. 'I bet they would have sat there and had a picnic and then gone out on the boat ...'

We stand in the same silence that I've stood in quite a lot these past few weeks; it's a silence caused by history weighing heavily on my shoulders.

The man waves his stick in farewell.

'Get a dog!' Steve barks. He turns to me. 'This is a kind of outlier of the Hughes trail,' he says, 'but I wanted to bring you here to show you how huge an attraction this could become.'

He's right; Ted Hughes, like the Brontës, has fans, people who would walk through this soggy landscape just to look at the pool mentioned in 'Pike'. Maltby could become the new Haworth and before we know it they'd be serving Crowburgers in the Queen's Hotel.

We're back in the car and heading towards the site of a very significant part of Hughes's life, a place that made him the poet he was, that helped him to define the countryside he loved. It looks like we're heading to a golf course, and indeed we are. Men of a certain age are walking in golf trousers that have been altered by devoted wives on rattling sewing machines so that the TV's volume is permanently turned up. We park by the side of the road. It looks like we're walking towards a neglected patch of grass at the side of the golf course, and indeed we are. I'm learning to look, look closely, and disregard the evidence of my senses that tell me I'm looking at nothing, nothing at all. Steve has taken his glasses off and there are jewels of rain in his beard.

'There's nothing here now,' he says. I could have told him that. '... but this was the home of John Wholey, who was Ted's best mate at Mexborough Grammar School,' and, as the men shout 'fore' and the golf balls fly, Steve tells me the tale of someone who feels a little like me, felt like he didn't quite belong, felt like he had to express his feelings somehow, using whatever materials came to hand. Ted Hughes chose writing. I chose drumming with knitting needles on large Tupperware containers. Later I chose writing, of course, but possibly only because my mam wanted her Tupperware back. Who knows where my career might have gone if she'd kept her Christmas cakes in an old biscuit tin?

John Wholey's dad worked as head gardener at what had been a country house and sporting estate but was now Crookhill Hall Receiving Hospital, a place where men and women were treated for tuberculosis for months and years until they either recovered or simply stayed. The Wholey family lived in a cottage in the grounds, the phantom of which Steve and I are now standing in front of, or perhaps in the front room.

John and Ted were inseparable mates in the early 1940s, cycling together across a layered landscape that on the one hand was as feudal as it had ever been, with forelocks tugged shiny, and on the other hand was in thrall to the new modernity of mining and railways and the idea that engines and machines would save the world. John and Ted cycled and fished all over South Yorkshire and the north Midlands, and on Lord Scarborough's estate they would have found the pool that we'd gazed at earlier today, Laughton Pond, full of fish like a netful of charity balloons.

As Hughes wrote in a letter:

> We fished, we shot, we made tree houses, damned streams, found a tree house and enlarged it, felled trees, made bonfires and did all the things that boys should be allowed to do but seldom get the opportunity.

Maybe that isn't rain in Steve's beard. Maybe it's tears.

We walk a little way beyond where the Wholeys' house would have been, to another small pond, badly silted up and full of reeds.

'This could be another source of Hughes's "Pike",' says Steve, and he pulls out a photograph of the young Ted and John Wholey sitting by the bank of what would then have been a bigger, deeper pond. My heart skips a beat. This is a bit like finding Sir Percival Cresacre's brooch behind a discarded lemonade bottle at Cat Hill. Things are clicking into place for me, here: Yorkshire is handing me small epiphanies about itself and the people who made it and the people and places who are making my reaction to what Yorkshire is and has been.

Steve is talking about his plan to get the pond restored to its former state, to get people to come and pay a few pounds to fish the waters Ted Hughes fished. He believes it will happen, and somehow I do too. If I can somehow turn this kaleidoscope I can understand this place. I can become Yorkshire Enough. The rain is receding.

A golf ball arrows past my head. We clamber back into the car to return to Mexborough where we park not too far from the newsagent. Steve has got his teacher's voice going again.

'So we see Ted Hughes, transplanted from a rural idyll in West Yorkshire to a noisy and dirty place like Mexborough; we've seen the place where Ted, with John, rekindled the love of nature that would pervade his poems. And now we're going to go to the grammar school, where he met the teacher who would get him interested in poetry, who would start him off on the road that ended with him becoming Poet Laureate.'

Mexborough Grammar School was, as I said earlier, seen as slightly superior to the rest of the schools in the area, including mine at Wath, just a few miles down the road. Steve surprises me by telling that it was fee paying, that those who went to the school would have to stump up £9 a year to go.

'Mind you,' he says, as we walk by the side of the cricket pitch to the main entrance of the school, 'not a lot of them paid. I've seen records where it says that a pupil would pay once, maybe twice, but then leave the school at 15 with the rest still owing.'

Ah, the 'How Much?' philosophy of private education.

The school hasn't entirely changed; there's a new academy in the town now, just a little way up the road, and the old grammar is a business centre that seems to have left everything just as it was. We go in and I feel like Ted Hughes might have felt as he walked in on his first day; we wander through the hall and our feet echo like the nervous sensible shoes of first-year pupils. Unlike them, we leave a trail of mud, much of which is the property of Lord Scarborough. At the back of the hall there's a corridor and we turn down it.

'This is a really important part of the Hughes trail,' Steve says, his voice echoing. We walk up to the door of the school library. 'This is where John Fisher gave Hughes the copy of *Tarka the Otter* that gave him a start as a writer, that gave him permission to become a poet.'

John Fisher was the visionary pre-Alec Clegg English teacher who inspired generations of Mexborough children including Hughes and Mexborough's other great poet, the forgotten genius Harold Massingham, who was a master of the unexpected image with his description of his Aunt Cassilda Adams's Yorkshire Puddings as being like 'wet window leathers' and Old Denaby's chimneys 'smoking like snuffed candles' and who ended up writing crosswords for the *Listener*, his churning brain only coming to rest when it hit upon the interface of the perfect clue with the perfect solution.

Ted Hughes stayed in contact with Fisher for many years and credited him with getting him into Cambridge by sending a portfolio of poems to Pembroke College; it's hard to ignore the importance of moments like that for young minds, of Fisher handing Hughes *Tarka the Otter*, or Mr Brown giving me *Crow*. Steve and I stand by a big window and Steve points out the next station of the Hughes's Cross, Old Denaby. He waxes lyrical about the fact that Hughes could see the countryside from here, that his paper round would take him across the canal into an area far from the muck of Mexborough. My metaphor-seeking brain tries to make something of this, tries to see this as an example of many Yorkshire people looking for the Other Place, either the place they remember as a child or the place that's not Yorkshire that they'd like to get to. My musing is constantly interrupted by two men who are sitting at a table by the window and discussing job interviews. Words like 'experience' and 'eye contact' and initials like CV keep floating into my reverie. Practical language will always swamp poetic ruminations, of course. Specially round here.

We leave them to it and walk by the side of the canal, imagining the squeaky wheel of Hughes's bike as he cycled by the water in the early mornings before school with a sack of news. There used to be a ferry across the Dearne at this point that the miners (and Hughes on his bike) would catch when they crossed to Denaby Main Pit. We cross a new bridge as the Trans-Pennine Express crosses nearby, connecting Manchester Airport to Cleethorpes for all its worth.

Steve's telling me that in this part of town, this semi-rural settlement that feels a world away from Mexborough, Hughes could indulge in the country pursuits he loved.

'He liked to catch mice and skin them,' he says, making elaborate gestures that replicate the catching and skinning of a mouse. 'He'd have liked to catch bigger animals and skin them, but there were plenty of mice to hand.'

I imagine rows of skinned mice hanging on a wire fence like pale notes for some kind of night music.

'The local fisherman used to buy the skins off him and use them as gloves.'

Now he's just being daft; now we've slithered into some kind of parody *Cold Comfort Farm* netherworld of people standing by a canal with hands that look like pet shops. He catches my quizzical look.

'I didn't believe it myself,' he says, as we walk up the lane to Old Denaby, 'but I checked with somebody from the Mexborough local history group and they said it was true.'

Yes, well; just because it's true doesn't make it any more believable. He points to a field.

'This is the field where he got chased by the horse that appears in his story "The Rain Horse".' He points to a scattering of trees. 'He'd walk through those woods with John Wholey and so many of the poems were born there.' It starts raining again. 'Ted Hughes weather!' he shouts with a kind of soggy joy.

We stand at the top of a hill and gaze down at Mexborough. I have a sudden memory that there used to be, and perhaps there still are, tropical fish in a tank in the ticket office. I don't tell Steve because I don't want him to reveal that Ted Hughes used to catch them and skin them and sell them to people who caught mice.

My face is so cold that it appears to belong to some-body else. I'm having difficulty speaking through a mouth that won't do as it's told. My voice, when I do speak, either clatters off into the air like a crow or hunches close to the ground like a pig.

'What's Yorkshire about this?' I ask. I'm asking myself as much as Steve. 'What makes this a Yorkshire scene rather than a Lancashire scene, or a scene from anywhere else in the country?'

Steve's cold too, so he does some eloquent pointing and some minimal speaking. He points to Mexborough town centre, split by a bypass, dominated by a cavernous Wetherspoon's in a building that used to be the Market Hall, struggling to survive in the harsh economic weather.

'This!' he shouts. He turns and points to the woods. Birds escape trees. A squirrel appears busy but is probably just cold. A man walks across the horizon, dragged by a dog.

'That!' Steve shouts. I think I know what he means.

I wish I'd got some mouse-skin gloves.

'FROM ... TO': ON THE TOURIST TRAIL

THE M62 CUTS through Yorkshire east to west, and two roads slice through Yorkshire north to south, the M1 and the A1; the M1 and the M62 are functional and get you from A to B via M. They aren't the Silk Route or the Way West, although the M62 does have a certain bleak beauty, particularly where the road divides to accommodate the farmhouse that they couldn't knock down when they were building the motorway, and also where Yorkshire pans into Lancashire and Lancashire cross-fades into Yorkshire, marked by two stone mini-obelisks that look like milestones.

Decades ago, when I was in a performance poetry group called the Circus of Poets, our Volkswagen Dormobile, the Versewagon, broke down right on the cusp of the two counties in driving rain and horror-film mist. It was almost as though the front wheels were in Yorkshire and the back wheels were in Lancashire. The Versewagon had broken down through a lack of water and we didn't have any, and we didn't have any kind of receptacle to collect water in apart from the four colour-co-ordinated plastic mugs we took on stage with us. Mine was red with white spots because I wore a red shirt on stage; maybe you had to be there, in the vortex of the early 1980s cabaret poetry scene where these things mattered almost more than life itself. We pushed the Versewagon into the side of the road and two of the lads held their mugs under a trickling stream that dripped and drenched down into the side of the road to try to fill them up. I took more drastic action. There were no cars coming. There were no planes flying low overhead. I began to wee into my cup, mainly because I wanted to get home. A police car arrived, silently and unexpectedly. Remember that because the times were as they were, with a sense of frustration and violent opposition in the air, particularly in the north, groups of young men driving around late at night often got stopped by the police. I know that doesn't happen now.

I zipped up and put the cup down. Thankfully the coppers didn't seem to have spotted my splashy liquid crime.

'So, what are you up to, lads?' one of them asked in a voice of silky Scouse.

We explained about the gig in Blackburn and the performance poetry and the co-ordinated outfits and the matching cups. They didn't seem impressed. The second copper, also from Liverpool, asked us to open the boot. We knew that we were about to almost die of embarrassment and we almost died of embarrassment when he got the tennis racquets out and held them up with aggressive disdain.

'What are these for, eh?' he asked.

I explained that part of the act was a poetry version of a heavy metal song and that we pretended that the racquets were guitars.

I made the mistake, in the heavy weather, of aiming for a tone of levity, saying, 'We've got a lead tennis racquet, a rhythm tennis racquet and a bass tennis racquet and I don't have a tennis racquet because I pretend to play invisible drums. It all makes a bit of a racket.'

There was a silence that seemed to last the length of a European sleeper train's journey and then the first policeman said, 'I bet it's really funny when you're on stage, sir, with the lights and the music and the makeup and that.'

I didn't have the courage to tell him we didn't wear makeup and later, in the comfort of the Versewagon, I wished I'd said, 'What division are you in, Officer, the irony squad?', but I'm glad I didn't. The 1980s were weird times on the Yorkshire border.

The A1 is the more romantic of the roads through the county, and when you're on it you feel like you're on a journey rather than a trip. It's to do with the fact that there aren't junctions on the A1, except when it inconveniently becomes the A1M; there are just turnoffs. You can slip off and go to Burghwallis if you want, or Darrington, or Upton, and you haven't got to wait for the formality of a roundabout. I guess it's like the difference between staying in a B&B and having a night in one of those hotels where a bloke in a top hat spends all day whistling for taxis. The A1 used to go through Doncaster, indeed it used to go through the town of Bawtry near Doncaster, and there was a house at the extreme end of the main street on the cusp of the boundary with Nottinghamshire called Number One Yorkshire, because it was the first, or last, house in the county. I should live there.

The A1 is the road that I associate with days out in Yorkshire. My dad would sometimes say, when he tired of his normal Sunday afternoon trundle in second gear past Great Houghton woods and on to Brierley Crossroads for a Danny's ice-cream, 'Let's have a run to North Yorkshire,' because, as I'm finding time and time again in the writing of this book, that's the kind of place people associate with their idea of what Yorkshire should be. Indeed, when my dad's relatives came down from Scotland to visit, we would take them to what we called North Yorkshire, even though it was actually mainly West Yorkshire, because my parents were convinced there would be nothing to see round our way, despite the fact we lived in an almost Lawrentian idyll of pit villages that rubbed up against the country. Not the countryside, note: the country. They're two separate states.

Yorkshire, or as I prefer to call it, 'Yorkshire', is indeed a place that people love to visit. Some recent statistics, compiled before the 2014 Tour de France that turned the county into a seething mass of people shouting and waving, tell me that in 2009 10.6 million people came from different parts of the UK to spend at least one night here. That's a mountain of tea- and coffee-making facilities that could stretch as far as the asteroid belt. That's a lot of gurning selfies taken in front of beauty spots. That's a long queue of couples in craft bakers choosing granary loaves. People visit different places for different reasons and, somehow, there may be issues of class here. Just to note, you realise; not to unpick. Hen and stag parties flock to Leeds and Hull in minibuses and stretch limos; people who read big newspapers go the Yorkshire Sculpture Park and nod and say words like 'intriguing'. People walk through the RHS gardens at Harlow Carr and feel that somehow the experience is doing them good, and it probably is, and Goths flock to Whitby every October to be with their own kind and have darkly gothic fun.

So I decide to take a day trip up the A1 and into the kind of Yorkshire that qualifies as Tourist Yorkshire. Maybe, once I've been, I'll try and use my literary skills to make a new Yorkshire-wide slogan to attract even more people, or a series of tiny, jewel-like sloganettes to push people in the direction of a town or an attraction. I often think of these slogans as advertising haiku, trying to say as much as possible in just a few words.

In 2014 Calderdale Council had to defend itself from criticism aimed at its new 'Pretty Gritty' slogan, but I like it: it's descriptive, it's pithy, and it rhymes. In the past, Yorkshire has been 'Alive with Opportunity' and Leeds has experimented with 'Leeds: Live it, Love it' which steamed with alliteration and which made people alliteratively angry when it was found to be almost the same as the slogan for Hong Kong which went 'Hong Kong: Live It, Love It'. I see what they did there. Bridlington has been 'Beautiful, Bracing Bridlington', which could be haiku-speak for 'Bring a Cardigan', and in 2003 Rotherham, a town I like very much, described itself in a brochure as 'Perfect for Short Breaks', which in some ways it is.

It seems to me that Yorkshire is trying to sell itself as all things to all people which in itself would make a serviceable if bland slogan. 'Yorkshire: All Things To All People.' The other linguistic way to sell the county, of course, is to use the 'From … To' template beloved of the writers of press releases. You could move from the general, 'Yorkshire: from the West to the East, from the North to the South', to the perhaps too specific, 'Yorkshire: from Mushy Peas in a Ceramic Ramekin at Harry Ramsden's to Sunsets over the Wolds on Thursdays in October.' I'm not only going on the tourist trail, I'm going on the slogan trail.

The only problem is that I can't drive. I had a couple of lessons when I was 17 with a man from the Pennine Driving School in Wombwell who was more nervous than I was, and since then I've gone everywhere by bus or train or I've begged lifts. I remember the instructor's hands shook and he wore flapping sandals the size of industrial waste-paper bins. After a few minutes I knew that driving wasn't for me. It was the way he looked like he was going to weep every time I turned the wheel.

To go by public transport to the bits of Tourist Yorkshire I wanted to visit would be difficult, and anyway the idea is to take the route that many visitors take, to find out what intrigues them, what drives them, as it were, up the county's spine.

I recruit Iain the Artist, who has recently passed his test and is eager to drive anywhere, everywhere. I see him driving through Darfield to the library and the paper shop and we wave our artistic waves, wishing we were somewhere on Cat Hill.

He picks me up at home on a cold, bright day and he gestures to the back seat, which is full of maps and menus for the Chinese takeaway he delivers for.

'Where are we going?' he asks. 'Because I've got loads of maps.'

I shake my head and tell him that we won't need the maps because we don't really know where we're going.

'We're going to go up the A1,' I tell him. There's a pause as we trundle past Cat Hill.

'And then where?' he asks.

'Anywhere,' I say. 'We're going to pretend to be Comforts.'

Ah, Comforts; the universal slang word for visitors adopted by residents in all Yorkshire tourist spots. They've only comfor't day, you see. Now there's a slogan waiting to be coined: 'From Friday to Sunday? No, there's plenty to see in Yorkshire even if you've only comfor't day!' I might write that one down.

Iain looks dubious but I explain that I really want to recreate the idea of the day trip to Yorkshire, even though we're in Yorkshire. I want us to be two of the millions who do it every year, to the Dales ('Dales is Best', according to the Yorkshire Dales Millennium Trust) and the Wolds (the East Riding Motto is 'Tradition and Progress' which asks questions about when a motto becomes a slogan and when a slogan becomes a strapline).

We roll up the A1 past a parked truck in a field with the words PREPARE TO MEET THY GOD written on it, which is a kind of slogan. Well, we're going to prepare to meet our Yorkshire. Now there's a slogan! This is getting addictive.

There's a matrix sign above the road warning us of strong winds but real day trippers wouldn't mind about this. They're going to make the best of it. They've brought a Rainmate and maybe some elastic to fasten their cap on with. 'Bring on your strong winds: we've Comfor't day!' I want to somehow arrange to put that phrase on a matrix sign but I guess that would spoil the anonymity I'm travelling under. These small packets of language get to the heart of selling a county to those who might want to visit it but are unsure. Many years ago there would have been no choice: the mill hooter went and everybody in Bradford would go to Morecambe and when the pit cage got to the top of the shaft everybody in the South Yorkshire Coalfield went to Cleethorpes. These days, confronted by the world as a playground, Yorkshire has to sell itself and I'm determined to help.

I need to define where and what Tourist Yorkshire is, though; to work out how soon you leave the part of Yorkshire that tourists wouldn't really want to go to, and how soon you enter the place they would. There won't be a barrier, of course, no border control with surly guards and a sign saying YOU ARE NOW ENTERING YORKSHIRE, even though you're leaving it as well. Iain says it's probably Ferrybridge Power Station, and I think he's right. Power stations, with their huge cooling towers, dominate much of this part of Yorkshire. They have names that sound like the names of lesser-known Viking gods: Eggborough, Drax, Ferrybridge; well, maybe not Ferrybridge, and there's something majestic about the way the steam from their towers clouds the sky on a clear blue morning.

We ponder the idea of the Acceptable Yorkshire as we drive past Askern, a pit village that used to be a spa and perhaps encapsulates all the divisions and diversions I'm unpacking in the county. Askern sits on the border of South Yorkshire and North Yorkshire, physically and conceptually. In the eighteenth century it became known for the medicinal properties of its waters, although one Dr Short, in his contemporary bestseller, *Mineral Waters of Yorkshire*, refers to the waters as having a most unpleasant taste and odour, although that's never done the pump rooms at Harrogate any harm. It wasn't a bestseller, that book. It had a limited market. I feel inexplicably grumpy. The Darfield waters must be getting to me.

During the early to mid-1800s, Askern's reputation as a spa grew, and visitors came from all over the north of England to splash in its healing waters. Hotels and guest houses were built, and people who would now be known as tourists came and strolled round the lake and often paused to breathe in the sweet and edifying air. In this alternative history view of the country, Askern could have been Harrogate, could have been Bath. Imagine that: people with parasols and clean, bright faces would have come down to Askern from York. A genteel leisure industry would have grown up around water that tasted like bad eggs. Yorkshire in general and South Yorkshire in particular would have been a very different place. 'Askern: from water to gentility.' It works, or it would have.

And then, with that unbendable sense of inevitability that we've encountered before, in the late nineteenth century, coal was discovered and the landowners and entrepreneurs realised that coal was more profitable than water-cures and the spa's importance dwindled until, by the start of the World War I, it had more or less faded away to one person walking slowly with a broken parasol on a grey afternoon in autumn. Askern became a busy and crowded pit village and eventually the closed Coalite plant meant that the area had a most unpleasant taste and odour. Not many people comfor't day these days.

At Ferrybridge Services the A1 meets the M62; turn left and you can go to Leeds and Bradford and Huddersfield and beyond to the place where I pickled into a coloured cup. Turn right and you'll go to Pontefract and Castleford and on to Hull. But carry on up the A1, going north, and you'll end up in Day Trip Yorkshire, familiar Yorkshire. I guess it's like saying that America is the Grand Canyon or Ireland is one strip of bars in Dublin. North Yorkshire is the Reyt Grand canyon of the north.

This is a Yorkshire of tea rooms and galleries, of walks by rivers and visits to castles and museums. It's a Yorkshire of scribbled postcards popped in postboxes in tiny villages, and of people who are only too happy to give you directions or simply to pass the time of day with you as you wait for the little shop to open after lunch or, as I believe they call it round these parts, 'dinner'. And yet, and yet, isn't this the Yorkshire I've mainly been writing about already? Didn't I have a nice cup of tea in Saddleworth? Didn't I chomp a marvellous pork pie in Horbury? Didn't I serve a toasted teacake in Darfield Museum? It's a dilemma. Which is the real Yorkshire? Maybe in the end it's all down to slogans and straplines.

We pass the services at Ferrybridge and Iain turns to me and says a devastating word, a word that's part sneeze and part sneer, a word that sounds particularly devastating in his small car with its maps and shiny takeaway menus: 'Posh'. He changes gear and says it again.

'Posh. This part of Yorkshire is posh, and that's what makes it different to Barnsley. The people here are posher, they've got more money, they've got better jobs, better houses. Their dads didn't work down the pit or if they did they got out. That's the difference.'

I'm surprised. I don't use the word 'posh' a lot, and I certainly don't use it much in connection with Yorkshire. I think of the lazy TV parodies and stereotypes of the Yorkshire person and the word Posh doesn't spring to mind. When I was in Leyburn and Settle that didn't feel posh; touristy, certainly, doily-tabled, for sure. But posh? Not really. The faces of the farmers were too hewn. The Shawl felt a little desolate. But maybe now we're entering into a different part of the county, a part that requires new ways of thinking to try to describe it.

'Where shall we go, then?' Iain asks. 'Somewhere posh?'

Well, let's just go and see what we can see. It'll probably all be posh although, crucially, it wouldn't say it was, and of course there's a difference between Posh Yorkshire and Real Posh that's like the difference between Vintage champagne and home-made elderflower champagne. 'From vintage champagne to elderflower champagne: That's Yorkshire!'

We turn off the A1 and go to Wetherby, best known for its racecourse. When I was a boy we would always get stuck on the A1 at Wetherby on our way back from visiting the Scottish branch of the family on Easter Tuesday because the races were just turning out; my dad's face would go pale as we inched along and the car threatened to overheat and he'd had one too many sips of tea from the flask. Perhaps when we got closer to home he'd be able to find a convenient hedge. Like father, like son. These days there's a service station just off the A1 at Wetherby and in the early days it was going to have the slogan, 'Your environmentally friendly service station'. Needs work.

Today there's no race meeting so we enter the town without fuss and our way isn't blocked by any stumbling racegoers walking against the odds.

'Prosperity,' Iain says. 'There's an air of prosperity here.'

He's right. I despise the word 'austerity' with its cosy image of all-in-it-together allotment-digging and vest-darning, but this is the northern end of Austerity England (and the midlands of Austerity Britain) but it doesn't seem very austere. There seems to be a sense of murmured comfort. The streets are quiet, which could mean that most people are at work. Iain isn't sure where we are.

'Are we near Leeds?' he asks.

I assure him that we are.

'This could be Leeds overspill,' he says, and we wander down to the river, presumably to see if we can find people talking in Leeds accents. Legend has it that the town is halfway between London and Edinburgh, so it really is in the midlands, and as such it's always been an important staging post on the A1, with mailcoaches and stagecoaches carrying passengers with smocks speckled with travel-sickness calling off here and taking refreshment and hard beds for a night or two. The old Great North Road used to come through Wetherby on its way from Doncaster and

Bawtry and, like any settlement with a bypass, it feels a little bit as though things are passing the town by. Things like Time and Noise.

Wetherby is also part of the marvellously named wapentake of Skyrack, which sounds like a character from the sort of science-fiction trilogy that gets presented to me at Writers' Workshop evenings by keen lads with goatees and black flat caps and lots of pencils in the top pockets of their jackets. A wapentake is an old word for a meeting place, often near a crossroads or a river, and Yorkshire is festooned with them, including the wapentakes of Gilling West, Whitby Strand, Osgoldcross and Hang East. I for one would like to revive these names, to give the county a certain gloss and fizz. Surely it would be better to live in Skyrack than Leeds? That would bring the tourists in. 'Wetherby: That Halfway Wapentake.' That sings.

Iain and I think we're walking to the river but in fact we're just getting stuck in a car park. We can see the river, we can hear it, but we're just strolling between cars. The odd thing is that the car park is full, and yet the town feels empty. There's a teashop at the end of the car park, but it's closed. WINTER HOURS, the sign says. So where is everybody? Is there some kind of wapentake meeting happening in a giant underground bunker that we don't know anything about?

We find an open café and sit down. I'll test out one of their espressos, place it in an espresso hierarchy that goes back years. Mmm: quite good; a zing to it, a blackness and a crema. Opposite us are four people, two couples, who couldn't be from anywhere else from Yorkshire for reasons that it's actually quite hard to put your finger on. One of the men has got a mane of white hair a bit like mine, but longer and more mellifluous; another of the men is going bald and has admitted it. You get the sense that he tried a comb-over for a while but then one day, after a walk in a stiff breeze on the front at Filey, decided that enough was enough and sliced the strands away. Their wives are dressed as though they've been dipped in Marks & Spencer from a great height then hauled back up to the ceiling. The two men are wearing ties, not because they've just come from court appearances but because they're the sort of men who always wear ties.

Not for them the flinging away of the hated tie on the last day at work. The tie is essential, they'll tell sceptical great-nephews, to keep your neck warm. To them it's as simple as that, just as it was for my dad, who used to change into a different tie, a green one, when he went out into the garden to dig.

But so far, so universal. These could be any four people in any comfortable town. They're having tea, and one of the women is pouring. One of the men is having a toasted teacake and he's stuck his serviette down the collar of his jumper even though it makes his wife tut. When they open their mouths, though, it's obvious that they're from Yorkshire. It's not that the accents are strong. It's that they're talking about the price of things. I know that part of the mission of this book is to deal painful and possibly fatal blows to the myth that Yorkshire people are tight, because as far as I'm concerned we're generous and free-spirited, but this quartet are making a liar of me. Sadly for the cause of investigative non-fiction I can't hear everything they're saying but from the snatches I can hear I can confirm that the naturalistic dialogue is of a fiscal nature.

It's frustrating not to be able to catch it all. Despite my best efforts at leaning over until my head is almost on the taller woman's lap, and despite pretending to drop a spoon so that I can get closer I can only pick out certain words but they're the important words.

'He doubled the price,' the man with the teacake says. There is mumbling that I can't decipher. 'They wouldn't take a cheque,' he continues.

There is muttering that cannot be notated, even by a man with a mind sharpened by espresso. There is a lot of inaudible talk but I can tell by the way eyebrows go up and down, lips are pursed, hands are run through hair, a mobile phone is checked for messages and a hand is patted with familiarity, that financial considerations are at the top of their list. Why else would Yorkshire people waggle their eyebrows or purse their lips? Unless they were caught in a hurricane, of course. At the counter a young man makes clattering music as he washes up a phalanx of those metal teapots that always leak all over the tablecloth.

There is one of those sudden moments of crystal silence that sometimes descends on rooms like this; by a kind of cosmic coincidence everyone has stopped talking and clinking cups and scraping chairs back and scratching their heads. Everyone is silent and everyone is listening.

Except the man with the toasted teacake and the tucked-in serviette. He's finishing off a sentence that pins him down geographically like nothing else could: '... and you could get it down the street for 50p cheaper!'

I want to cheer but stop myself by grabbing the free biscuit from my saucer and thrusting it sideways into my mouth, painfully. Nobody notices because they're all nodding in agreement. I write the phrase down. I'll pass it on to somebody at Visit Yorkshire: motto, strapline or slogan? I'll let them decide.

The noise begins again. Iain and I sup up. Time to leave. We wander aimlessly down the main street as though we are a couple looking for somewhere to live and gainful Yorkshire-based employment. In a charity shop we look at scarves because Iain says the scarves in a charity shop are a fine and meticulous indicator of poshness. I feel a bit shivery just saying the word 'posh' in Yorkshire because our USP is that we aren't posh and yet this feels posh. Or if not posh, then psh, or osh.

Because Iain's an artist there's no point going round a gallery with him especially if, like me, you don't know much about art but you know what you like. Like all artists he'll point to a painting and say, 'Now that's really good,' and then he'll shift his gaze a little down the wall and say, of what to my untrained eye appears to be *exactly the same painting,* 'Now that's rubbish. They should chuck it away,' and it's the same with the scarves in this little shop.

He holds one up.

'Posh'.

He holds another copy of the same one up from further down the rack.

'Not posh.'

He holds another one up that looks like the first one. He lifts it towards me with an enquiring look.

'Flipping heck, that's posh,' I say.

'It's not posh at all,' he says.

I'm the same with words, I suppose. I can spot an authentic one a mile off and those false t apostrophes cut no ice with me, tha knows. 'Palimpsest': great word. 'Webinar': not so good word. Iain the Artist would think they were aesthetic equals, the fool.

Wetherby, it's not you, it's me. I don't feel right for you. I'm just a kid frum tarn and you're sophisticated. I know, I know: you'll tell me that I'm not digging deep enough, that if I looked harder I'd find deep wells of unsophistication. It's not you. It's me. Ours was just a short relationship; one drink and the possibility of a scarf. I'll be back, though. I just need to get my head together. My Yorkshire head together. I've got a slogan for you, though: 'Wetherby: Come off the Main Road and See Us!'

We drive out of town, which is better than being driven out of town, and we're still not sure where we're going. I suspect that the tourist industry of Yorkshire would like to be like my eldest daughter who always enjoys having a timetable whenever she goes away. The tourist industry would like me to amble from mining museum to media museum, from ruined castle to lakeside walk, from breath-taking view to Pub of the Year. I'm sorry, but I believe in the joy of encounters, the true value of serendipity against the fool's gold of the set-up meeting. So we decide to go to a village that we've never been to before and we trundle up the hill to Kirkby Overblow and here I find something important for this book and for my thinking about Yorkshire. And, appropriately for Kirkby Overblow, the wind is getting up. It's not only getting up, it's going out of the house for a long run up and down the hills.

My friends Harry and Lizzie live in an ex-silver mining village near Liskeard, in that part of Cornwall that was riddled with pits in the nineteenth century which tried their best to extract as much precious and non-precious metal as they could from the earth before it all collapsed. The place they live is an old silver miner's cottage but if they hadn't told me, the first time I stayed there in 1985, I would never have known. The point here is that I thought their Cornish village was posh; if it was a scarf in a Wetherby charity shop I would have called it posh. And yet it was like Darfield, it was an ex-mining village.

And would the bleak beauty of those Cornish hills have simply been bleak if the pits were still there? Does beauty arrive with disuse? And is it simply the fact that the silver mine near Harry and Lizzie's has been closed for many years longer than Darfield Main that makes the area worth visiting? I wandered down the tiny main street that first time and it wasn't like walking down a street at home; the past had been put in an envelope and posted to me, rather than still limping along as a shadow of the present. Maybe nobody in that village could remember where the pit bus stopped.

I only bring Cornwall in because I've often thought of it as an honorary southern Yorkshire, down to the mining and fishing and the brass bands and the post-industrialisation and the perceived isolation from the centre of things if the centre of things is London, which it isn't. It's Darfield, of course. And we've got a mining museum near Wakefield but somehow the old mining areas in Cornwall seem more exotic, more, and here's a phrase I invented a while ago and which seems relevant, *available for myth*. That's what I need for my Yorkshire: I need it to be Available For Myth, and this part of the county seems more available than my part, somehow, notwithstanding the Cat and the Man and the Owl in the Tower. Maybe it's harder to make myths about the place you live in. Mind you, I've made a living from that for 35 years. 'Available for Myth': print that slogan on T-shirts and sunhats because that's what the heart of tourism in Yorkshire is about.

I'm thinking of all this myth and mining stuff because Kirkby Overblow, perched on the top of a hill not far from Harewood House, used to be in the middle of an iron ore mining area. The beautiful word 'Overblow' comes from 'orblauers' or iron smelters, and there were probably iron-works there until the end of the seventeenth century. As always, history has put all its baggage on the carousel and not come back to claim it, and there's farms and housing over the places where people strained and sweated to make something from the ground.

As a poem on the cover of the *Brief History of All Saints' Church Kirkby Overblow* says:

Christian history is here enshrined
where in olden days, iron ore was mined
tho age takes toll of stone and written page
may we take care of this, our heritage.

Although that third line is a little too long to fit the rest of the poem, it's certainly true. Age weathers everything, even written memory, rendering words and ideas obsolete and quaint. In the 'Yorkshire is Texas' style, the leaflet tells me that between 1778 and 1803 the tower was largely rebuilt and fitted with a new clock ('said to have the longest pendulum in Yorkshire'). I love that 'said to have'; as if they were ever in any doubt. From the churchyard you can almost see Harewood House, which is another (another!) big house that dominates the surrounding area like a man in a big hat can dominate a cinema audience.

Once, when I was doing a poetry workshop with some junior school children from Bradford in the grounds of Harewood House, there was a particularly grumpy kid who didn't want to join in the jolly poem-making and who seemed determined to squeeze enjoyment from the act of not enjoying himself, in the Yorkshire fashion. As we wandered around finding things to write about he suddenly spotted a 10p piece on the floor and darted for it like a seabird after a lugworm. He pocketed it and I thought it might cheer him up, but it didn't. His lips remained a straight line in the unimpressed moon of his face.

Ten minutes later, in an enhanced repeat of the miracle, he found a £1 coin in the grass and pocketed that, too. It clinked next to the ten pence piece, making money-music. He still refused to smile.

At dinnertime we all sat around and ate our packed lunches. He'd got a bag of crisps and it was in the days when you sometimes got a cash prize in a little envelope in your

Cheese and Onion rather than a little packet of salt. He found one of the free gifts and opened it up: it was a tightly folded £20 note. He almost grinned, then stopped himself.

'So even if you're not enjoying the poetry, at least you've made a bit of money out of the day,' I said.

He didn't make eye contact with me and munched insistently, the £21.10p weighing heavily.

I've thought about that treasure incident a lot over the years, and I've welded a narrative to it about never being satisfied with the crumbs from the rich man's table, but maybe it was just that the lad had a really sad face and he was whooping with laughter inside. He hid the emotion well, because he was from Yorkshire.

From Kirkby Overblow we're blown by a breeze so stiff it must have swallowed Viagra, to Knaresborough, mainly because Iain has always wanted to visit Mother Shipton's Cave and also because he has a vivid childhood memory of standing on a bridge looking across a river and he's convinced that was in Knaresborough. I find that kind of memory snapshot happens a lot when I talk to people about Yorkshire: they recall something, a view from a bus window, a moment on a beach, a pint in a pub garden, a hat blown off in a hailstorm. For them Yorkshire is a glimpse of the past and maybe a hope for a return. For people like me, it's the golden sludge we trudge in. (Write that one down, and all.)

Mother Shipton's Cave is, like so many things in this county, as much an emblem and a symbol as a dank spot with water dripping from the roof. It's famous for being the 'oldest entrance charging tourist attraction in England', a phrase which for me works as a slogan, having extracted belm from palm since 1630. Mother Shipton was a seer, a prophet, who was said to have been able to foretell the future although as with all these predictions they're looser and baggier than actually pinpointing what might win the 2.30 at Pontefract. Mother Shipton, or Old Mother Shipton as she was known later in life, was born towards the end of the fifteenth century and became so well known as a lifter of the future's shirtlap that Samuel Pepys writes of how he and the royal family discussed her prophesy about the Great Fire of London in what was presumably a smoke-filled room. She was so famous that parodies of her were performed on stage to such an extent that she was thought to be a precursor of the pantomime dame, something that she really couldn't have predicted. Oh yes she was. One encyclopaedia dismisses her predictions as 'mainly regional' and many of her better-known and more sensational ones were later found to have been faked by a man called Charles Hindley, who published a collection, purporting to be of her prophecies, in 1862. Its slick/creaky couplets appear to foreshadow the internal combustion engine, the internet and the act of strolling around at the bottom of the sea for fun and profit:

> Carriages without horses shall go
>> and accidents fill the world with woe.
> Around the world thoughts shall fly
>> in the twinkling of an eye.
> … Underwater men shall walk
>> shall ride, shall sleep, shall talk.

Presumably, the accidents that fill the world with woe would have been caused by the coming and going of the carriages without horses. Although Hindley's versions of the crystal ball were discredited, a lot of fans of Mother Shipton still hang on to the idea that she was privy to a Knaresborough-based portal to the misty and ill-defined area known as the Future.

When I was a child the most tangible part of the Mother Shipton story was the petrifying well, where through a process of dripping water and calcification ordinary objects were indeed petrified into a kind of fossilisation. I remember going there with my family and being amazed by a petrified bowler hat, gleaming in the subterranean light. I liked bowler hats because John Steed wore one in *The Avengers* and if I thought about John Steed I also thought about Emma Peel and that made me very happy, in an awkward kind of way. In the 1980s, the magician Paul Daniels and his wife Debbie 'the Lovely' McGee bought a share in the attraction but stardust can't really help the fact that it's a well, a walk and a few predictions. It's a pleasant walk, mind you, and Iain and I were hoping to talk a stroll by the river and perhaps devise a few predictions of our own, but the gates at the entrance were locked and we couldn't get in. We should have predicted that, I suppose.

'It's Yorkshire,' I say to Iain and to anybody else who'll listen. 'You expect it to let you in with open arms but when you get there it's locked and the real Yorkshire is happening in a place you can't find.'

That's probably a bit wordy for a motto, but it might make a strapline.

We turn and walk back to the car. I wonder if Mother Shipton would have predicted this. She probably did, but we are too daft to read it and too thick to understand. Maybe I feel too close to this place to be a tourist here. I'd rather be in Askern, I think. I find myself saying the words 'Clockwork Yorkshire' aloud to nobody in particular. I'm not sure what Clockwork Yorkshire is, or where it really is, but I think it's any part of the county that I don't happen to be in, and that must make me Yorkshire Enough. I think the quest is coming to some kind of endgame, the last few overs of the match, the extra time that dwindles to its conclusion.

It's time I went to the seaside, the inner circle of all the circles that Tourist Yorkshire is made of.

UP THE HILL TO PARADISE

MUCH OF YORKSHIRE is coastline, of course, and in the past few years the North Sea has enjoyed being in close proximity to the land so much that it's started to bite it, chew it, swallow it and occasionally spit it out. Seasoned Professional Yorkshiremen like myself sometimes worry that, if we live long enough (and the Yorkshire air means that we probably will) Yorkshire will erode away until it's the size of Rutland, San Marino, or the Shetlandic islet of Papa Stour. It'll be hard trying to stick up for an area of land no bigger than your back garden, saying things like, 'This used to be the mighty county of Yorkshire,' as people point and snigger.

Over a number of decades I've built up a private hard-earned vocabulary of shorthand terms for each of the major Yorkshire resorts as a form of eccentric personal coastal defence. This is the first time I'll have employed them in public; let's see how they stand up to scrutiny. They'll be useful for Visit Yorkshire, I reckon: I'll parcel them up and send them on.

I call Bridlington, 'Dropped Pasty', because when I was there once as a young boy on a family day trip my parents insisted on buying me a Cornish pasty for my dinner even though I'd blubbered and wailed for a pork pie, their dubious and tissue-thin argument being that Cornish pasties were healthier. In an even more ludicrous attempt at persuasion my dad took me to one side and whispered, 'They eat them in Cornwall,' which is like saying that flight in a hot-air balloon is enjoyable and safe because it happens in the sky.

They gave me a pasty and I took it gracelessly, snatching and fumbling at the same time. It felt like a piece of skin that had hardened round the heel of a pensioner. My parents ate theirs with loud lip-smacking enjoyment. My dad put his thumb up after gesturing at the pasty. My brother said the taste of a pasty beat the taste of a pork pie any day of the week.

I held mine gingerly and, still trying to make my body shake with sobs, walked over to the harbour. The tide was out and boats balanced on oleaginous mud. I leaned over the harbour, pretending to look at the wading birds that pressed their long legs into the sludge. I dropped the pasty slowly and deliberately and it flopped into the mud and sank. I turned round and pretended to cry.

'I've lost my lovely pasty,' I wailed, unconvincingly.

'Well, you can't have another one,' my dad said, his voice implying that this was some kind of punishment.

Gulls laughed overhead, their mouths half-full of chips. If you wanted to use flat caps and headscarves as a crude indicator of social class, then I think you'd see Bridlington as about halfway up the ladder. There would be the odd trilby, and occasionally what looked like a hat from the Russian Army.

I call Filey, 'Pushing In', because when I was first going out with the girl who has been my wife for many years we were queuing up at the window of a shop for some candy floss when a person pushed in in front of us and got served first. To my eternal shame I didn't hit them with a shovel, which would have earned my wife-to-be's gratitude for my chivalric gesture; instead, I did what I always did in those days in any situation because I thought it was a funny thing to do: I quoted Groucho Marx inappropriately.

'What this store needs is a detective!' I said, wiggling my eyebrows like maggots and adopting a Marxist walk.

There wasn't a shovel handy, anyway.

There are slightly more flat caps and headscarves in Filey; in the old days slightly more club trips than private cars, and these days more minibuses full of extended families and slightly less young professionals.

I call Whitby, 'Tiny Caravan', because, after a family week in a large caravan, my dad decided that we should stay another couple of days because the weather was good and he wasn't due back at work just yet. We had to vacate the caravan we were in but the owner promised he had one just the same, in fact better, for us at the other end of the site. The four of us – my parents, my brother and I – drove down to the replacement caravan in the faithful blue Zephyr 6 with the registration number UHE 8, down to where the owner was waving us in like we were a hearse driving carefully into a cemetery. He indicated what seemed to be a toy caravan with a flourish. It looked about as big as one of those packet curries that were all the rage in the late 1960s. It was the sort Father Ted and Dougal ended up in. My mother looked disgusted and suggested that we go home straightaway.

My dad, always the optimist, said, 'I think we'll fit in okay; it's only for a couple of nights.'

The owner opened the door and put his hand inside the caravan to show us how deceptively large it was, but his hand seemed to take up most of the available interior space. I've been in bigger cardigans.

Once we were in, it took quite a long time, in the fierce Whitby heat, to get out. It was a bit like quads being born. My dad shook his head sadly and decided that we should go home. The owner, in an odd and unforgettable act of generosity, put his hand in his pocket and gave my brother a magnet, one of the ones shaped like a horseshoe. We played with it all the way home, sitting in the back of UHE 8 pretending to magnetise clouds and crows so that they'd follow us back to Darfield. In terms of social class, Whitby attracts the adventurer and the bohemian, the biker rather than the driver of the bubble car.

I call Scarborough, 'No Coffee', because, in the middle of the night during a weekend with the Darfield Bellringers in Robin Hood's Bay in 1973, I persuaded Dave Sunderland to drive there in his car because I was convinced, on no evidence at all, that there was an all-night café near the South Bay Gardens where we could get a cup of coffee and a bacon sandwich. We'd sat up far too late in the hotel bar and the conversation had ranged widely, from Grandsire Triples via Captain Beefheart to a half-hearted discussion of the Yorkshire coast we were on, and we came to the conclusion that it was all right for the older end but a bit genteel for go-ahead members of the church and chapel youth clubs like ourselves. The pegs at the bottom of the Robin Hood's Bay hotel stairs were festooned with flat caps, which proved our point.

Although the all-night café we were going to was completely a figment of my fevered late teenage mind, I described it to him in great detail: the green walls, the steam rising, the rickety chairs, the jolly fishermen and F. Scott Fitzgerald-style lushes who would inhabit it, the gruff but kindly owner whose moustache was caffeine-stained and who would have many a tale to tell. There may even be tight-trousered girls there who would giggle at our anecdotes, something that never happened in real life. I have no excuse for this except that I was a bookish boy with an imagination the size of an open-topped double decker bus.

We drove into Scarborough and the full moon was a badge on a game-show host's blazer. We progressed up and down the silent roads looking for the café which I finally admitted did not exist. I had another idea; we could go to a posh hotel and they'd serve us coffee. We pulled up outside the Grand Hotel but, in the end, we didn't dare go in. We were kids from Darfield who'd got lucky with our O levels but we thought we wouldn't be as posh as the people who were sleeping in the darkened rooms. We went back to Robin Hood's Bay and, the next day, elevated the trip into a catalogue of epic and glamorous encounters through the self-generating power of anecdote. The other campanologists didn't believe us. They thought we were pulling their rope.

*

And now I'm off to Scarborough again on a bright blue January morning, to see if I can find those people, the beautiful ones that I imagined clinking their espressos in that imaginary café with what turned out to be see-through walls. I hope it doesn't disappoint; ever since my quest for That Café, there'd always been a slight air of disappointment about the town.

I get the train to York from Doncaster; just as we're pulling out of the station the trolley man comes in. It's the one who's like a music hall turn. The one who likes to shout. I like him.

'Morning All!' he bellows, to the consternation of a gaggle of Japanese tourists who fish in the lanyards round their necks for their tickets. He points at them then points at himself then points at the trolley.

'This should give you a clue that I'm not the ticket collector,' he shouts, 'this big thing here that I'm dragging behind me.'

He rattles the trolley and the cans of lager shift. He then addresses the passengers as a unit.

'Ah, Doncaster: they don't bury their dead, they just send them to this carriage!'

I laugh, alone, like someone who has got the wrong end of an unsubtitled Ukranian epic in a suburban cinema in Kiev at the tail end of a long autumn afternoon. The train gathers speed and he hauls the trolley down the aisle, hooting gags and imprecations all the way.

At York the man bids us all farewell, standing on the platform and spreading his arms beatifically then pointing the Japanese tourists towards the station exit. A fellow passenger rushes up and shakes his hand saying, 'Top man! Top man!', to which the trolley gent replies, 'Yes, sir. We're all top men. And I mean that most sincerely! Missing you already!'

I clamber on the Scarborough train, which is busy, even on a January Tuesday morning. The woman on the seat beside me is on the phone.

'Just get out of bed and get the kettle on. I'll be there in 45 minutes.'

I guess that counts as a romantic invitation in Yorkshire.

A young, dreamy lad and a couple of women get on at Malton. The women discuss egg custard made with duck eggs, and the lad keeps looking out of the window and announcing things.

'The clouds are low,' he says, and he's right; it was bright earlier but now it isn't.

The woman from earlier talks on the phone again, quietly but urgently.

'Two sugars. Two, remember. Two.'

Just before we arrive at Seamer, the lad says, 'We are now arriving at Seamer. Change here for Bridlington.'

Everyone looks at him, startled.

'That's what they'll say in a minute,' he says, and they do, the posh automatic voice ringing out over the whole train, interrupting him as he speaks so he stops saying what he was saying and joins in the announcement.

I feel like saying, 'The clouds are low,' just to be sociable.

At the station I imagine sitting, or lolling, or lying, or setting up house, on the long-lost bench on platform 1 that was reputed to be the longest in the country, able to accommodate multitudes of the comfortable buttocks of Comfor'ts as they waited for their train.

I wander down towards the sea front; a busker is playing the saxophone to a pounding backing track and the wheeling seagulls overhead twist his music in a pleasantly avant-garde direction. The woman from the train passes me, hurrying towards her sweet tea. It's too early in the season for donkeys, and that's a shame.

I recall the tale told of the Working Men's Club trip from somewhere in South Yorkshire that went to Scarborough in the early 1960s and took hundreds of children to the beach for donkey rides. As the crowds of kids approached the donkeys, one of the donkeys broke away and began to run down the beach towards a rival set of donkeys and for no reason that anyone can fathom, except for a kind of pied piper effect, the children and many of the adults ran after it. The donkey was running like a racehorse and the club trip had difficulty keeping up. Somehow, in the air, there was an unstated and frankly ludicrous nervousness that if the donkey wasn't caught nobody would get a ride. Some of the children were whippet-thin; some of the adults were melon-shaped and were wearing braces. Caps fell off and may or may not have been picked up. It was a warm, some would say hot, day. Inhalers were produced from pockets and brandished in the sun; some were dropped in the sand and subsequent inhalations were gritty and smelled faintly of shellfish.

The donkey eventually arrived at the place where the other donkeys were standing around, closely pursued by the club trip. I like to imagine that there were ragged and breathless cheers. The donkey singled out one of the other donkeys and, to use a euphemism employed by somebody's cousin in the butcher's the next day, began to 'go on a date' with it. Vigorously, noisily and repeatedly. Eyes were averted; eyes were narrowed. A camera was produced but then put away.

'No Coffee' is known, much to the consternation of 'Dropped Pasty', 'Tiny Caravan' and 'Pushing In', as the Queen of Yorkshire Seaside Resorts, and it's certainly visually regal, with its two bays, two beaches, formal gardens, cliff lifts, and the aforementioned Grand Hotel dominating the view like a king on a chessboard. I walk along the front of the North Bay, by the sands, and even at this time on a bright but raw January late morning, people are eating fish and chips and trying to win cuddly toys with those grabbers that never did what they were meant to in a complete failure of nominative determinism. The sun has come out again like a hermit crab from a shell.

The North Bay and the South Bay are separated by a massive rocky promontory topped with a castle; I was once filming a documentary in Scarborough with some wrestlers and I stood by the castle with an imposing, muscular American whose stage name was The Dog and whose real name was, wonderfully, Al Green. Al isn't with us any more but I remember him as a gentle and thoughtful man, except when he was throwing me around and pretending to drop me on the floor but breaking my fall (as opposed to my ribs) just an inch before the unforgiving earth in a back room at the Grimsby Auditorium as the camera rolled and the soundman said, 'I think Ian's going to be sick,' as he moved his boom microphone out of reach.

I asked The Dog what he got out of wrestling and he said, in a voice that was so deep it reactivated dried-up springs deep below the ground, 'I see it as being like Shakespeare; you got the good guys, and you got the bad guys. And the bad guys seem to be winning at first but then in the end the good guys always win.' I wished I'd put that in my essay on *Henry IV Part One*. I might have got better marks.

Shakespeare was interested in duality, and I reckon Scarborough would be a great setting for a performance of *Macbeth*; after all, as the witches say, fair is fowl and fowl is fair, and sometimes when it's raining in the North Bay it's sunny in the South Bay and vice versa. These sudden shifts in Yorkshire weather could be metaphors, as The Dog knew, for Good and Evil; and they could also tell you it's time to nip in for a plate of chips or an hour on the slots watching your last 2p piece just fail to knock your penultimate, your antepenultimate and your preantepenultimate 2p's back down the chute and clinking into your purse.

As I walk down towards the Futurist Theatre where I saw Mike Yarwood and the Black Theatre of Prague on a double-bill in the mid 1970s, I encounter three of the classic Yorkshire Seaside Stereotypes that warm my heart with their inevitability and, yes, their wholehearted Yorkshireness.

There's the long-wed couple staring stoically into the middle distance as they eat their sandwiches from foil and sip coffee from a flask; they won't go into a café because they're not paying those prices. They never have and they're not going to start now. They sit in a silence that just, and only just, manages to be companionable, managing not to catch each other's eye or make any kind of sociable noise that might be construed as small talk. Maybe one of them forgot the milk. Maybe one of them said something that reminded the other of the sad and solitary death of Uncle Norman in a hotel room on what was meant to be a celebratory weekend for which he'd bought new pyjamas and a dressing gown monogrammed with a bright N. You could cut the silence with a plastic knife from a picnic set.

There's the fat bloke in shorts and vest who's sweating like a sponge and who keeps dabbing his face with a duvet-sized hanky, even though it's only January and it's not that warm to anybody else except him. He'll be from a small town in West Yorkshire and this will be the first time he's been to the seaside since last autumn and somehow, in his head, the weather will be the same as it was on that balmy September day, and that's why he's sporting the shorts 'n' vest ensemble. He should, if he was a normal human being, be cold but he's created his own micro-climate and he's living in it. He's a sort of Baked Alaska of the streets who lives with his mam who is lagging behind and calling out to him to slow down but he's seen a chip shop and he's a lard-seeking missile. He passes the couple eating their sandwiches and he says, 'By, it's warm!' They don't reply, unless chewing stolidly is a reply.

'I'll tell you this,' he says, 'if this is that there global warming I'll have it!'

Just behind the fat bloke in shorts there's the couple with the mardy kid. In fact the kid is beyond mardy; he's, to use a wonderful South Yorkshire word, maungey, with a soft 'g' like Geoffrey. If you're maungey you're whining and sobbing, you think the whole world is against you, your eyes are strawberry red with tears, you've lost the ability to enunciate consonants and a constant vowel-soup keens from your wobbling mouth. Think of me when I wanted that pork pie.

The couple are doing their best to pretend that the child is not theirs. They stare straight ahead or they look out to sea where a boat is bobbing like the child's emotions. After a while the mother comes out with the old Yorkshire phrase that's used by parents who have reached the end of their tether and have gone far beyond it: 'Wait till ah get thi ooam.'

The demotic gives it more power, don't you think? Almost Shakespearean? They pass the sandwich-chewing pair who roll their eyes.

I accelerate to overtake this White Rose diorama and pause by the Central Tramway; Scarborough once had five cliff lifts but the Central Tramway is one of only two still in use. The Central began life as a steam operated funicular in 1881 and after converting to electricity in the 1930s, continues to deliver a genteel version of powered flight to anybody too bad on their legs to ascend or descend the cliffs on foot. There's no doubt that being on a funicular, particularly for the first time, is an amazing sensation, like parachuting from a top bunk or being a fledgling launching yourself from a nest. In the 1970s, people falling off platform shoes must have felt they were on a funicular. Shakespeare and The Dog would enjoy the duality of it, the upper and the lower stations, the top and the bottom, the toffs and the rude mechanicals.

The townspeople might disagree, but Victorian times were the golden era for Scarborough and places like it. The edifice that is the Grand Hotel was built in 1867 and designed by Hull architect Cuthbert Broderick, who was a real Yorkshire landscape-modifier, being responsible for the town hall and the Corn Exchange in Leeds, both of which slice up the sky in a dramatic way that suggest majesty and the potential of wealth. The Grand Hotel is a huge bow-tie on Scarborough's dress shirt and when it was opened it was one of the biggest hotels in Europe, riding on the waves of people who came to sample the waters of the town's spa; some of the hotel's bathrooms had two sets of taps so that guests could wash themselves in what that couple with their sandwiches in gleaming foil would call Proper Water, after they'd bathed in seawater. It's said that at one time it had four towers to represent the seasons, 12 floors for the months of the year, 52 chimneys for the weeks and 365 bedrooms for the days of the year. So if you didn't want to use it as a hotel, it would make a useful diary, except in a leap year.

Scarborough could have ended up being the Askern of the east, of course, had not the black gold intervened; the two of them could have slugged it out for the restorative water market. It's January so the cliff lift is closed, which is a real shame; now I'll have to walk.

Before I go aloft, I turn back to the amusement arcade. I feel like I haven't given this aspect of the town enough attention. Am I too posh for amusement arcades? I sincerely hope not. I'm at the seaside so I decide to test my passion at a Passion Testing machine by the front door of a gaudy flashing and winking emporium of delight and disappointment. For 50p you can put your hand inside and the interior workings of the device will work out how passionate you are. As I've discussed in this book already Yorkshire people in general, and Yorkshire men in particular, and South Yorkshire men in even more particular, are known to be undemonstrative and it can be said they lack passion in certain areas of their lives that don't include football, Rugby League or cricket. I look round because I don't want to test my passion in front of anybody; it's a private thing, like shaking bits of dried skin out of your socks onto the mat in the kitchen. Doesn't everybody do that?

I put my money in. I put my hand in. I stand there. It's like waiting for the results of a blood test. I try to think passionate thoughts and my ears go red, which may just be from the cold. I think about the numbers of visitors that have strolled down here for decades: in 2012 the footfall in the town centre was over four and a half million. I don't know if that means that four and a half million people visited Scarborough, or four and a half million feet pounded the pavements, but either way it's an impressive number. Multiply that number by a hundred and you get an almost unfathomable number of visitors to this part of the Yorkshire Coast and I have to come to the conclusion, not being very good with statistics, that everybody has been to Scarborough and that some people have been twice. I keep my hand as still as I can, letting my passion flood out as I think about the numbers.

There are several levels of passion listed on the machine. For men the most passionate is Super Stud, followed by Sex Mad and Hot Lover, with the least passionate being Useless and Needs Help. For women, Burning is the top of the passion scale, with Man Mad and Hot Pants close behind and Useless bringing up the rear again. Useless is unisex; it does not discriminate. The words sound like the sorts of nicknames that workmates give each other in private that sometimes slip out through social media. I guess you could use the Passion Meter as a device to find if you and a potential partner were suited. After all, if you were a Rude Girl, you wouldn't want to go out with a man who was Innocent. Maybe likes should attract here, and Super Stud could go on a hot date with Burning, and leave Useless and Useless to enjoy a night in with mugs of cocoa and reruns of *Gilligan's Island*.

I'm pleased, though not too pleased, to say that I'm not Useless and I don't Need Help. I'm way up from that. One up from that: I'm Harmless. I know that Yorkshire people are meant to be quiet lovers whose concentration is easily broken when in a romantic situation. I know research has shown that during a session involving kissing and murmuring on a couch they'll drift away mentally and start trying to name the team that got to the quarter-final of the League Cup when a fox ran on the pitch. But Harmless?

Surely that's an insult to my Yorkshirehood? My hands must be cold from the sea air. Yes, that'll be it. What a waste of 50p.

I walk up through the gardens to the top of the cliff and stare at the beautiful sea, trying to imagine how those Victorians would have seen it all those years ago.

'We tried Askern,' they'd say, their voices full of the excitement of an era that believed anything was possible if you could harness steam to power it and people to make it, 'but we prefer Scarborough.'

I like both, but that's because I'm trying to understand them both, and not just for the purposes of this book: for the purposes of my life in Yorkshire.

I love the contrast of the two halves of Scarborough, from the Hot Pants of the South Bay to the Nice Lover of the North Bay. Once you're up at the top of the cliff looking over the South Bay you're in a kind of Bath on Sea, with a regency crescent curving across the landscape, taking the eye to somewhere beautiful and unexpected. There are hotels and an art gallery on the crescent now but walk around it with your eyes half closed like I did, almost bumping into the car of a man who was sorting out his receipts as he sat in the driver's seat, and you can imagine how it was; the talk will have been murmured and muted and fine hats will have been held on to against the strong wind as a monocle glints. The crescent really is a fine example of regency architecture and the past seems to hang there in the air; what is so impressive about this end of Scarborough is that, like a tune you can't get out of your head, it goes on and on. Except that this is a beautiful tune like a piece by Philip Glass that incorporates tiny changes when you think you've got it fathomed. Behind the crescent there are more streets of older, beautiful houses, many converted to hotels and flats but still retaining the idea of Scarborough being a place you take your time in.

Scarborough's a great place for the memorial bench, too, that part-sculpture, part-poem that invites you to sit and think. There are many that remember people 'who loved Scarborough' and who possibly requested a bench in their will, but my favourite is a very simple one that just says, 'In loving memory of John Clark Parks Superintendent of this town from 1922 to 1951 He loved the beauty of Scarborough,' although of course the actual plaque is all in capital letters which makes it seem as though it's shouting, and you wouldn't want that on this quiet morning.

In a county that's shaped by wealthy men with big ideas of how to make more money, John Clark (because of the lack of punctuation on the inscription, I'll always think of his full name as John Clark Parks Superintendent) was a man of vision who was determined to make his end of Yorkshire more beautiful and more accessible to people who wanted to come there to breathe. Peasholm Park, at the top end of the town, is one of his crowning achievements. As a child I remember going there to watch the miniature sea battles that were enacted each evening, and we filmed The Dog and I walking and pretending to talk by the lake for what the director called Beautiful Rembrandts that I could do voiceovers over later.

Clark was a Scot who moved to Scarborough in 1921 to work as an assistant to the visionary Harry Smith, the town's chief surveyor and engineer, who created the idea of much of what we know as Scarborough today but who wouldn't have managed it without the practical help of John Clark.

The *Scarborough News* says that:

Smith had the strategical vision, but Clark the tactical know-how; one was the engineer of genius, the other the supreme horticulturalist. Their partnership made Scarborough's parks, gardens and new streets unrivalled ... They were determined to make the whole of Scarborough a floral, tree-covered paradise by the sea.

I think that deserves a memorial bench. They should have called him Capability Smith.

I wander down towards the sea through the South Cliff Gardens that a friends' organisation is working very hard to restore; these gardens were part of the municipal reinvention of the town as the spa trade fell into decline and the tourist trade picked up. The restoration of lost and neglected gardens is a delicate thing; they aren't like buildings that can be remade and repainted. They rely on rain and sun and nurturing. A man runs up the stairs past me, panting like a dog. I'm going down, he's going up. Good job I don't see symbols everywhere or I'd see one there. History shifts like a pile of leaves blown about in a breeze. I need a café to help me gather my thoughts about this complex county.

And I find one. Bay View, with its view of the bay. I feel a glow, not just from the brisk walk and the interesting breeze.

I feel that somehow I'm starting to understand something about how this place, this county, can survive and thrive in the twenty-first century. I was worried when I first started writing this book that I'd end up pacing more and more slowly through the sticky mud of the past, eventually being unable to move, my cries for help becoming feebler, dwindling to nothing. Now, here on the east coast, I feel that Yorkshire really is embracing the new century, taking the lessons from the past and applying them to the present.

I glance at the menu, ask for an espresso and get a reaction I've not had for a while.

'Are you sure?' the man behind the counter asks.

I nod. I'm discovering that my face is so cold it's hard to frame words or, once framed, utter them.

'Do you want a glass of water with it?' he asks.

I've noticed that these days you're often offered a glass of water with an espresso as though this makes it more bohemian and/or more palatable.

I shake my head.

He must think I'm a Russian tourist who has no grasp of English and is relying on universal gestures to get through the day, like a man directing traffic.

'Sit down and I'll bring it over to you,' he says, slowly and clearly as though I'm a deaf Russian.

I surprise him (and, I must admit, myself) by speaking.

'Could I have some beans on toast, too, please?'

I must seem like a very strange espresso-sipping-beans-on-toast-eating Russian with a Barnsley accent.

I sit and gaze at a lighthouse. The beans on toast come on a rectangular plate which gives them a certain *je ne sais quoi.* I wish I'd bought a postcard so that I could write on it, 'I am eating beans on toast and drinking espresso. I can see a Yorkshire lighthouse. All is right with the world.' I'd post it but I wouldn't put an address on it, I'd just let the postman enjoy it when he came to empty the box.

A couple are sitting at the next table and the man brings them their lattes.

'I've tried something different,' he says. They look at their cups with what can only be described as Yorkshire Concern.

'You've drawn a heart on it,' the woman says. 'That's new.'

I'd add that to the message on my postcard if there was room. And if I'd bought a postcard.

I don't care if I miss my train home. I want to stay here. I want to join the Friends of South Cliff Gardens and do my bit. Mind you, I've had this feeling before, in Brompton. It's time to go.

I walk out of the café and back in the vague direction of the station. Then I see a sign that points me to the Old Town and I feel that I have to go. I love Old Towns and anywhere I go with an Old Town will find me mooching around in it. There's something about the light reflected from a cathedral wall across the outdoor table of a café that melts my heart. Also, I have vague and shimmery memories of ringing the bells in the church at the top of the hill on the bellringing weekend that led to me and Dave Sunderland's coffee failure all those years ago.

The key word here is 'hill'. It's a steep walk upwards past older houses, tight streets, model ships in windows. I realise that I'm employing a kind of industrial-strength version of the Yorkshire walk here, leaning as far forward as I can without falling over, pumping my thighs and breathing like a sea-creature dropped on land from a great height. I'm getting closer to the St Mary's Church and I'm being overtaken, as usual, by women. They're going in through the main door and I'd like to join them but I feel I can't. I turn a corner and have a memory as sharp as a cheese and onion crisp of walking up this same hill many decades ago to ring the bells, making their iron mouths sing all across the listening bay.

I spent a lot of time ringing bells as a younger man, all the way across Yorkshire. Subsidence from the coal mines had meant that the bells at Darfield were silenced from 1954 until the early 1970s when the National Coal Board agreed, reluctantly as it always did, that it was liable for the restoration of the tower and the bell fittings and a local teacher called Mike King gathered a gang of local teenagers, including me, around him to get the bells going again. It seemed like it might just be more fun than table tennis at the youth club.

King's great passion was the restoring of old bell towers that had fallen into disuse and there were a number of them all across the former coalfield. Many of them hadn't gone silent because of subsidence but simply because, in small farming villages left behind by the wash of history and often the clamour of war, there weren't enough people to ring them. The other reason for the silencing of the bells was that a lot of the smaller towers only had three bells in them, and that meant that only a certain number of changes could be rung on them. You could ring the first bell, then the second bell, then the third bell. Then the second bell, then the first bell, then the third bell. Then the third bell, then the second bell, then the first bell, and so on, although the '… and so on' doesn't go very far. Ringers like to ring changes on six bells and above, to give them something to get their teeth into and their hands around, to satisfy their need for complex and euphonious mathematical patterns before they all go to the pub to talk about bellringing.

Consequently, during many weekends and school holidays, I found myself carrying sacks of pigeon-droppings down rickety ladders in a kind of Duke of Edinburgh's Award Scheme of the mind. Pigeons would find their way into bell towers through holes in walls or gaps in wire netting and would squat there, literally and figuratively, for years. I had an unusual and privileged view of parts of Yorkshire from above, seen through bell-chamber windows or sometimes, if we were feeling particularly daring, from the tower roof itself as the birds flapped and grumbled and we flicked bits of their own decades-old detritus back at them. We'd visit bemused vicars and tell them we could get their bells ringing again, and if they didn't want us to do that, we could at least clear their towers out. We tried to sell the benefits to the community of ringing for Sunday services, for weddings and for funerals. Sometimes the vicars were robustly enthusiastic, sometimes they were querulously dubious. Some brought us cups of tea and fanned a few biscuits out on a plate and some left us to it.

At the end of the 1970s, when punk had lit bushfires under all kinds of assumptions and the Thatcherite revolution was just about to rip up all kinds of certainties, me and Dave Sunderland and Noel Marsden and Andrew Fawcett got to see a side of Yorkshire where the church was still a kind of mistily defined centre of rural affairs, where flower rotas went up as if by magic and someone would arrive on a bike to tend a much-loved grave. There was a whiff of the feudalism that still covered much of the county like a groundsheet, and a hint of older hierarchies in the box pews and the Christmas trees and baubles packed into cupboards at the bottom of the tower.

If you like an odd and eccentric way of mapping a place, then this is it. St Helen's, Marr (three bells), not far from Darfield near the A1, had a stumpy bell-tower that won the gold medal for chicken-poo, and as we shifted bag after bag of it the unchanging pitheap-and-farmyard Marrscape became visible through the bell-chamber window. Frightened pigeons circled, seeking permission to land in an improvisation of feathers and feet. One of the bells has the words 'Jesus be our speed' inscribed on it, and the excitement I felt as we brushed the words into the light was comparable to the feeling when the second draft of a poem begins to shape itself on the page.

St Michael and All Angels at Skelbrooke (three tiny bells) further up the A1 towards Ferrybridge had been silent for years because local rumour had it that the tower was unsafe and if the bells were rung it would crash to the ground. We tried to prove to them that because the bells were the size of blackbirds' eggs (I'm exaggerating, but only mildly, for comic effect) no structures were in danger, but they remained sceptical. As we spoke to the verger in the churchyard, the A1 hummed with purpose, making the village seem even more isolated than it actually was, more encrusted with history. And in one sense it was just another Yorkshire village with another hall, now a private house, hiding behind the trees.

Three bells at Hickleton, one of them the oldest in South Yorkshire, cast in 1490 probably at a foundry nearby.

Three ringable bells at Hooton Pagnell just down the road, where the church also has a carillon of nine bells that play tunes every three hours, even the idea of which seemed to fill Mike King with a mixture of disgust and rage because they weren't, in his words, 'proper bells rung by proper ringers'.

Wombwell was even odder: it had a number of bells but rather than being in a bell-chamber they were situated on the roof, exposed to wind, rain and late-night singing from the Little George at the other side of the car park. Nothing can rust a bell more than 'My Way' sung off-key, experts have noted.

Of course, at least once in my bellringing career, as I gripped the tail-end of the sally and rang a half-muffled quarter peal, I was responsible for pulling too hard and making the stay crash into the slider and break against the headstock thus resulting not only in a failure of esoteric and specialist language but an accident which, waiting to happen, happened. I'd be thrown around the ringing chamber like a bungee jumper in a farce as fellow-ringers ran forward to help then ran away without helping me; to an observer it would have looked like I was the centre of a flower being blown about by the wind and they were my petals coming out and going in. That sort of thing happens to all ringers at least once; suddenly the thing you were in control of is in control of you, which is how I feel about my expanding and atomising ideas about Yorkshire.

I carry on up the hill in Scarborough as fast as I can without running because I hope it'll make me feel fit and in control. My breath is arriving more quickly than I intended it to, as though it's falling downstairs. The women are piling into the church and I don't feel that I can go in; perhaps they're going to the funeral of a friend. Then, wonderfully, as though I've planned it and I haven't, I turn onto a street with the best Yorkshire name I've ever seen.

Paradise.

The street is called Paradise.

Not Paradise Road, mark you, or Paradise Avenue.

Paradise.

I suppose Paradise Close would be just round the back.

Later, I read that there's a blue plaque on Paradise House, at the end of the street, telling me that Sir George Cayley, 'The Father of Aeronautics', was born there, but I don't notice that. I stand and gaze at the one word on the wall: PARADISE. I'm in Yorkshire and I've found paradise. I glance down the hill at an enormous dog that barks scarily at passers-by. Of course Paradise would be guarded by a dog as big as a fitted wardrobe. This is Yorkshire, after all. There's no point giving it a biscuit. I say it aloud, which is a bit silly, a bit Not Yorkshire Enough: 'I've found Paradise.' The dog looks up, then looks away.

I stand by the sign and grin and mouth the word Paradise to myself once again. That's a slogan. That's a strapline. That's a motto.

CITY LIGHTS: LEEDS AND BRADFORD AND YORK AND TIME

'M ON LEEDS station standing aside to let a flood of commuters rush by me and I'm contemplating once again the idea of Yorkshire time; it seems to me that if I'm to make any headway in understanding this place I'd better have a go at getting to the bottom of this county's peculiar time zones.

People from Cornwall are often characterised as having a hazy notion of time and punctuality with their wonderfully evocative West Country version of *manana*, 'directly' often shortened to 'd'rectly' because it takes less time to say to give you more time for chewing pasties, and there's a Yorkshire version of that locution: 'in a bit'. This is just one of several layers of Yorkshire time which can be filtered down to two opposing camps, one of which is 'in a bit' with the other one being 'gerron wi it'. One implies a casual relationship with the clock, a relationship that is sometimes intimate but mostly respectfully distant, and the other speaks volumes about running to the bus stop in the hope that the previous bus might be a few minutes late so that you can catch it before the later bus rolls up on time.

Between the two is a set of time frames that would baffle Dr Who. These include 'when I say so', which implies to the waiting child that the seconds and minutes will pass as slowly as treacle down the side of a tin, and 'frame!', an old mining word, always uttered with a sense of urgent despair, sometimes lengthened into, 'Will tha frame?', which means, 'Do it now or before now if that is possible.'

The ancient industrial South Yorkshire day could be divided into zones like segments of an orange that were at once flexible and immovable: Pit Time led to Breakfast Time which led to Ah'll Gerrof Then which led to Graftin' which led to Snap Time which led to Graftin Ageean which led to Ooam Time which led to Darn't Allotment which segued into Bed Time, and there were pre-industrial variations on this which relied on different jobs (planting, harvesting) but which still danced to the same rhythms of the day.

There are three Yorkshire cities that seem to live in different time zones, and that's why I'm standing here like a rock in a river of Loiner urgency before I go to visit all three. Leeds seems to inhabit a space that is simultaneously today and tomorrow; Bradford exists in moments that are cut off from linear time and hang in the air like dust-motes in a sunlit space; York is today and yesterday and the day before yesterday and the day before that, lurching backwards to infinity or at least to a place where everybody smelled the same as each other and the animals they slept beside.

Each of these cities would say they were the best in Yorkshire and perhaps in their own way each of them is;

imagine them as boxers about to take to the ring in a three-sided boxing match, gumshields in place, gloves up. Waiting for the bell; waiting for Time to shift.

If you lived ten Leeds years, they'd be different to ten York years and a Bradford decade; I think the Leeds years would go more quickly, the York years more slowly, and the Bradford years might not be years at all but may well just float to the surface of the calendar as bundles of hours.

I'm marvelling at how stylish this Leeds crowd seems to be; these suits are so sharp you could slice parsnips with them. These haircuts are so stylish they come from the week after next. Most of the women are power dressed and the ones who aren't are wearing those disconcerting jeans with the holes in the knees, as though there's been a mass fallover on the streets of the small towns that feed the great hungry commercial machine that is Leeds. I step even further back, and back, trying not to be carried along by the mob and dumped in an office and told to make a cup of spreadsheets and fax some estimates or whatever it is that people in offices do.

As I step further back into a little nook near platform 1, my memory conjures up the sound of bagpipes. I look around but of course there are none; they're just playing a strathspey in my mind's ear.

A few years ago, around the time I was poet in residence at Humberside Police, I was also Poet In Residence on Northern Spirit trains, the precursor to the unloved Northern Trains that we rattle about in now like dried peas in a tin that smells of Doritos and Zero Hours Jobs.

It was the perfect job for me, rattling around the north and writing poems: it was what I did anyway, but I didn't tell them that.

Someone from the press office rang up and said that they were starting a new service from Leeds to Edinburgh and could I write a poem to mark the occasion? I said that I would and that I'd try and think of lots of rhyming words for Leeds and Edinburgh, thus presenting myself with a hostage to fortune the size of a bison. Leeds is easy enough but the rhyming possibilities of Edinburgh are limited. There hasn't been a station in Jedburgh or Sedbergh for years.

The plan was that I would recite the poem and then a piper would play a tune and then some VIPs would get on the train, go as far as Shipley then come back and have a good lunch featuring the best of Yorkshire and Scottish cuisine, presumably a haggis in a Yorkshire Pudding.

I got to the station early, holding my poem like it was important.

I was met by the PR person who told me where I was to stand.

'Is the microphone coming later?' I asked innocently, straining my voice above the busy station din and already knowing what the answer would be.

'Oh, we didn't think you'd need a microphone,' the PR person said. 'You've got a good big voice.'

That's true but it's not as big as the 10.45 225 electric train to King's Cross calling at Wakefield Westgate, Doncaster, Retford, Newark, Grantham, Peterborough and Stevenage.

The piper turned up; he was a huge man in a kilt that flapped and flared in the wind, threatening a McMarilyn Monroe moment. He tuned the pipes, a phrase which some people would regard as an oxymoron but not me. I find them beautiful and evocative, but they're also loud. Very loud, and not to everyone's taste, I admit.

The train was due. The VIPs arrived and white roses were pinned to lapels with a brittle combination of haste and care. The piper and I stood like spare makeweight suspects in an identity parade at a suburban police station.

With a sense of rueful inevitability, a sharp PR person conveyed the news that the train was late. Watches were consulted and muttered muted conversations were had behind clipboards.

'You'll have to read your poem as the piper plays,' someone said.

'Good job we didn't get a microphone,' I replied, and the irony fell silently from my lips and rolled down a grate.

The train was on its way into the platform; at a signal from a man wearing huge glasses, the piper began to play and I started to recite my poem.

I was like a fish, opening and closing my mouth in a bowl. I was like a ventriloquist's dummy being made to create the sound of bagpipes at an open-air talent contest. I stopped reading the poem and I may as well not have started.

The VIPs piled onto the train and the piper and I shook hands. His pipes moaned orgasmically as he folded them up and put them into a bag.

'Cup of tea?' I asked, but he couldn't; he had to get to a wedding.

'I'm on with a chimney sweep,' he said and wandered away majestically.

I often think of that little story when I think about Leeds, and today it strikes me that it tells us quite a lot about the city and its attitude to time, in miniature. Put a poet and bagpipe player on at the same time on a noisy platform? Things will work out for the best. Train is late? Things will work out for the best. The two things are happening at once? Well, that's fine because it saves us time and that's the best thing to do with time: bang two pieces of it together to see if they stick. Leeds's version of Yorkshire time has been built in recent years on the initially novel concept of the 24-hour city, born from a conference hosted by the council in 1993, and which felt like a natural progression for a place that liked to position itself as a major European hub. Leeds has always felt economically confident with a manufacturing and industrial base initially built, like much of the region in the eighteenth century, on textiles and coal. The city saw a huge growth in population in the nineteenth century as the old industries competed with newer ones like brewing, printing and the making of off-the-peg clothing. Marks & Spencer began as a stall on Kirkgate market and until 2011 Joshua Tetley's Brewery made millions of gallons of a beer that drinkers would tell you, 'didn't travel well, like bananas'.

The idea of the city as a Barcelona of the north didn't really catch on, mainly because of the weather, but it still makes great strides towards being a city that never sleeps because, after all, sleeping is a waste of time. No sleep till Garforth, at least. East Garforth, preferably.

Like Sheffield, the city is awash with students and this helps with the image of somewhere that's always on the go; at the station, I seem to see more young people than I've seen in other parts of Yorkshire and that bloke reading his *Yorkshire Post* in the house by the side of the Shawl in Leyburn would look and feel out of place here.

I wait until the crowds have gone and I step out of the station and begin to walk into the city and as I walk I can feel time going more quickly, clipping minutes off the hour like slices from a loaf. I feel like a rube from the sticks venturing to New York for the first time in a John Cheever story as people push by me to get to whatever important money-spinning deal they've got lined up.

There was a PR-spun furore in 1996 when the upmarket store Harvey Nichols opened a branch in Leeds and at the time it really did feel like the 24-hour city would become a reality. I popped in there once and saw the footballer Trevor Sinclair carrying an armful of clothes to the checkout like he was carrying someone from a smoke-filled building; he didn't know who I was but he winked at me as though we were fellow conspirators in on some elegant game to change the perception of what Yorkshire could be. On the day of the store's opening BBC TV's *Look North* got the poet Simon Armitage to comment on it, which he did with characteristic wryness, but the idea that the store was some kind of art installation stuck in the gallery of the city stuck.

I walk by Harvey Nichols and turn to go up towards the town hall, a gorgeous shining white landmark designed and built in the 1850s by Hull-born Cuthbert Broderick; like Sheffield City Hall and Huddersfield station, it's a symbol of civic confidence and pride, a concrete (or limestone) way of saying to the other cities, particularly those in the south, that we're every bit as good as they were.

I'm going to the town hall to relive one of my great time-based humiliations; I was booked on the Monday of the first week of January a few years ago to give a talk to 2000 GCSE students who were studying poetry. It was part of a regular series that went on all over the country; a number of writers would deliver talks that consisted of half an hour of wit and erudition and then another writer would get up and do the same; the advantage for the young people was that if they didn't like you it didn't matter because there'd be another bard or scribe along in a minute, and the advantage for the writer was that after half an hour you could stop.

Some writers felt nervous at the idea of rattling to vast crowds but I've always enjoyed it. It's when I'm on stage talking that I feel most alive and, interestingly, most Yorkshire, even though Yorkshiremen are meant to be dour and tight-lipped. It was my first booking after a very quiet Christmas and I was looking forward to that peculiar time-stretch that happens to me when I have to speak in front of a big crowd. It may be half an hour in reality but once I stand up the half hour goes in the blinking of an eye even though the minutes before I shuffle onto the stage edge by like tortoises.

On the day of the gig I noticed how oddly quiet it was on the walk up to the town hall; I put this down to the universities still being on their Christmas break. Normally, when you did one of these events you passed loads of school children, some in uniform and some not, some in a crocodile and some freeform, some teachers harassed and clipboarded and some casual and texting. The streets were movie-set quiet.

I got to the town hall and it began to dawn on me that time or the calendar or my diary were playing tricks. Nobody was playing chess on the giant chessboard in front of the town hall and a man was strolling across the squares like a bishop. The main doors to the town hall were locked. I rattled them feebly, hoping that they would open to reveal my attentive and eager audience. Nothing happened. Leeds time was swallowing the morning without chewing it.

I went round the side and by now it was obvious to me that I had turned up on the wrong day, that my Darfield time didn't coincide with Leeds time. I'd got Barnsley-lag.

A man was sitting behind a desk staring into space.

'Is there a conference on? A conference of young people?' I asked.

He peered at me with Christmas still in his eyes.

'Not here,' he said, gesturing round. 'Are you sure it's the town hall you want?'

I was; I fished out my letter of confirmation and showed it to him.

'I think it got cancelled ages ago,' he said, and I felt myself plunging into a vortex of time where 'ages ago' was so far away that it didn't register on the still surface of now.

I went outside and almost ran across the chessboard back to the station.

Now, years later, I stand in front of the town hall and listen to a man almost shouting into his phone.

'I need to alter the face-to-face,' he says in awkward poetry. 'The face-to-face has to move. See if you can get him in a situation where he has to tie himself down to later in the week.'

Ah, tying yourself down to later in the week. That's Leeds for you. I wander back to the station to take a train to Bradford, Leeds's great rival in the 'best city in Yorkshire' stakes. Some people who aren't from Yorkshire have, in the past, said ridiculous things like, 'Well, they're all part of the same conurbation, aren't they?' and from the architect Will Alsop in the early years of this century to the current idea of a Northern Powerhouse, there's been talk (or rather wind and breeze) of a mega city stretching all across the M62 of which Leeds and Bradford would merely be component parts. You may as well argue that Lewis is part of Harris or that Laurel is part of Hardy.

Bradford was once one of the richest cities in Europe, creating impressive cityscapes funded by wool, an incongruously soft and gentle substance on which to metaphorically build huge chimneys like that of Lister's Mill, round the top of which it was rumoured you could drive a coach and six horses, and the town hall, which could be in Genoa or Milan. I never wanted this book to be about decline, but Bradford mirrors places like Hull and Sheffield and Barnsley in that it's been falling away for years in terms of wealth and influence but it was one of the first places in the country, perhaps after Telford, to realise that industrial architecture could be worth a day trip, or a weekend, or maybe a week-long guided visit. Bradford bridges that gap I've come across again and again in the writing of this book, the chasm between the Yorkshire that tourists love to browse through, and the Yorkshire that the rest of us live in.

'Bradford: A Surprising Place', was a promotion campaign from the 1990s that put places like Lister's Mill chimney and Sir Titus Salt's village at Saltaire on huge posters in the hope that people would stop there on the way to somewhere considered beautiful. At the same time that Leeds was promoting its 24-hourness, Bradford was taking snapshots of the past and wanting you to come and look at them and spend your money in the gift shop, and it worked, to a certain extent. Saltaire is a UNESCO World Heritage site and the locks on the canal at Bingley are a wonder to behold, their combination of water, light and engineering never failing to make me gasp. Bradford time, though, doesn't run like Leeds time does. It wanders; it takes, if this isn't too tautological, its time. It's a canal rather than a fast-flowing river.

Bradford's fall from prosperity was steeper than that of Leeds; in 2012 the wonderfully named local paper the Bradford *Telegraph & Argus* published a piece about a report that showed that Bradford had faced the second biggest decline of any city in the country in the previous century, using measures including skills levels, population, employment and wages. For a city built on hard graft this is hard to take: like Leeds, it grew rapidly, its population exploding from just 5000 in 1801 to more than 100,000 50 years later. And over the years a lot of the people who worked in the mills and factories had come from all over the world; there's a part of the city called Little Germany named after the incomers from that country, and from the 1960s onwards workers from India, Pakistan and Bangladesh added to the layers of cultural complexity that are a major part of what Bradford is and what it may become.

I catch the train to Bradford Forster Square, rebuilt in 1890 to include the fantastic Midland Hotel where the great actor Sir Henry Irving died in 1905. It's fitting that a person from an age when acting often involved shouting and gesturing should die in a county that loves shouting and enjoys gesturing more than most. Maybe my thinking about Yorkshire time and its variations comes from the fact that I live a time-based life: because I can't drive I'm always on the train and if you go for the 08.56 at 08.58 that's no good whereas if you were in a car those two minutes might not make a great deal of difference.

The railways sealed the idea of universal time in the nineteenth century because before there was a set time, people would go out at their own version of 08.56 to find that the train had left at what it understood to be 08.56. What I'm finding is that these hyper-local time zones still hang on in Yorkshire, clock-fossils telling the people of Leeds to hurry along there and the people of Bradford to just stop for a moment and gaze at this building that filters light through history.

Leaving the station behind, I begin to stroll up to Manningham Lane because it feels to me that I'll find some version of the essence of Bradford Time here. Manningham bristles and jostles with business: Asian and Eastern European shops clamour for your trade. I stand outside a Polish hairdresser's and stare for a little too long at the women who are getting their perms done. I step past a man who is glugging from a can and singing something that reminds him of home, wherever that is. A car passes, playing loud rap music and the driver sees me and gives me a complicated hand gesture that could mean absolutely anything, anything at all, and because of the frame of mind I'm in I think that his hand is like the hands of a clock. Yorkshire has always been an inviting place and Bradford has wonderfully opened its doors to the world more often than many places.

I'm trying to find the place where, with the drummer Satnam Singh, I came across a bouncy Taj Mahal outside a shop. I'm trying to find the café where, with my brother-in-law Terry and his mate Omar, I had the best curry I've ever had: a curried partridge sitting with its legs splayed on a big white plate, for all the world as if it was sunbathing. Omar kept pointing out older men in amazing headscarves and trousers and saying, 'Look at that beauty. Will you just look at that beauty.'

I walk past the back of Valley Parade, home of Bradford City Football Club and where I once sat next to a man at a Barnsley V Bradford match who turned to me and said, 'Versus is right: I can't stand any women, except my mother.' I'm still trying to come to terms with that one.

Barnsley's first game of the 2006 season was against Bradford City and my son and I went on the supporters' coach in the August sun to watch what would undoubtedly be a wonderful game and the gateway to a season to remember. In the end, the season wasn't too bad but we lost that game 4-0 and my son and I left the game early. As we walked round the back of the huge stand, the sun threw whole streets into shadow. A lad ran by clutching a samosa. 'Four-nil!' he shouted cheerfully. I hope the samosa was too hot and I hope it burned his fingers.

In July 2001 a combination of industrial decline, gatherings of particular ethnic groups in particular parts of the city, far-right activism and a swirling pool of rumour led to riots between white and Asian youths; tensions exploded and buildings burned. Since then much has been done to restore and rebuild and in some cases create racial harmony in the city and, although austerity is kicking Bradford hard, it still comes back for more. All my thinking about Bradford is crystallising into mental Polaroids that could be stills from a film: The Moment at Valley Parade, The Bouncy Taj Mahal, The Spreadeagled Partridge. They could be pub names.

I'm looking for my moment, my defining Bradford time-based moment. Across Manningham Lane, some lads are having what to many people might sound like a row but to the initiated is just a heated discussion.

I nip, as I always do when I'm looking for something to bring the day into focus, into a coffee shop. A young Eastern European girl is taking a coffee and an enormous slice of cake to another young woman at the far end of the café, in the half-darkness. She's wearing the most beautiful headscarf I've ever seen: it's pink and piled high like candy floss or a waterfall caught in a frozen second. She's staring into the air and her stillness is astonishing. I stand and take it in, this version of Yorkshire that's as delicate as porcelain and as strong as steel. I'm trying not to stare. Time has stopped. Yorkshire time: T'ime. The two women are laughing and in my foolish and innocent world I think they might be laughing at the joy of being alive, but they're probably just laughing at me. I don't mind; this is Yorkshire, this is a representation of time and I feel I'm getting somewhere. I feel that I'm getting somewhere slowly and imperceptibly, like a glacier does.

I wander back to the station and take a train to York, the third of the triumvirate of cities I'm trying to clock. I've marvelled for years at the way York has reinvented itself within living memory. When I was a child, York was a northern city with walls and a Minster but in many ways it was just a northern city, speaking with a Yorkshire accent that was distinct and different to many other variations of the template in that it called itself Yark. At Low Valley School we talked about the fact that the Romans had lived here and I got a star for knowing that it used to be called Eboracum in those days, a fact that I'd got from a quiz in the *Sunday Post*. Now, over the decades, it has become a major stopping point on the global tourist trail, a sit down on the three-piece suite with matching footstool that also includes London and Stratford upon Avon and Edinburgh.

York is, in many ways, the perfect tourist destination because most of its attractions can be wandered around in a manageable amount of time, whether on your own or in an organised group following somebody who is carrying a raised umbrella through the sunshine. VisitYork, the agency that oversees the 'Big Attractions Group', noted that in 2013 the top five attractions had started to recover visitor numbers after the crash of 2008, and each of these burgeoning attractions offer you a view of York time, it seems to me.

There's the National Railway Museum with its platforms-full of engines and carriages and memorabilia, all of them based to a greater or lesser extent on that sliver of Time when the whistle blows and the train begins to move.

There's the Castle Museum which presents you with the Yorkshire past, or a version of it, in a series of images and pieces held tightly by time so that they can't wriggle forwards or backwards.

There's the Jorvik Centre, a triumph of presentation that was one of the first interactive museums in the country to give you the idea that the Vikings and the other ancient inhabitants of York, were they still around, would look like this and sound like this and smell like this and, crucially, that they were probably quite a lot like us and this is Time as a blanket or a net, catching everybody and keeping them warm.

York Boat takes you up and down the River Ouse and this is perhaps the most subtle representation of York-based Yorkshire time; the river is never the same, the breeze is never the same, the crowds crossing the bridge and waving at you are never the same but the sensation of moving along this water is timeless and connects you straightaway to the past because you are feeling like those nameless people would have felt all those hundreds and thousands of years ago. They wouldn't have had a watch, of course: they would simply know that it was time to move over the water and that time was moving as they moved over the water.

I'm on my way to the greatest and most sublime of all York's attractions, the Minster, walking across the Lendal Bridge towards an articulation of light, space and sound that dominates the skyline and which is an emblem of this city's (which we mustn't forget is the county town) relationship with Time.

There's something I must do first, though; Time has caught up with me and all this wandering means that I haven't had time for a haircut for ages and while I'm here I think I'll go in somewhere for a trim. It feels like a bit of a betrayal of Mad Geoff, especially as I've heard he's not been well, but needs must: I'm feeling and looking a bit wiggy. I want to appear my best in the Minster's sacred and musical atmosphere.

I go into a place called Jax on the corner of Gillygate that I've been in once before, years ago. As I go in, the barber is just going out.

'Have you come for a haircut?' he says, and I bite back a witty and cutting reply and say that I have.

'Sit down,' he says. 'I was just popping out for a minute but it'll wait.'

I sit in the plush chair and remind him that I've been in before; he doesn't remember. I tell him that last time we talked about when he had a branch in Doncaster and local hairdressers kept undercutting him until they were only charging 50p for a haircut and he couldn't compete with that.

'That's cheaper than Shaky Pete!' I say but he doesn't respond. I'd forgotten that not all Yorkshire barbers know each other, that they don't all live on the same street and go on outings together on a bus driven by a bald woman.

He starts to snip and, obliquely, the conversation turns to the passage of time, as I knew it would on this day that I've found myself obsessed with it. He tugs at my quiff.

'You've got a good head of hair,' he says, and I tell him I'm 59 years old. 'You'll have that hair for evermore,' he says, as he cuts bits of it off. 'You'll have that hair when you're 75.'

Suddenly I have a vision of myself as a very old man: my hair is even whiter than it is now, it's the colour of a snowman. Everything else about me is diminished and feeble, but my hair is still the hair of a younger man, like Ronald Reagan's used to be, except mine is real. I see myself tottering around like those images of older people on the road sign and I see myself still trying to finish this book, or one like it, still trying to put the pieces of Yorkshire together or take them apart to see what makes them tick, with my hair flowing majestically in the wind.

'Do you reckon having all this hair will make me look younger when I'm older?' I ask.

It's an intimate question but barbers are used to intimate questions. Barbers and opticians touch you in places that only lovers normally touch you. Especially in Yorkshire.

He gives a noncommittal reply.

'I reckon it's all to do with the neck,' I say, warming to the subject. 'If the neck goes scrawny or floppy then people will know that I'm old, but if I can keep my neck youthful then I've got a chance to cheat the calendar.'

He smiles as though he's heard all this before from blokes my age: the babbling that comes from the knowledge that Time is sharpening his razor. All this thinking about the distant and recent past is giving me an insight into the flow of time: am I Leeds-tomorrow, Bradford-moment or York-past? I'm not sure.

He's finished. He shows me the back of my neck in a rectangular mirror and my eyes prickle with tears: the back of my neck is the back of my dad's neck. That square line of hair. That odd empty field of skin poking out from the sensible jumper. I am my dad, I am stuck with being him, stuck in his time, stuck with his Scottish grammars and syntaxes deep in my Yorkshire soul, my Not Yorkshire Enough soul.

I pay up and leave; time to go to the Minster. The trim is more than twice as much as it would have been in Geoff's but I don't mind; this is York, not Darfield, there's more money swirling around and anyway, I've learned a valuable truth, or I'm inching towards learning a valuable truth: Yorkshire time may not really be any different to any other time. We grow up, we age, we grow old and decay. And the backs of our necks look like the backs of our parents' necks, and further back to our ancestors' necks. We are them and they are us. Time will beat us.

I leave an overgenerous tip but it's my way of being grateful for the lesson; I just hope I can articulate it. Death and rebirth, something like that: Yorkshire as a circle. Will t'circle be unbrokken?

It's getting dark as I walk towards the Minster. It's almost time for Evensong, that aching moment in the day when afternoon turns to gloaming to the accompaniment of heavenly singing. An Australian woman confronts me.

'I can't find the door,' she says, urgently.

I point to a door as big as a cruise liner.

'I've tried that,' she says, shaking her head. Does she think I'm young or old? I wonder, but I don't say anything.

We see other people going into a side door and we follow them. As we enter, two rows of people in surplices and robes cross the floor: the choir. I stand and gaze around me, marvelling at the mixture of reality and fantasy that the space is made of. The Australian woman and the others follow them, but I sit alone in the middle of Yorkshire time.

The Minster is the largest gothic cathedral in Europe and there have been structures for worship on the site since the seventh century AD; parts of the current building date back to the thirteenth century and, astonishingly, took over three centuries to complete; throughout the decades after that the fortunes of the Minster waxed and waned like a stone moon but from the 1960s to the present day, interrupted by a fire caused by lightning in the year of the Miners' Strike, there have been concerted efforts at restoration and now the building feels, if not complete, then alive.

The voices of the choir rise with unbearable passion. I bow my newly shorn head, not in worship of any god but in awe of time. Each of the three cities I've visited would claim to be the best in Yorkshire but all of them are caught in different interpretations of the passing of the years. The future, the recent past, the present, the future. Are those tears on my cheek? They are.

I'll just sit here for a section of Yorkshire time and think about the back of my dad's neck.

BAHT 'AT

'VE BEEN A little obsessed, if you can be a little obsessed, with the dirge-like and glacier-slow Yorkshire National Anthem, 'Ilkley Moor Baht 'At', for years; as a young man, I wrote a poetic variation on it called 'Hatless on the Moor', trying to turn it into something post-modern, which maybe it was all along. It feels like an eternally resonant folk-tale about love and regeneration and it contains a simple Yorkshire truth, one of the Yorkshire truths that I've been trying for ages to unpick from the county's vast cardigan: if you don't wear a hat you will die. Stark but logical. Shocking but true.

And I've long harboured a plan to turn it into an opera or a play or a free-form jazz wigout. It feels like the kind of narrative that can take any kind of interpretation because of its deep and profound simplicity. In AGM bullet points it retains its shimmering straightforwardness.

A man goes on the moor to court Mary Jane but he forgets to take his hat. The rest of the verses pose an alternative and terrible future for him. He catches cold and dies. He is eaten by worms. The worms are eaten by ducks. The ducks are eaten by the dead man's friends. The dead man's friends (including, I like to think, although this is

326

never made clear, Mary Jane, who, in an unwritten verse, turns to one of the company and says, in a voice almost breaking with emotion, 'There's something terribly familiar about the taste of this meat') have therefore eaten the dead man. They have 'etten thee'. It's nutrition, in a circular way, from the soil. I'm surprised it's not been adopted as a theme song by the Provisional Cannibal Wing of the Green Party.

It's a cold, clear, late Friday morning and I get off the train at Ilkley in the company of about a dozen youngish men who are dressed in versions of what some people who wear suits all day at work consider to be casual clothing. They're the opposite of the people I encountered on Leeds station. They are wearing jeans or, to be more precise, they are 'wearing' 'jeans'. They all have the same hairstyle with a severe-to-angry side-parting which matches the creases on their legwear and they are evidence that at least the local gel factories are still operating at full tilt and taking on extra staff. There is one youngish woman in the group who can be identified by her different haircut and the youngish men swarm around her trying to attract her with schoolboy banter and laughter. She looks wary but that may just be her high heels and the uneven road surface. They swarm into town, moving like wine flung down a restaurant wall and I follow, trying to work out who they are and where they're going at this time in the morning. If it was later in the day I'd say they might be a stag party with somebody's sister tagging along but this feels a bit early, even for stags. There's a rugby match on the TV later, but not for hours.

Maybe they're going to the match; maybe they're going to get on a coach, a coach identified as a luxury coach because it's got a toilet you climb down steps into, and go all the way to Cardiff to sing off-key in the faces of people dressed as daffodils. It figures, I guess, because Ilkley is more of a Union town than a League town. They turn a corner and I turn another corner. Like Union and League did, in fact, in that hotel in Huddersfield in 1895, 15 men down one corridor, 13 men down another, side partings shining in hissing gaslight.

I've got a thought-out plan and I'm on a final mission. I want to do something symbolic to mark the climax of this quest of mine to try and define Yorkshire. I have to admit I've not really got very far despite all the strolling and tramping and trudging and note-taking and sitting in cafés: I thought that by the time I'd got to this stage, an image of Yorkshire would have solidified in my head like a city comes into focus when the glitter in a snow globe settles. All I know is that Yorkshire is a mosaic and collage and a kaleidoscope and maybe I could have guessed at that before. I wouldn't have had so much fun, though. Or drunk so many espressos. Or got so wet and cold. Or ended up down so many blind alleys.

So I'm going to walk up to the moor and I'm going to take my hat off. I will be, literally and symbolically, baht 'at. I'm not only going to take my hat off, I'm going to tear it from my head and fling it away, woolly litter spinning through the cold, cold air. I'm going to leave the hat for somebody to find and maybe, just maybe, they'll think it might be the hat of the man from the song that's been coughed up by the earth after a tiny shuddering tremor. Maybe I've had too many espressos these last few months: I do feel a bit shaky, a bit ill-defined.

I turn up through the town and begin the ascent towards the moor, feeling the pull of it in my middle-aged legs. I've been coming to Ilkley for years and it was one of the many influences that defined and shaped me as a young poet; I read at open mic sessions at the Literature Festival in the 1970s and eventually got booked to read my poems on bigger stages in front of some people I didn't even know, which still comes as a shock. I saw the Liverpool Poets here, and the great poet of Yorkshire landscape, Pete Morgan, who once stopped me as I was walking back towards the station and said, 'How's town?' which for years became a catchphrase of mine that only I understood the importance of.

During the Liverpool Poets gig, as Brian Patten was making his steady musical way through a love poem, a church bell rang the hour and *Brian incorporated it, making a reference to the bell in his poem.* I italicized that because at the time I thought it was just the most poetic thing I'd ever seen and heard, and in many ways I still do: I've waited 40 years to do the same but by some odd temporal non-coincidence, a bell has never rung as I read a poem out to a small but keen crowd. There's still time. How's town?

I bought one of my first poetry magazines at the Ilkley Literature Festival in 1973; the magazine was called *The Urbane Gorilla* and the man selling it was a gentle but scary-looking giant called Tom Owen. He stood there shouting, 'Who wants to be urbane?' in a way that I found devastatingly anarchic and frightening and thrilling, especially in a genteel place like Ilkley.

There was a stack of copies beside him on a table and I leafed through them and one fell to the ground with a slapping sound. He looked at me coldly.

'If you don't want to buy one, don't handle the fucking merchandise,' he said. This was even more devastatingly anarchic and frightening and not quite so thrilling. I bought four, counting out change from my man-purse, which in those days would have been a boy-purse.

And now here I am again, making my way up the hill towards the moor, my hat pulled low over my face in an attempt to thwart the wind's permanent reshaping of my facial features. Years after the *Urbane* encounter, I was booked to give a reading of my work at the Craiglands Hotel as part of the Literature Festival; I got off the train and was briefly unsure as to where this iconic establishment, which had been a key part of Ilkley's development as a spa town, actually was. Luckily TV's Alan Titchmarsh, the Ilkley-born writer and gardener, was walking by with a sense of loam-based purpose.

I have to admit that for years I thought he was called Alan 'Titch' Marsh like Dave 'Boy' Green, and that he was really Little Alan Marsh so I smiled as I asked him where the Craiglands Hotel was. He pointed vaguely up a hill and said a sentence that included words like 'left' and 'right' and walked away. I set off in what I thought was the right direction but which turned out to be the left direction.

All these decades later, I'm sure that Little Alan wasn't deliberately sending me the wrong way but I found it interesting that, wandering back streets in an attempt to find the hotel, I passed the iconic Yorkshire prose king, David Nobbs, walking the other way. We nodded to each other and to this day I wish I'd asked him if Alan had given him vague directions too. I like to think he had.

This morning, the further up the hill I get, the more I can see of Yorkshire laid out like a dropped invitation to a marvellous event. Ilkley, like Askern and yet so much not like Askern, was a spa town in the nineteenth century where people would come on the new trains to renew themselves in its healing waters. Visitors included Madame Tussaud and Charles Darwin and an image of a railway carriage with those two in would make a wonderful caption competition.

The enormous Ben Rhydding Hydropathic Establishment was a palace of healing on the edge of the town, founded by former Mayor of Leeds, Hamer Stansfield, in 1844; under Hamer's roof, cleanliness was very much next to godliness and guests read the Bible every morning after breakfast, often whilst sitting in the room into which moorland air was pumped and which was known as a 'fresh air bath'. Presumably too-vigorous pumping would result in pages from *The Book of Habakkuk* fluttering like holy moths. The Turkish baths at the Hydropathic Establishment were a wonder of the Victorian age and in their own way a bricks and mortar representation of 'Ilkley Moor Baht 'At'.

First you went into the Frigidarium, or Cooling Room, to prepare your body and your mind for the temperature-based experiences that were to follow. The Frigidarium is like the opening of the song: the hat is not worn and the protagonist begins to shiver. The bather then made their way to the Tepidarium, which was maintained at a constant temperature that was enough to make you sweat but not enough to make you shout out in agony and run weeping from the room. The Tepidarium was like the singer dying on the moor; an event of great significance but not in any way foreshadowing the horrors to come, which in the case of the song is human-on-human ingestion and in the case of the Ben Rhydding Hydropathic Establishment was the Caldarium, the hottest room, which maintained a constant temperature of over 150 degrees.

I thought about the Caldarium as I made my way up the hill; I was in a fresh-air bath of my own and it felt like iced fingers of wind were being pumped into my vicinity from the outskirts of Novosibirsk. I fancied just a few minutes in it, just to get the feeling back into my knees. As the nineteenth century ground or bounced along, depending at which end of the social scale you sat, the popularity of healing waters declined, but luckily Ilkley had enough Yorkshire nous to partially reinvent itself as a fashionable inland resort for those with enough ready money to get somebody to iron their newspapers. I suspect that the people taking afternoon tea in the hotels were secretly pleased that they didn't have to sit swathed in warm wet blankets from head to toe in the name of health.

The only remaining hydropathic spa is the white-walled White Wells, a cottage that stands out above the moor's wind-brushed green. It was the first of the town's spas and Charles Darwin visited it; I like to think of him

suddenly coming up with the whole of his theory of evolution as a result of a volume of freezing water being
sloshed down the back of his neck; I picture him standing
up in delicious agony and making his way across the
room in a halting representation of that illustration that
shows primitive man emerging from the shuffling gait of
the long-armed ape.

I walk towards White Wells behind a couple from the
Midlands who are discussing emojis. The man is baht 'at
and his bald head shines in the sun; he's playing that faux-
naif game of pretending he doesn't know what an emoticon
is, pretending that his mind is wired for higher things like
BBC4 and avocados. The woman is enjoying explaining
them to him, putting him in his place. It would be too easy
to say that the back of his head looks like an emoji that
denotes confusion, so I won't.

'So you're telling me they're those little smiley-face
things that people put in emails?' he says, like a badly
written character in a radio play.

'That's right,' she says, brightly, 'and not just emails.
Tweets as well.' The wind is getting stronger. My hat wants
to fly, I can tell.

'Oh, I don't do Twitter,' he says, the words 'because I'd
rather be watching BBC4' unsaid but obvious.

They're examples of the tourists I've encountered and
attempted to pin down as I've written this book; they come
to parts of Yorkshire for a reason and perhaps that reason
is that those parts aren't much like the place they live, and
they avoid parts of Yorkshire because they're too much
like the places they live.

I accelerate past them, partly through irritation and partly because I'm desperate for a wee. There's a free toilet advertised, which of course attracts me as a Yorkshireman who's been known to vault over those toilets in stations that try to charge you 30p for unzipping rights.

As I pass them, he is saying, 'They're mainly for children, though, aren't they?' I go into the whitewashed toilet and there, in a little dish by the sink, is a beautiful arrangement of old soaps of different colours, shining like a still life at the first meeting of an art class. I'm oddly moved; I've been looking for symbols of what Yorkshire is all the way through the freezing and rain-lashed winter of writing this book, and somehow, in an obscure way that I can't define, this feels like one. Perhaps it's because it's about making do and mending, never throwing anything away, about wanting to make yourself clean after a hard day at the pit like my father-in-law used to do with those big cakes of green soap marked PHB for Pit Head Baths.

I photograph the little soapscape just as the emoji man comes in. He looks at me suspiciously like I'm some kind of health-and-safety officer concerned about the possible trip and slip hazards of soap shards.

Now I'm out on the real moor; the emoji debate has rumbled away, and I climb and climb. This feels like a version of proper Yorkshire, ancient and modern at the same time, celebrated in song and fringed with commercialism and tea shops. True, there are no mills or steelworks on the horizon, but I know that I'm walking in the bootsteps of generations of workers who've come here to breathe some clean air and to fortify themselves for the Monday-morning knocker-up and the rattling snap tin.

If Yorkshire is a fortune cookie I want to get to the motto; if Yorkshire is a cracker I want to get to the joke. If Yorkshire is a whodunit I want to get to the denouement and be surprised when a minor character walks out of the shadows with a smoking gun and if Yorkshire is a musical I want to go out whistling the 11 o'clock number. If Yorkshire is an outdoor bonfire event I want to get to the fireworks. If Yorkshire is a fairy tale I want to get to the bit where Goldilocks is found and somehow, somehow, the bears forgive her and they all live happily ever after.

Maybe that's the point of all this: maybe I want to find out why Yorkshire makes me happy, because it does. This county, with all its ridiculous sense of superiority and know-ingness and piss-taking and history and accents that easy to parody makes me deliriously happy. I feel that when I'm here I somehow begin to understand the concept of the universal in the local, the idea that profound and moving things can happen in a place where the vowels are as flat as the caps.

Speaking of caps, I can't wait any longer. The hat must come off. I'm hesitating because it feels like a significant and silly moment at the same time. It's like me in that respect; it's like this county in that respect. It lurches towards significance and trips and falls as often as it doesn't. Maybe the launching of the cap will make me Yorkshire Enough. Probably not. I think that what I really want is for somebody to come up to me once I've slung the hat and say, 'You'll catch your death of cold,' but that's not going to happen.

I grip the hat's soft wool. I pull, hard. I swing the hat round my head, whirling it and whirling it.

I'm sorry, all those places I never got to in my search for the essence of an indefinable county: sorry, Tingley, Bingley, Batley, Ossett, Wetwang, Hedon, Gomersal, Acomb and Tong. Sorry, Portobello, Drighlington, Beverley, Thorne, Marsden, Robin Hood's Bay, Aysgarth, Hubberholme and Hawes. Sorry, Bentley, Bishop Burton, Pateley Bridge, Skelmanthorpe, Ripon, Bedale, Crackpot and Idle. Sorry, Luddenden Foot, Staincross, Scholes, Scholes, Cottingham, Addingham, Terrington, Otley, Morley, Lofthouse and North and South Dalton. Sorry, Parkgate, Friendly, Yeadon, Ward Green, Giggleswick, Flockton, Frickley, Farnley, Farsley, Queensbury and Thornton Rust. Sorry, Uckerby, Ugthorpe, Dungworth, Netherthong, Upperthong, Dinnington and Denby Dale. The litany of place names says so much: each of these are little Yorkshires, little histories, little compendiums of stories and repositories of dialect words that don't exist outside the village boundaries. All those books waiting to be written. Sorry. I'll be back, though, because I'm still here. I'm not going anywhere unYorkshireish any time soon.

I let go of the hat and, carried by the wind, it flies high in the air, making a temporary eclipse as it passes the sun and looking, yes, like an emoticon. A Yorkshire emoji: part-smile, part-grimace, part-wink, part-imperceptible nod. My head is suddenly chilly and I start to shiver. I'm a sentimental man easily moved to tears and I'm moved to tears now. Yorkshire is still a mystery to me, and maybe that's how it always will be and maybe that's how I want it. Now I'm being ridiculous. Now I'm crying in public about something that isn't sport and isn't my mam. I'm not behaving like a Yorkshireman. I blow my nose with a sound like a foghorn and begin to make my way back down the hill.

IN MY BEGINNING
IS MY END

I T'S FIVE PAST six in the morning. We're in Darfield, a village in the heart of the old South Yorkshire Coalfield, about five miles from Barnsley and ten miles from Doncaster. It's that time of year and that time of the morning when spring is shifting the sky from glow to gleam and as I walk I can almost feel the light on my face like a cobweb. The early bus to the distribution warehouse slows down and picks up a man who has been frantically scratching a scratchcard before he chucks it away through the door of the bus. I haven't had my Not Yorkshire Enough dream for a while, possibly because I've been thinking so much about the meaning of Yorkshire that there hasn't been room for it in my brain.

This is a sad morning; in the last couple of days we've had the shudderingly awful news that Mad Geoff has died; it's as though a clock in the village has stopped forever, mid-tick. Bu stopped me on the street yesterday to tell me as I was walking back from the museum, and someone pushed a note through the door in the early evening. Big Martyn stopped his taxi and shouted the news to me through the driver's window. 'And he was only working on

New Year's Eve,' says Bu, his voice choking and breaking. He looks at me steadily. 'He was a legend, a legend,' he says and walks away. In the paper shop I saw a notice that said that Geoff's funeral cortege would pause by the shop for a few minutes on its way to the crematorium on Thursday for people to pay their respects. I'll be there, my head bowed, my grey hair just that little bit too long in the afternoon light.

I walk up the road and a taxi passes, bringing last night home to bed. I'm not sure how much I've learned in this autumn and winter of strolling and digging; I've gone further into my own past than I thought I would, that's for sure, and I've started to work out how much this place means to me and how little I really mean to this place. This county really is built of story and myth, memory and fable. If Mad Geoff is a legend then he will take his place alongside the Valley Ghooast and the Owl in the Tower as part of the web of oral history that reverberates around the Ridings until you can hardly hear anything else.

Yorkshire will carry on, with or without me, that much is true. It has changed, subtly and imperceptibly, like light through a stained-glass window, even during the writing of this book. The house up the street that was for sale for ages has been sold, my old neighbour who has been away for a while has come home, and I can hear the comforting sound of his TV through the wall. The huge waves that hit this part of the county in the 1980s are still making their presence felt and I stand at the top of the Inkerman Fields and look towards Manvers, formerly one of the biggest coking plants in Europe and now an archipelago of golf courses, call centres and fast food outlets and I remember a time when, as a young man fired up by two pints and a bag of crisps at the Bridge Inn, I stood with my mates at midnight looking out at Manvers belching smoke and we pledged that we would stay here and make this a better place or if we left we'd come back and make this place a better place. Of course, none of us did anything so noble or far-reaching, but that's just the folly of youth.

Yorkshire persists; it changes and it stays the same. It is eroded and it regrows. It is a place to visit and a place to live in. It is a place that I still cannot work out. It is a place unlike any other. It is a place I will spend my life trying to figure out. In the clear early morning I am tempted to whistle 'Ilkley Moor Baht 'At' but the moment passes quickly.

Time to go home and put the kettle on.

THANKS

THANKS TO THE people who helped me tell this tale, including John Tanner, Iain Nicholls, Ian Beesley and Steve Ely.

Thanks to Andy Goodfellow at Ebury who had the notion that I might be able to write something longer than 500 words with a gag or a rhyme at the end, and Liz Marvin who made sure the fat was hot before the puddings went into the oven.

And endless thanks to my wife, children and grandson for putting up with me and my daft ideas.